Intercarnations

Intercarnations

Exercises in Theological Possibility

Catherine Keller

FORDHAM UNIVERSITY PRESS

New York 2017

Copyright © 2017 Fordham University Press

All rights reserved. No part of this publication may be reproduced, stored in a retrieval system, or transmitted in any form or by any means—electronic, mechanical, photocopy, recording, or any other—except for brief quotations in printed reviews, without the prior permission of the publisher.

Fordham University Press has no responsibility for the persistence or accuracy of URLs for external or third-party Internet websites referred to in this publication and does not guarantee that any content on such websites is, or will remain, accurate or appropriate.

Fordham University Press also publishes its books in a variety of electronic formats. Some content that appears in print may not be available in electronic books.

Visit us online at www.fordhampress.com.

Library of Congress Cataloging-in-Publication Data available online at http://catalog.loc.gov.

Printed and bound in Great Britain by Marston Book Services Ltd, Oxfordshire

19 18 17   5 4 3 2 1

First edition

CONTENTS

	Introduction	1
1.	Returning God: Gift of Feminist Theology	15
2.	"And Truth—So Manifold!": Transfeminist Entanglements	35
3.	*Nuda Veritas*: Iconoclash and Incarnation	47
4.	Tingles of Matter, Tangles of Theology: Bodies of the New(ish) Materialism	60
5.	Confessing Monica: Reading Augustine Reading His Mother. *With Virginia Burrus*	83
6.	The Becoming of Theopoetics: A Brief, Incongruent History	105
7.	Derridapocalypse. *With Stephen D. Moore*	119
8.	Messianic Indeterminacy: A Comparative Study	136
9.	"The Place of Multiple Meanings": The Dragon Daughter Rereads the *Lotus Sutra*	147
10.	The Cosmopolitan Body of Christ. Postcoloniality and Process Cosmology: A View from Bogotá	164
11.	Toward a Political Theology of the Earth	174
12.	The Queer Multiplicity of Becoming	193
	After/Word Intercarnate	209
	Acknowledgments	211
	Notes	213
	Index	249

Introduction

I

Any body, opened for closer observation, might break into a multitude. It already participates in all that composes it, that nourishes and enlivens it, that rejects or interests it, that asks ever more of it. It turns into a life, a garden, a collection, a collective, a movement, an earth, faster than you can say its name. It gets into you, into the flesh and the force field of you. It morphs right now into print. And still, so many bodies later, it registers as *some* body, not just anybody. So particular in its participations that it appears as just this one.

The one and only? No, this is not a book about The Incarnation. *Intercarnations* will not conduct a return to the core Christian dogma of the exceptional descent of God into that one body. Intercarnation—a singular concept plural in effect—does not signify the one and only Incarnation relationally softened up and diversified for flesh-affirming postmodern Christians. It offers not a recuperation but a redistribution. Sometimes, of course, the incarnational exceptionalism has already broken up in the distribution of its own corporeal elements. And then the collecting bodies begin to buzz with an ancient shalom. But as theologians of the body put it graciously, "an incarnational faith is no guarantee that bodies will be treated with respect, given dignity or seen as sources of divine revelation."[1] The historical body of Christ, even in its self-distributing multiplications, its participatory disseminations, suffered early sabotage by its own success. Routinely thereafter the sovereign Lord claims His monopoly on religious truth. Intercarnations, the multiplicity of them or the singular text, can only be named in resistance to the incorporated orthodoxy of The Incarnation—to *Christ, Inc.*

Intercarnations, however, is not a polemic. To put its theological task positively: It witnesses to the multiplication and entanglement of any and all becoming flesh. Affirmations of the corporeal, the carnal, the mattering of matter, of all its materializations are, in the meantime, proliferating promiscuously in theory. In practice "materialism" is intensively contested ground, between its old Marxist and its latest corporate brands, its old Newtonian and its new posthumanist models. Its theological forms convulse with decades of urgency, yielding cosmological, feminist, ecological, and queer innovations of the signifiers and affects of materiality itself, ourselves. And on occasion, in the process, renewals of that "becoming-flesh" gets signified as incarnation.

Intercarnation would signal one more verbalization of the disunified communion of a boundlessly entangled materiality. If attention to this entanglement before and beyond the human takes theological form, it does so neither by the assertion nor by the reduction of the body of Christ. Far from obsession with the singular guy incarnate, this theology is preoccupied with just about everybody else. Like he was (she adds piously). So the present collection attends asymmetrically to theological bodies diversely female, animal, vegetal, mineral, religious, irreligious, cosmic, and cosmopolitan. Getting into flesh happens precisely not as an exceptional episode or a last-ditch rescue operation. For if what theology calls God is nowhere and never *not*, no hard line can be drawn between creation and incarnation. A deity who is "through all and in all" (Eph. 4:6) is pretty much by definition pan-carnate. But no doubt with such differences of reception, of intensity, of *mattering*, as to break up any simple God-world One.

Intercarnation highlights the intermittencies, the intervals and interdependencies, of *world* relations. Does it transcribe a panentheism of all flesh in God and therefore God enfleshed in all? Perhaps not quite so neatly. For only in the twists and tangles of creaturely becoming, which is always a becoming bodily, does the subject matter of theology matter now. Or, then, ever. The carnal manifold of the world may indeed compose a living all, *pan*, not as the unity of all bodies but as the innumerable entirety of "the flesh of the world."² But the turbulent diversity of all that vulnerable flesh, the entanglement of all creatures in their neighbors and in their strangers, mostly involuntary, demands now relentless attention. In the perspective of all of that intercarnational activity, the ancient incarnation does not matter less. On the contrary, it may matter all the more when we emulate its own shift of attention from itself.

2

Despite its claims, Christ, Inc. has never held a monopoly on Christianity. So some of its worst violence was directed against differing Christians. It took more than three centuries for Christianity to consolidate under the sign of one cross, one sword, one religion. And so it took that long for the figure of the becoming-flesh to settle into the exclusionary substantive of Incarnation. This history, carrying the distortion and its Christological alternative, is not the subject of any one of the essays in this book. So let me touch upon it here.

Right in the privileged text of all Christological exceptionalism, hidden in the plain view of standard readings, a far more complex becoming comes into play. If, according to the prologue of Gospel of John, "the word became flesh and lived among us," it is precisely that word through which "all things came into being." And the same verse emphatically clarifies what is far less cited: "What has come into being in the word was life" (John 1:4). All of it. Nonetheless tradition soon managed to abstract that word from the life of "all things"—to separate the life of that one man from the life of all matter, the life of the creation. Mayra Rivera finds here a "strange carnal poetics," in which life and light circulate and materialize, as flesh and bread: "The bread that I will give for the life of the world is my flesh." Therefore "an emphasis on exchanged and transformed flesh structures a collectivity in terms of the mutual imbrication of those who participate in it."³

If the distribution of flesh as bread, as the material life of the world, expressed itself in the life of one Jewish body, it was as a life exposing its own entanglement in the life of all the living. It was from the start easy, temptingly easy, to mistake the distinctiveness of his hyper-gift as an absolute exception. John has Jesus himself respond to the accusation of blasphemy: that "you, though only a human being, made yourself to be God" (John 10:34). The author of this gospel, in which Jesus owns his messianic identity and announces that "the Father is in me and I in the Father," had reason to take seriously this suspicion of blasphemy. Startlingly, Jesus disarms the charge by quoting Psalm 82: "I said, 'You are gods.'" So then he succinctly argues—while the crowd, rocks in hand, prepares to throw—that "if those to whom the word of God came were called 'gods'—and the scripture cannot be annulled" how can you say that I (doing all these works, these healings) am "blaspheming because I said 'I am God's son'?" (John 10:33b–36). In other words, the gospel of John is radically redistributing divinity itself. (And he slips away that time.)

This is not just one fleeting text. In the prologue itself "all who received him" receive "power to become children of God" (John 1:12). To become a child of God, daughter or son, means, in other words, to take part in the god-family: to become divine. A relational capacity is conferred, not a natural or supernatural status: a possibility, not a guarantee, for a becoming, not a being. The becoming flesh of God does not just make possible the becoming divine of our flesh. It looks back to an ancient Hebraic history—not identifiable with so-called polytheisms—witnessing to this divine multiplicity. Of course, these Johannine attestations to an incarnational manifold, the dissemination, the lateral distribution of divinity, of multiple humans becoming gods, are not among the bits of John blasted on billboards and otherwise over-quoted. (He comes to what was his own—all those John-quoters—and still "they did not accept him.") Psalm 82 did, however, serve as one of the major proof texts of the ancient tradition of theosis, or theopoiesis: the becoming-divine of the human. "God became human that we might become divine."[4]

The prologue of John's gospel may be read as announcing—not as a monopoly but as a novel disclosure—the logos, *principium*, word, of all materialization. It is always already included in all things, as the condition of their possibility and the mattering of their life. It comes exemplifying the life of the universe: the cosmic exemplar, not the sovereign exception. In its own historical context, the enfleshment of the one God in a particular body enacted a radical provocation, finally intolerable to the sovereign powers.

Of course, the notion of incarnation provoked tension from the beginning within Abrahamic monotheism. But it can only be said to drive the anti-Judaic supersessionism as Christ became the brand of the Roman Empire. It took a much longer interval for the symbol to occlude, in one of the more tragic self-contradictions of human history, its own really embodied Jewishness.[5] And the separation of Jesus from his Jewish body produces, as J. Kameron Carter demonstrates, the whole modern drama of "race": first, in the racialization of the Jews, and subsequently, of Africans.[6] Christ, Inc.

Introduction

looked paler and paler. Yet at the same time the contemplation of that vulnerable flesh, sacramentally entangled with other bodies, retained—contrary to the metaphysically Greek devaluation of matter—messianically Jewish elements. For which bodies matter.

And so, for example, at a particular moment in history—not as exception but precisely as exemplification of a deep history—intercarnation means: black bodies matter. The particularity of that claim—which is not in practice helped but neutralized if one adds "all bodies matter"—bursts in its revelatory moment like the singularity of Jesus in his. And that makes it no less entangled in the utter density of theopolitical relations and ecosocial materializations that compose the space of a shared time. Particularity does not trade against the world in which it participates and which takes part in it—cannibalistically or commensally. Particularity is always only a *relationship* of difference, a relation to that from which it differs. Relations of difference in its asymmetries, inevitable or oppressive, cannot all be addressed at once, nor once for all. But neither can they be denied. In our moment, here, now, for example: it might be relations of race that call us to a new becoming-flesh. And at the same time, in the name of justice, race does not clip blackness from the variegated spectrum of tawny bodies, nor from matters of sexuality, gender, class, climate. The intercarnation here holds the doctrine of the incarnation accountable to the messianic mattering of all flesh.

3

No number of messianic comings or theopoietic becomings will cleanse from human history the apocalypse-soaked entanglement of the three Abrahamisms in each other. And in almost every other *other*. Nor will secularization accomplish the purge. What sometimes can be called postsecularism lets us instead recognize how all secular liberation echoes the first Exodus. The prophets haunt every just critique. This is no ground for a new theopolitical triumphalism. Ghosts do not ground. They solicit self-questioning. But theology cannot advance the self-questioning of its own secular contexts unless it is at the same time questioning its own ancestral complications. Indeed, precisely as questioning, as quest—*fides quaerens intellectum*—theology might now shut itself down. *If*, that is, it does not come to terms with the thorny multiplicity of its biblical undergrowth. Confusion could never be avoided. From the start, within the sacred texts themselves, that rhizomatic complexity was always exhibiting too many genres and moods: songs and stories, amoral legends and moral codes, prophetic rages and conciliatory wisdoms, messianic resistance and patriarchal assimilation. And then it gives rise to the vociferous history of orthodoxies vs. heresies, of Platonisms and pragmatisms, of rationalisms and reformations, unifications and divisions, establishments and dissidents. And it was always tangling with the traditions that preceded or confronted it, with elemental goddesses and golden calves, critical philosophies, secular sciences, imperial sovereignties, social revolutions . . .

All, really all, still participating in the body of theology. This carnal multiplicity can no longer be kept out of sight. So any discourse that backs itself into some messianic corner of purity—even of liberative gender, race, sex, or class—within the faltering institutions of liberal Christianity will soon be muttering to itself. Yet these theologies of social movement in their many waves are still finding their voices. So we might just admit: This exposed mess of multiplicity either takes theology down or stirs its unpredictable becoming. If, then, theology can muster the "wild patience"[7] that will bear with its own webby chaos, we may find in the uncertainty the possibility of theology itself. But that might mean theology not as the discourse of any single community but as source of possibilities for the living world.

In the complications that link us to mixed histories and impure achievements, that enfold multitudes within our very bodies, there germinates even now the chance for a wider justice and a healthier earth. The possibility, not the likelihood. The twist of the impossible into the improbable. Which means it is possible. We earthlings can do it. After all, the canny Nicholas of Cusa already in the fifteenth century named God the *posse ipsum*—the possibility itself, the *can* do of every creaturely doing.[8] The doing is not for God but for creatures to do. To do is nothing but to embody—to make actual in the world something that might have remained just possible. So if multiplicity exposes the interlinked differences that we singly and collectively embody, it exposes them as possibilities for new doings: new bodies of thought, provoking and provoked by new planetary materializations. So theology must, *can*, help to keep more honestly in view the movement between multiplicity and embodiment that is relationality itself. This means that it requires of us all cannier embodiments of what we may call *entangled difference*. Whatever they call it, the essays in this book all *do* some version of entangled difference: Indeed, the phrase may be considered a paraphrase of intercarnation. This difference, not to be confused with separation, is nothing but the relation between irreducible particulars. Their particularity is nothing but their mode of participation in one another. Their almost always unconscious "mutual immanence," as Alfred North Whitehead put it.

With theology itself, as the formalized discourse of the Western religions, in question among most thinking people, difference cannot be appeased by various feminist or materialist or ecumenical supplements. The questions go way down, to the geologos of creation; they go way up, to any theologos. So now the questioning drives the very possibility of theology, which includes the possibility that theology is not the answer. Christianity, for example, may reach consummation in its self-deconstruction. Of course the cannier autodeconstruction does not confuse itself with autodestruction. It knows that questionability offers its own answerability.[9] And what is this self-questioning but a perennial symptom of the prophetic iconoclasm? Without confrontation now in earnest with the possible death of the bodies—conceptual, institutional, habitual—of old-line religion, there is no possibility that theology can be answerable to the living, indeed, even to its own livelier constituencies.

In the meantime, the questionability of theology to itself has yielded a half-century tradition of the theology of the death of God. It has gone far to break up the common sense of Christ, Inc. In league with the secular and then the postsecular, the break up continues, and it gains nuance: theology of the death of God becomes theology "after the death of God," or the radical theology of the insistent but inexistent God; or God again, *Anatheism*, "God after God."[10] But then the question hardly confines itself to "Does this One exist?" Let alone His (oops) Son? The purity of the Death of God, the rendering of a divine something as nothing—*nihil*—has been hard to sustain, even under the heading of the "nihilism of grace."[11] Upon closer observation, is it a Christ-shaped nihil that deposits its clean void, right in the space where the single Body had ruled? Perhaps something messier than "death," indeed livelier.

The institution in its old-line North does, at any rate, seem to be collapsing under the weight of a tired, distracted incredulity on the one side, a radical self-questioning on the other. It was always prone to dematerialize anyway. The body of Christ, though initially offering a superb figure of entangled difference, got tragically disentangled from its planet's life. Or rather, it laid claim by conversion to the human lives of much of the planet, but only as it sealed itself into the institutional way station for an afterlife. But this collapsing may not be revealing a void but something more interesting. What appears instead suggests a chaotic decomposition, the return of the Body to the earth, the dissolution of the One into the all, the all too many. Too many spirits and spiritualities, options, channels. Too many perils, too many humans, too many migrants, too many galaxies. And the decompositions that become visible, audible, touchable, smellable, within this return will not lose the whiff of death. Amid too many fragrances.

And yet composition is also underway: improvisational self-compositions of the multitudes themselves, compost piles amid loss. Rotting and gestating, dissolving and resolving, these entangled manifolds of the earth may respond quite differently to us if we respond to their bodies and ours with less fear. And more canniness. We would become better artists of the possible. Unexpected alliances might arise, not awaiting salvation but actively, amorously salvaging. They would intensify planetary resistance to the global corporations that now threaten the corporeal ground and climate of our shared life. New assemblages of entangled difference will not arise without the realism of fear, the politics of outrage, and the temporality of lament.

The recomposition of our world is triggered, first of all, by desire: by what Laurel Schneider calls "promiscuous incarnations."[12] And yet it is never just a matter of embracing all our relations, of blessing multiplicity. Our polydoxy is just as selective as any orthodoxy. It seeks its own right teaching and finds its elements amid both the orthodoxies and the heresies of the world. So this promiscuity is proving itself oddly discerning. But the spirit at play in intercarnation recognizes a multiplicity of spirits—not all of them—as trusty. Because bodies matter, we discern the spirits: some of them wreak casual violence against bodies, some work a discarnate indifference. In this instance I like the King James translation: "Beloved, believe not every spirit, but try the spirits whether they are of God. For many false prophets have gone out into the world" (1 John 4:1). To discern is to try: We try and we are tried, we test, we try on for fit, we suffer trials, we risk experiments, we feel out desire. Then the decision to act, to cut through the impossible multiplicity, can happen—and happen cannily.

To try the spirits, to give them a try-out, to test them—we do this mindful that they all seek embodiment. Not because they pre-exist matter but because they are energized possibilities verging on realization, haunting voices in conflict with each other, virtual bodies needing our discernment—as to just what we will next materialize.

4

Sometimes it is just some text. This one gathers together a few experiments in specifically theological possibility—the possibilities theology fosters and the possibility of theology itself—hoping to encourage new ones. *Intercarnations* is made up of a dozen essays written for a multiplicity of occasions over the past decade or so. *Essay* as it happens, comes from the French *essayer*: "to try." These essays all try spirits stirred up by some specific question, in a particular context. They come between the more solid bodies of monographs; they form their own intermittency. They test possible answers and stir up some more spirits. Usually they are discussing neither the neologism of intercarnation nor the paleologism of the incarnation. Often they are exercising a more directly feminist theology than my books of this millennium have signaled. They have been selected because upon rereading them I find they test out, they discern something still or again surprising to me, and they collect with enough coherence to live out their lives under one cover. Or shall we call it one skin—recalling the vellum that enfolded older manuscripts, when books were mainly theology? And before that skin turns virtual, before its flesh turns back into screen, it iterates the title of another book, *Word Made Skin*, which teaches that a delicate surface, if it lives, may offer all the continuity that a discourse needs—or can bear. "Language and body are communicative, outreaching and indrawing. But they are also, importantly, constitutive—constitutive of ourselves."[13] In the indrawing, we—in logos and in flesh—fold our world into ourselves. And outreaching, we unfold it otherwise.

These essays do not do their unfolding in a necessary sequence. They may be read in any order and are not arranged by chronology or architecture but by neighborliness. They form a certain sequence by way of their thematic affinities; but their resonances cross horizontally through them all. As occasional pieces, they repeat elements of each other and of my monographs. I have not masked their contextual eventiveness nor have I sought to update them artificially.

The first essays of this collection enfold the legacy of feminist theology, which has destabilized the foundations of theology and inserted itself into any live future of theology. It is one way of unfolding an ancient history of language and body otherwise. Does that history, in its Christian force field, still open a black hole of betrayal? Or does it open, in its dramatic shifts of gender, like a gift? "Returning God: Gift of Feminist Theology" considers how the much touted "return of God" is both helped and hindered by the demand for gender and sexual justice. Perhaps the particular cunning of feminist theology is that it returns the God-gift to its givers, refused? What kind of return of God would not poison the flesh of its female and queer recipients? Initiating the deconstructive trajectory of this book, this essay enjoys the conversation on "the gift" circulating between Derridean thought and its religious reception. But can a gift circulate, return? And what does feminist theology—a name many of us who embody it do not frequently use now for ourselves—have to give?

The next essay heightens the tension of any rigorously relational thinking: that between entanglement and difference. As difference multiplies, the tension intensifies. And as gender folds into sexuality, into race, class, and ecology, into materiality, it resists reduction—as each of these issues do—to a mere issue among many. Instigated by a poem of Emily Dickinson, "'And Truth—So Manifold!': Transfeminist Entanglements" hopes to keep feminism from getting either transcended or stuck in a certainty of its own. Multiplicity begins to insist upon its own truth—and therefore upon a corollary unknowing: "An Ignorance beheld/Diviner than the Childhood's."[14]

In truth, the spirits of feminism want ever more flesh. So "*Nuda Veritas*: Iconoclash and Incarnation" offers a brief visit to a museum in Vienna. Here a bold, protesting nude of the early twentieth-century Klimt demands our attention. Her gilded gaze—citing in all irony the icons of Byzantium—sends us off to another exhibition, that of Bruno Latour's *Iconoclash*. To honor matter, iconoclasm is never enough. And such honor is what John of Damascus directed, against an imperial iconoclasm, to the incarnation, "the matter which works my salvation."[15]

The next essay takes us deeper into matter, right back through its mottled Christian materialist history and down, deep down, into its nonhumanity. "Tingles of Matter, Tangles of Theology: Bodies of the New(ish) Materialism" contemplates a bodily becoming neither human nor divine but entangled in both. In conversation with Karen Barad, quantum entanglement discloses the relational ontology—the "agential intra-activity"—of which every body in the universe is woven. I demonstrate the proximity of Barad's to Whitehead's responsive materiality. Intercarnation might here have turned to *intra-carnation*. But then there might seem to be a single mega-body inside which all enfleshment takes place. The point, however, is that creatures, micro- or macro-, do not pre-exist their relationships. If the new materialism is new, it is in the fluency of a universe vibrant—quite spookily—in its every embodiment.

The creativity of the universe in its unfathomable fluencies had not escaped the attention of Aurelius Augustine. And in the *Confessions* that awareness cannot be dismissed as Platonic dualism cum ecclesial patriarchy. Written with Virginia Burrus, historian of Christianity and late antiquity, "Confessing Monica" reads Augustine reading his postmortem mother. In his tears for her, she morphs into the oceanic deep, *tehom*, of

Genesis, the "something-nothing" or fluency itself. His deconstruction of the (Augustinian) master narrative of the creation of matter from nothing at all seems to open up as the womb of all bodies. For a churning moment, a de-oedipalized respect for Monica stirs the "multiplying matrix" of an alternative. I have elsewhere systematically linked the *creatio ex nihilo* with a masculinized omnipotence, while deriving its oceanic alternative from the poetics of the creation narrative.[16]

When, however, we return poiesis to its ancient meaning, that of making, creating, a doubling of theological creativity comes into play: that of language and of its matter. Theopoiesis means not God's making but a "making God," or becoming-divine. In "The Becoming of Theopoetics: A Brief, Incongruent History," a pre-Augustinian spiritual practice comes into uneasy relation with a modernist theopoetics. The latter turns out to have a surprising pedigree, closer to death of God theology than to any ancient mysticism. But certain recent embodiments of theopoetics link its insistent poiesis, beyond deconstruction, to a cosmological creativity. The becoming-divine signified by theopoiesis now flows through the divine becoming of "the poet of the world."

In the standard narrative, however, the genesis of the world is answered by its end. The gift of the creation gets taken back. Yet biblical eschatology is not summed up by the apocalyptic Messiah. Nor is the apocalypse summed up by "the end." Entering with the New Testament–scholar Stephen Moore into an encounter with Jacques Derrida, "Derridapocalypse" reconsiders the "gift" of the messianic coming. Stimulus both of the revolutionary movements of the West and of our fundamentalisms, the Book of Revelation offers the perverse eucharist of "God's great banquet, to devour . . . the flesh of all, whether free or slave, small or great" (Rev. 19: 17–18). Yet participation in the flesh of everybody finally yields to the new creation: a shadow play of intercarnation that unfortunately may continue to require, even to merit, our attention.

The next essay persists, in an altogether different register, with the question of messianic politics. "Messianic Indeterminacy: A Comparative Study" reads comparative theology within the Abrahamic rhizome as inseparable from political theology. The darkness of the messianic anointing is no more that of its frequent destructiveness than of its unknowable indeterminacy. Freed of any certain outcome or homecoming, the messianic hope breaks open a temporality of collective becoming. As messianic indeterminacy thereby darkens into "the nonknowing of a not-ending no-one, the naught of our now entangles us indirectly in everyone—without untangling us from the direct demands of some one tradition."

Comparative theology in the Abrahamic modality is then supplemented by a quick trip to a much further East. In "'The Place of Multiple Meanings': The Dragon Daughter Rereads the *Lotus Sutra*," a radically other sensibility, other spirit, other textual body enters the conversation. And it is a wisdom of multiplicity in extremis—"countless ages," "innumerable buddhas," who use "innumerable skillful means." Indeed, the means of this beloved sutra epitomize entangled difference: the buddhas "know that nothing exists independently,/And that buddha-seeds arise interdependently."[17] These far-flung intercarnations effect here some unexpectedly current entanglements.

The final three essays profile a planetary politics for a theology in search of its future. "The Cosmopolitan Body of Christ. Postcoloniality and Process Cosmology: A View from Bogotá" arises in postcolonial Colombia. In the context of an engagement between process and liberation theologies, it proposes a cosmopolitanism with *cosmos*, a "cosmovision" (Sylvia Marcos) hearty enough to support the vibrant materializations of the populations most subject to the depredations of economic globalization. Indifference to the differences—of human and biological diversity—of the Global South calls theologically for the skillful means of a densely decolonial cosmology.

Of course, the entire globe is now enfolded in the warming atmosphere. Unfortunately, this shared crisis is not likely to produce an answering, planetary solidarity. But it might. "Toward a Political Theology of the Earth" considers such deterritorializations as might make it possible. Seeding an alternative to the political theology of exceptionalist power, the intercarnation fosters "the new people and earth in the future."[18] Won't the possibility of that future, irrepressibly eschatological, be better fortified if its own political theology—the prophetic eco-justice alternative to imperial sovereignties—is not repressed? But then the possibility of theology itself becomes inseparable from the possibility of the earth's and, therefore, our own future.

Finally, in the scene of a lecture in Berlin happening at the moment of the Paris climate talks and of an exacerbated Western Islamophobia, the assigned topic of "genders and faiths" twists into "The Queer Multiplicity of Becoming." It unfolds a relationship between the Christian, the sexual, the national, and the anthropocentric exceptionalisms. A windy eros breathes some life and hope into the entangled multiplicity of our stressed earth, our shared flesh.

If intercarnation offers itself as a transient trope for the mattering of our entangled difference, it only hopes to stir up more becoming practices.

What calls itself theology now, here, in its diffraction of pluralist-feminist-socio-ecological multiplicities, has not been tried for long. Its novelty knows itself parasitical on much that is old, passing, passé, impassible. But whatever its aporias, its trials and tests, by whatever nicknames it travels, theology has not lost life, spirit, and affect. Its questions still gather force. Its poetics pick up where logos disappoints. Of course, we will keep falling into silences of unknowing, of doubt or of horror—and hopefully not at those moments when our strong speech is needed.

Apophasis may swing in and out of apocalypsis. Even as theology folds in and out of the impossible. But amid these experiments, we might hold this thought: In religion and outside of it, we have, as a species, barely begun to recognize our differences *as* our relations. On the verge of too late, we may just be starting to take responsibility for the planetarity of our life.

CHAPTER I

Returning God: Gift of Feminist Theology

Doubling Back

In Christian culture there is something menacing about a return, a *second* coming. The Lord should not have had to come twice. He was nice the first time, he tried love, he healed and fed us, and see what happened to him. We threw his gift in his face. The Book of Revelation warns of what a different mood he will be in when he comes again: He is gonna kick some butt. The storm will not stay in the desert this time, it rains shock and awe upon Babylon, that whore. Her beasts of terror are everywhere; this war must go to the ends of the earth. The re-coming one, the *revenant*, has eyes "like a flame"; its protruding tongue is hard, "a sharp two-edged sword" (Rev. 1:14, 1:16).[1] Or word. This Word is a WMD. It will cut down the

---

"Returning God" was written in its first form as an address at the "Feminism, Sexuality, and the Return of Religion" Conference at Syracuse University. The proceedings were published in a book of the same name, *Feminism, Sexuality, and the Return of Religion*, ed. Linda Martin Alcoff and John D. Caputo (Bloomington: Indiana University Press, 2011).

enemy empire. But first it will penetrate and destroy the traitors within the churches, like that Jezebel, that woman who dares to lead and prophesy. "I am throwing her on a bed . . . and I will strike her children dead" (Rev. 2:22). Was she teaching too free a love?

"Love" does occur in John's Apocalypse, once: "I reprove and discipline those whom I love" (Rev. 3:19). The last letter of the New Testament apparently counterbalances the excessive love not just of Jezebel but of Jesus. And yet we have to admit that the difference between the love gospel and the apocalyptic rage, the *différance* between the love unreserved and the love deferred, has been politically indispensable. That tense messianic expectation has charged the revolutionary movements of the West, democratic and socialist, as Ernst Bloch magisterially demonstrated, with threat and hope.[2] The apocalyptic utopia also encodes certain movements Bloch does not discuss, movements of women, such as the Saint-Simonniennes of the early nineteenth century, with whom Claire Démar founded a journal with other working-class women announcing (in her upper case): "The word of the WOMAN REDEEMER WILL BE A SUPREMELY REVOLTING WORD."[3]

Let me then admit that the first religious icon that really got my attention was a bit of feminist apocalypse. I was sixteen. It was a poster tacked up in a Massachusetts coffee shop, featuring a formidable female with long red hair, minimally covered by a bearskin and holding a staff. The caption (capitalized) read: GOD IS COMING, AND IS SHE PISSED. The full force of the pronoun hit me for the first time and forever; I knew that *She* was pissed because *He* had usurped her place, He and his armies of butt-kickers. (I was spending time at anti-Vietnam demonstrations.) I did not know that Her Coming presaged the coming of feminist theology, let alone of my going to seminary to assist Her return. I sensed she had been around before. She had given love, she was nurturing, she fed and healed and embraced. And see what happened to her, to her incarnation in and as woman, women. Oh, the menace of her return was exciting: a second-wave feminist apocalypse, rocking with sex and rage. Of course this returning she-God soon settled into more dignified theological and ecclesial debates. But *she* never enjoyed unambiguous status, not even as a pronoun, not even within feminist theology.

If feminist theology exists as such, if it is not just the residual oxymoron of an enthusiastic explosion, it lives by the begrudging tolerance and the avowed need of theology. And therefore it lives—so ambivalently—by the grace of its institutionally durable, textually deep, not altogether inflexible but certainly masculine *theos*. The attempt to spell ourselves the*a*logians was half-hearted. Its difference does not preach any better than, say, the Heideggerian distinction between theology and the*i*ology. Besides, no effort at feminization quite frees itself of its patriarchal mirrors. And of course the specter of a female divinity—a ghostly revenant of mythic goddesses—has necessarily provoked feminist ambivalence about any possible symbolic content, historical antecedent, fabricated icon, let alone archetypal and indelibly straight essence of femininity. "The feminine" projected to infinity—*She* spooked feminists almost as much as she spooked patriarchs, or as patriarchs spooked us. Feminist theological ambivalence always wielded its own double edge.

Looking back and forward, I do not hope to avoid the slashing tongues/word of the apocalypse, only to disarm it temporarily. Might its double edge then morph into the ambiguity—grammatical, sexual, theological—of "the return of God"? Is it God returning or *being* returned? Like a gift unwanted? Does the double genitive symptomatize the problem and the possibility—the menace and the hope—of religion itself? And might this exercise in return, as first of all a return of, or to, a feminist theology that has long taken itself for granted, prove at least therapeutic? The grant may otherwise run out. As the politics of a "gender" so densely problematized, complicated, intersectional, embodied, planetary—feminism in and around theology may still be giving its gift. As is every tradition that recognizes in itself "the very historicity that presupposes a tradition to be reinvented each step of the way, in this incessant repetition of the absolute beginning."[4]

To Return: Transitive or Intransitive?

What, then, is the relation of the "returning God" of a half century of feminist theology to the return of religion? Feminist theology, where an intensive secularization meets an ancient discourse, surely counts as one symptom of the so-called postsecular. But is "God" returning or getting returned? Might we now receive the gift of a return, a coming again? Or do we perform the return of the gift to its religious givers? Is our returning God, who comes by way of a few decades of creative struggle about His/Her/Its names and effects, a blessing and a renewal of the language of God? Or a symptom of its demise, of a final dissolution played out in the projection of theological language for progressive political ends? A transformation of God-talk or a late modern form of its well-intending manipulation? What kind of gift is She?

Of course from the start, feminist talk of God was confronting the limits of language. And transgressing them. We—and I am pronominally possessed in this paper by the ever faltering "we" of feminist theology—have tried altering those pronouns: She rather than He? The hiccup S/he? Alternating She and He? Or: "God ain't a he or a she, but a It." Thus Alice Walker's classic para-scripture: "Whenever you trying to pray, and man plop himself on the other end of it, tell him to git lost, say Shug. Conjure up flowers, wind, water, a big rock."[5] Amen. Go to the nonhuman. At the same time, we did not want to forfeit the chance, after not centuries but millennia, to glimpse our own female faces in the *imago dei*—which is to say, as actually *human*. The experiment in inclusive language allowed us to renegotiate the biblical stories, to retell them with higher-pitched voices and more laughter. The returning God of feminism was never just an apologia for women's leadership. It was not just the return of divine Daddy in drag. Or as Nelle Morton put it three decades ago, "Yahweh in a skirt."[6] Beyond God the Father, sisters in the wilderness, new woman, new earth—we wanted new ancient metaphors. Spirit Sophia, Mother Sophia, Jesus Sophia by the eminent way of negation and affirmation.[7] But with the quiet blessing of his post-oedipal, protofeminist potentiality? No doubt we wanted the impossible. Which is to say: a metonymics of the possible.

All of this intensity about the naming of God was cannily cultural, practical, liturgical, political. But it was at the same time altogether *theological*. It surely counts as evidence for an unexpected return. Among one subset of progressive thinkers, it energized with its argumentative passions a return not just of a vague religiosity but of an engagement with the old thematic and disputatious questions of theology. It effected a renewal of God-talk just when thinkers intent on speaking truth to power, or on deconstructing the truth of power, had deemed God truly dead. Whatever His liberalizations and deliteralizations.

In this way can feminist theology be said to have infused a few decades of life force into the God question, into God him/her/itself? This would be a great gift to theology: a gift of life. But the gift retains—along with the German word for poison, *Gift*—its double edge.[8] The interruption here and there of progress toward atheism by feminist theology not only complicated cutting-edge solidarity among secularists. It could at the same time work like poison on mainstream Christian male defenses—sometimes neo-orthodox, sometimes liberal, sometimes even liberationist—of the God of the tradition.

Indeed, if the grammar of the *returning of God* turns on itself, in the double genitive, then of course one might doubt that feminist theology really promotes the coming or coming again of any God. Have we in fact been *giving God back*? Returning God to the shop, like a dress that does not fit? Perhaps demanding a refund? Returning him to his producers? (As Calvin said, the human heart is a factory of idols.) We feminists in theology tried to feminize, womanize, neuter, queer, or pluralize God. We have fought with each other and with the lords of patriarchy to open a space for the gifts of women within theology and in the pulpit. But as both sisters and patriarchs sneered knowingly from the start: no matter how much we adjust and supplement and deconstruct and reconstruct God, He will remain pretty much He. Even when there is a generous willingness to use only inclusive language about the deity in newly written texts, prayers, liturgies—and that is a huge and rare concession—still God brings with him/her/itself the archive: the historical trove of scriptures, prayers, creeds, songs, doctrines. Theologies. And that archive is punctuated percussively, in relentless elegance, with its *He*s, *Lord*s, and *Father*s. In every new class of seminarians someone will say (not meaning to reprise Mary Daly's sarcasm): "but the masculine language about God is just metaphoric. We know He isn't a man." I do not break into tears or laughter; I love my students, they have come far and grow further. And exactly what supersession would I lay on them? Communicating around the turn of the millennium with an Austrian friend just learning about the minefields of the US feminist theological discourse, he emailed back in mock exasperation: "Holy she/he/it!"

After all, after generations, after so many fresh starts and subtle transgenderings, is the aporia of feminist theology just an oxymoron: God remains a guy no matter how we dress him, double and triple him homoerotically? Does not the leadership of church, synagogue, and mosque still, overall, compose a boys' club for those made in His image? Is the impossible dream a low-grade nightmare, the kind one grows accustomed to, full of familiar clichés and family poisons? In this impasse, many of us who are feminists in theology quietly—sometimes so quietly we can hardly hear ourselves—have said thanks but no thanks. We return the gift. The verb becomes transitive. We may be performing an honorable role, not unlike that of death of God theologians; we are exposing the idol of monotheism within His own household.

We do not then return the gift out of ingratitude but out of exhaustion—as though our alchemy had finally failed to transmute the poison. As though the gift was always after all the "gift of death"—of an Abrahamic sacrifice that, as Derrida notes, remained, though the public drama was played out between males, "at its very basis an exclusion or sacrifice of women."[9] Does this return of the gift that is the gift of death happen always too late? Or is it interrupted by the grace of a ram? But no substitutionary suffering has long mitigated the organizing violence of the patrilineage.[10] Another return on the sacrifice is demanded, another double return: The Christian God demanded payback for human sin, to be paid back in the human blood of his divine Son; and the believer who receives its gift of salvation is in it precisely for the final payback, in heaven if not sooner.

From this mournful vantage point, the religion that has been returning across much of the planet appears to be pretty much what it appears to be: the return of this or that patriarchy with a vengeance, whether it is militantly imperial or militantly anti-imperialist. The inviting exceptions at the self-deconstructing fringes of old-line religions would prove only to be proving the rule.

So it should not be surprising to remember that some of the first voices of feminist theology were carefully keyed into the death of God movement. Naomi Goldenberg, for instance, recognized in 1971 that "we women are going to bring an end to God." Yet she felt "there was a magnificence attached to the idea of watching him go" and returned with glee to "graduate school to study the end of God."[11] And it is in a curt salute to Thomas J. J. Altizer and company that Mary Daly's crucial chapter in *Beyond God the Father* is named "After the Death of God the Father." Is it the death of the deified male, we were asking? Or of God Himself? What is the difference?

In the rhetoric of the death of God and its intellectually fecund aftermath, ambiguity persists. Is the dying God *any* God that is person-like enough to be called and called upon as God? Or is the dead One precisely the opposite, the impersonal, immutable abstraction? Or then again a fusion of the God of the theologians and the God of the philosophers? Feminists in religion were quick to recognize in the classical fusion of a disinterested abstraction (*ontos*) with an invasive nearness (*theos*) the Western hypostasis of a self-interested masculinity. Also, we soon recognized the indifference of death of God theologians, absorbed in the thanatological grandeur of their task, in the gender difference, and, ipso facto, in the particular struggles—institutional, grammatological, sexual, political—of women.

More to the point, we were not declaring the death of just *any* God. We were particular indeed. We were preoccupied with difference. At least this turned out to be the case for those of us who had variously effected our own return of religion, often even of Christianity. Unconvinced by Daly's total feminist "exorcism," haunted by unrealized promises, we exposed ourselves to a theological *revenant*.

Wavering Women

Within Christianity—with at best inexact parallels among the other branches of the Abrahamic patrimony—a spiritual gulf opened early between those feminists who made an exodus first from the patriarchal church, then from any church, from theology itself, who returned the idol and with honor refused any return on their lost investment, and those of us who remained in some intentional way associated with a religious institution and its symbolic archive. We on this latter side accept its gifts and expose ourselves to the poisons; we partake of the dying of traditions and institutions where God is talked. However ambivalently, however critically, we conspire more with the theologies of exodus than with the exodus from theology. Feminist theology cannot—except when our anti-essentialism fronts for our whiteness—dissociate itself from the traditions of *theology*, which is to say, of liberation and Black and LGBTQ and ecological theologies, of what Cornel West calls "prophetic Christianity" as it gets mobilized against the "new Constantinianism."[12] Under the imperial regime of the first years of this millennium, the call to a prophetic Christianity intensified as it became more apparent among progressives that a secular response is inadequate to swing votes and perhaps even to keep ourselves *progressing*. Even a few writers in the *Nation* began to realize that the religious left may be of some use in countering what George Lakoff called the "strict father" paradigm, that theocratically tinged paternalism that had returned with an Islamophobic (not to mention Islamic) vengeance.[13] But apart from strategic concessions, and despite a suggestive theory of the postsecular, our colleagues in other fields presume a transcendent secularism.

Under the threat of this two-sided sword—of secular progressivism and of the politico-religious right—feminist theology not surprisingly displayed occasional symptoms of apocalyptic hysteria. Repent, for this end of this (phallogoanthropoheterowhite) world is nigh! Feminist theology in and well beyond the academy has strained to translate logos into flesh, wisdom into work, theory still in process into action still undecidable. Our ecclesial contexts hold our conceptual feet to the fires of an evangelical populism that US progressive thinkers disregard at (all) our peril. At the same time, we struggle at the shifting shorelines of our own finitude, where our still historically speaking young traditions fumble even as our generations pass. Our language sputters and falters, it shifts with our priorities. Our activist positivism wavers before the evident constructedness of our strategic God-talk. We can no more cash that constructedness into a smug post-Christianity than we can evade the challenge posed by the post-God guys.

Will our waver—lacking now the decisive either/or of Pascal's wager, let alone Kierkegaard's knight of faith—bring on the death of feminist theology? Or activate a constructive uncertainty? Deconstruction would not solve the problem; it can only defer solution, per se, and thereby offer us back our own difference. The deconstruction of God, ipso facto of God-talk, is precisely not its destruction but its desubstantiation—and Derrida soon recognized the kinship as well as the difference of deconstruction and what is called negative theology.[14] Not far from this recognition, a feminist apophasis, an "unsaying of God," began to appear. The ancient apophatic strategy, arising from key sources of ancient Christianity, neither erases nor kills God. It returns Him, indeed any projection of a person, an entity, an *ontotheos*, to the abyss. And so fertilizes the abyss. But a mystical solution to feminist problems, given the embeddedness of negative theology in Christian Neoplatonic hierarchies, would be premature. In this way the deconstructive engagement of apophatic theology may lend protection against a merely deepened patriarchy, a He beyond His names.[15] It defers God-talk in the very name of God.

At the edge of this interchange—never an identity—to say with Derrida "the divine has been ruined by God" becomes its own theologoumenon.[16] If there is a specifically feminist apophasis, it has been hovering with both positive and negative wings over the face of the abyss. For the abyss, upon closer meditation, is not an empty void awaiting a word of différance but our always already differential, always already engendering, *fluidity*. To associate this fluent circulation with the abyssal chaos of beginnings, with the deep of Genesis that is the Hebrew *tehom*, is to accept the gift of the creation in the very deconstruction of the metanarrative of one omnipotent origin.[17] The mystical oscillation of those wings over the face of the deep does not escape the world and its aching turbulence. It does not even escape gender politics.

For our language—feminist theology in its constructive self-consciousness, or the God-word chasing its male tail, language in all its circlings—comes upon the evidently fabricated political world of our common embodiment. The *logos* bumps up against its own constructions not just of *theos* but of *kosmos*. Not because there is *no* world, no flesh beyond our language, no body beyond discourse, but *because there is so much of it*. The boundless flowing matter, its *khora* that precedes and exceeds language as surely as any God, floods and short-circuits any common language.[18] It confronts us in our species' *un*common stylizations of gender and of gender enfleshed in the multiple contexts of ethnic and racial difference. On the path of deconstruction Ellen Armour pleaded for "whitefeminist theology" to give up on a unifying narrative and to instead "keep woman open as a site of contestation on which and through which theorizing and theologizing differences between women can take place."[19] "Keeping woman open" suggests a fluid space, a space churning with the waves of *tehom*, and thus a chance to waver at the boundary between identities, between certainties. When was not the abyss already fertile, cosmic compost, no precreation nothingness but a khoric space of possibility?

In the opening of and for us, women, gender cannot be abstracted from sexuality. So despite decades of fruitful theorizing, we still slip and slide between "gender" and "sex"; is sex what I *am* or what I *have*, or might not; or do we *do* sex, like gender, even if we are not having any? How many sexes and/or genders would we have to choose between? Coming into a similarly principled uncertainty, Judith Butler in a retrospective mood writes: "We try to speak in ordinary ways about these matters, stating our gender, disclosing our sexuality, but we are, quite inadvertently, caught up in ontological thickets and epistemological quandaries. Am I a gender after all? And do I 'have' a sexuality?"[20] These quandaries of sex/gender performativity propel and exceed academic queer theory. They push up against the unspeakable, the apophatic. But Butler rarely has the dilemmas of God-talk in mind. And even the most negative, the most apophatic, theology would not usually expect to encounter God's ineffability within this fluid opening between sex and gender.

Under the Sheets

In her satiric novel *White Teeth*, Zadie Smith captures the sexually unspeakable getting spoken in a conversation between three immigrant women in London: one Afro-Caribbean Jehovah's Witness and two Pakistani Muslims. One of the latter, Alsana, is arguing against her niece's feminist insistence upon sexual honesty between partners.

> "All this talk, talk, talk; all this 'I am this' and 'I am really like this' like in the papers, all this revelation . . ." about sex. When really "you do not want to know what is slimy underneath the bed and rattling in the wardrobe."
>
> "'Moreover,' says Alsana after a pause, folding her dimpled arms underneath her breasts, pleased to be holding forth on a subject close

to this formidable bosom, 'when you are from families such as ours you should have learned that silence, what is not said, is the very best recipe for family life.'

For all three have been brought up in strict, religious families, houses where God appeared at every meal, infiltrated every childhood game, and sat in the lotus position under the bedclothes with a torch to check nothing untoward was occurring."[21]

"What is not said" here signifies no classical apophatic reserve: Alsana's theology keeps sex, not God, unspeakable. But the glimpse of an immigrant Pakistani Allah in lotus position certainly thwarts the orientalism of our tantric icons. For this God under the sheets encrypts instead a common denominator of the Abrahamisms. At the end of the novel, the Jamaican protagonist's mother sits on a folding chair with the other "formidable Witness ladies," holding "a banner between her knees that states, simply, THE TIME IS AT HAND-REV 1:3."[22] Smith published her apocalyptic novel (with a comically counter-apocalyptic conclusion) in 2000. It was there to contest the millennial return of a multiply monotheistic and all-too-knowable patriarchy.

When it is the sexually censorious God who returns, the one who sniffs out our sex acts, the breaking of silence about sex and the breaking into theological speech by the second sex become a single double-edged project. What discourse can unseat that God of the bedroom flashlight? Straightforward atheism?

Too straight, replies feminist theology. We want an imaginary that gets back under the sheets of theology. A discourse that sends the prohibitive logos rattling against itself rather than mounting an opposing prohibition. A strategy that seduces rather than silences theology itself. Rather than a heroic atheology, feminist theology may be negotiating—under the cover of the sheets—a kind of metamorphosis. Thus the theologian Marcella Althaus-Reid, as satiric in her genre as Smith in hers, declares the queer God of an "indecent theology," flashing her light upon a Trinitarian orgy of love. Instead of omnipotence, she exposes "the omnisexuality of God." Her parody is revelatory. Behind it, but coming up close, very close, lies the multigenerational tradition, passing through a great diversity of gender and sexual voice, of an embodied divinity—of a "return [of] the lost presence of the polyamorous body to its theological discourse."[23]

That return is to the discourse of the incarnation. Its so-called scandal smacks of indecency: the embodiment of a disembodied God who might paternally patrol bodies but certainly is pure and free of flesh Himself. The passion of its excessive love was soon, however, funneled into apocalyptic vengeance: If God became flesh it was to pay off our debts. And we did not repay Him with due thanks and worship. Is that not why he is returning to give us what we deserve? The Jews would not admit he was God, the pagans never got it, the liberal oversexed Christians lost it, and they are all gonna get it. Gift indeed.

No doubt.

And yet there may be another, a less poisonous, return, another way of picking up where that lone incarnation left off. It may still be possible to receive that single overused, endlessly regifted body as a gift—indeed, a gift that, strange to say, has barely been opened. For it got wrapped hardly a century after the swaddling clothes in the doctrine of an absolute metaphysical exception, that of the one-and-only, once-for-all clothing of God in human *carne*. The exception proved the rule: the rule of the discarnate deity over all the rebellious carnalities. What if we make the oddly orthodox move of reading that singular body as a primary disclosure of something unspeakable about God—of what Paul found scandalous for his monotheism and foolish for the Greeks and that, for a moment, was tantalizingly new. The body of God incarnate morphs between the body of one Jew and the corpus of a radically diverse community. But Paul's church-body, with its multigifted interlimbed corporeality, began early on to define itself by its exclusions of sexually improper bodies. Clearly an indecently fleshly public was showing up to ingest the incarnate One.

And if the church fathers then soon offered up that provocative newness on the altar of an absolute singularity, they did so first wanting to protect the novelty of the Christ-event. But then to guard it from all competing novelties, they swathed its unspeakable flesh in Christological exceptionalism. The Christ could henceforth be endlessly regifted, in an orderly fashion. At least this was the hope. Otherwise the love that rains and shines on the just and the unjust alike might grow wild, wanton, out of bounds. Unspeakable effects were materializing in the early churches and particularly, it seems, in women, as signaled by John of Patmos's threats to "Jezebel's" congregation and Paul's warning to the Corinthian women prophets.[24]

Carnal Apophasis

Yet what would the divine love, the love that *is* God, *be* if not love out of all bounds? Its boundlessness got recognized in the apophatic tradition first as infinity, the not-finite not reducible to finite language.²⁵ It would not unfold in indifference to all the not-Jesus bodies but in intimacy with them, through them, *as* them. Job's ostrich and Leviathan, Jesus's sparrow and lily, hint at the amorous return of a divinity that had never left. Where would she/he/it go? Out of the bounds of monotheism, perhaps. Or of the triangulated trinity. Or of our mind. But boundlessness admits of no mere absence. Christendom in its dominant thrust reproves and disciplines the amatory imaginary. By opposing the exceptional incarnation to our routine carnality, the body (*soma*) to the flesh (*sarx*), the One to the Others, one might say that the regifted Christology in effect puts a stop to further divine enfleshment: *incarnatus interruptus*.

So one might in response call upon a marginal but tenacious subtradition from which feminist theology has sometimes drawn, according to which the distinctive incarnation that was Jesus reveals a boundless process of divine embodiment. It has antecedents in every mystical panentheism, from Irenaeus and Dionysius through Nicholas of Cusa and Angelus Silesius; even in John Wesley, when he designates as "practical Atheism" any denial that God is the soul of the universe, the *anima mundi*.²⁶ It has taken the form since Charles Hartshorne—mobilized for ecofeminist theology by Grace Jantzen, Sallie McFague, and Ivone Gebara—of the God whose body is the universe. Incarnation no longer reads as ontological exception but as cosmic rule. An unruly rule: The doctrine of the incarnation refuses to be abstracted from its *carnality*. This divinity embodied in all the flesh of the world materializes under cover in all manner of unchristian and irreligious activities. It can be found under the sheets, taking pleasure in our pleasure. And suffering our sorrows. Might it unseat the One with the flashlight more effectively than a straight non-God?

The polyamorous deity would inhabit a boundless multiplicity of embodiment. It suggests a species of panentheism, which, more than pantheism, allows room for interplay. If the God-trope is still inviting, it will no more reduce to the *totality of bodies* than to a *single body*. The divine would neither be exhaustively incarnate in all nor in anything; yet nothing would materialize outside of it. For the margin of the unknowable, which reserves difference in the midst of intimacy, even transcendence in the midst of—and so not transcendence of—immanence, remains inexhaustible.

The logos thus poetically written into the flesh of the universe is not limited to any revealed word. It may lure language from the darkness that enfolds every body; in that darkness, in its invisibility, pulse waves of possibilities. They extend oceanically to the horizon of the impossible. The possibilities offer themselves for a multiplicity of embodiments. Jean-Luc Marion suggests possibilities already realized in Christ the eternal logos, which we may receive as a pure and unilateral gift. Perhaps the possibilities of a multiple incarnation, mingling in the impure reciprocities of the world, look more like the *posse ipsum* (possibility itself) of Nicholas of Cusa, like Alfred North Whitehead's "primordial nature of God" or Richard Kearney's *God Who May Be*.[27] Its attractive power would gently and precisely take the place of omnipotence. But precisely in its margin of difference it opens a way, as the Black church says, where there is no way, a possibility in the face of the impossible.

The trope of God will in this sense invariably signify some personal relationship to the possible, a relation that collapses the impersonal infinity, like the quantum wave-function, into a particular actualization. But is not this relationality just what insults the projection-busting intelligence? God, however we translate Him/Her/It/We/They or You, will not come free of the trace of personality. In effect, the metaphors of personhood protect an otherness that is as such ipso facto infinitely impersonal. Yet the personhood that presumably protects the fluent alterity of God is never quite *other* enough. It soon gets refrozen in its high- and still literally Heness, his personal pronominality and his ontotheological nounhood. He reigns, dead or alive, as the substantive of substance metaphysics. Neither apophatically transcendent, for unquestionable verbalizations are confused with faith, nor boundlessly immanent, for He brooks for Himself no flesh besides Jesus.

The answering iconoclasm may be driven home by the very *iconoplasm* of She-signifiers: the constructivity of God-talk *shows*. But at this edge of projective personhood, feminist theology always and rightly falters. Is our divine gal-pal any freer from the person-problem than the guy in the sky? Indeed, would any widened range of metaphors, picking up where the interrupted incarnation left off, overcome the intimacy of what is called "a personal relationship with God"? They may get loose from the reified *person*, praying with Meister Eckhart (and Caputo next to him) for "God . . . [to] make me free of 'God.'"[28] But then if the feminist unsaying of the divine patriarch were finally to yield a bottomless uncertainty as to any theologically or politically or, heaven help us, queerly correct names, whether new or ancient, would we just fall silent again? Will feminist theology turn out to be the women's auxiliary of the death of God brotherhood after all? Ironically, then, not so different in theological effect from its mirror opposite, the tradition that "women should be silent in the churches" (1 Cor. 14:34).

The Gift of Possibility

To return to the opening question: What gift does feminist theology offer in this returning of religion? This, at least: In our struggle with and within the *theos-logos*, possibilities keep opening where they were none before—in an indeterminate space, between sex and gender, between theism and atheism, between language and silence, between too much and too little. In this space nothing we say of God, including the presumption of his/her/its existence, can be said to be just *true*. But God might remain a gifted metaphor for the space itself, the opening in which truth can be told. "In spirit and truth" (John 4:23). As Gianni Vattimo says, in the same Johannine spirit: "The truth that shall set us free is true only because it frees us. If it does not free us, we ought to throw it away."[29] In the interest of liberation, feminist theology has done a lot of throwing; we seem to be returning God to His makers, over and over. Over a couple of generations, we have never rested with any single naming strategy. We return our own names ever again, restlessly, nervously, creatively. As though each image, *eikon*, might at any moment turn to idol. Nonetheless, some of us find "God" returning. Even through the porthole of that gendering *o* of *theos*.

Will the returning deity perhaps swing both ways—received as gift, returned as idol—always? A waver without end? Maybe the gift can only be received if we can claim the double return as a possible strength. The strength of this possibility seems to appear only as we face its improbability. Up close, like the medieval "cloud of unknowing," the *aporia* itself evinces a certain *porosity*. Reading Derrida with a little help from Caputo, this might be the point where "the borders of the kingdom become porous."[30] His exegesis of the *basileia tou theou* echoes the passionate priorities of prophetic Christianity. And yet every pore threatens to close again: How can we linger long with the term "kingdom"? And who wants a "queendom" but for a term or two? And anyway, the translation of the kingdom of God into "the commonwealth of God" requires yet another pore or path.[31] (The linguistic wavering exasperates and illustrates.) Nonetheless, as Caputo was saying: At the point of hospitable porosity, the borders waver "in a kind of 'holy undecidability' between theism and atheism, among Christian, Jew and Muslim, between theology and a-theology . . . religion and religion without religion, and this precisely in the name of the God who loves the stranger."[32]

It is the Hebrew tradition of the love of the stranger that seems to have served as Jesus's hermeneutical test and key, opening up the stranger love of the indecent and of the enemy, love not performing self-martyring masochisms but amatory excess. The deconstructive undecidable is insistently not indecision. It marks the pause, the uncertainty as to our own certainties, by which we give some alien voice in or beside ourselves a chance. If as feminist theologians (for instance) we accept the undecidability in our work as precisely our receptiveness to the excess, the unexpected, the gift, then it does not paralyze action. It may *free* us to make our uncertain decisions. In grace—with Luther for a moment—to sin boldly. Even to go ahead and do theology.

The gift, then, is neither the undecidability itself nor the impossible as such. It is something unfolded from the indeterminate, and a fold, as the German *Falte* reveals, falters. The gift to unfold, to open, would be the particular possibility that offers itself, that lures us to receive it, to *realize* it. To embody it. But we do not escape the aporia of a return of that which had never quite come. For it has not yet quite been received. Christendom, as its feminists, along with about two millennia of other Christians have noted, did not "get" Christ. The Incarnation, like "the gift," has been neatly packaged in its substantive singularity—this one beautifully boxed gift and no other. But if the coming, the other who comes, is not to be the *same* returning with a vengeance, then in the difference of this coming the pores of possibility open. Sometimes anxiously, sometimes adventurously, ever amorously.

If the very notion of gift and its possibility comes to us afresh, if it comes by the grace of deconstruction, it may also need to resist a certain deconstructive gesture of purification: the impossible purity of the gift, aligned with an absolute alterity, or a messianicity purged of any embodied messiah, signifiers cleansed of the marks of matter, ground, earth, flesh. Or a utopic democracy pure of our paltry experiments so far, the absolute "to come" of a pure gift, a gift without *return*. Is it the imagined *purity* of the gift that renders it the impossible, that threatens to reify the impossible as the ideal, to dream the impossible dream? *The impossible surely does confront us; but it is the possible that lures us.* That offers its gift. Left in a hyperbolic dream of purity, the gift becomes the impossible itself; for the gift supposedly brooks no return, not even that of gratitude. So "return" in the currently unavoidable gift discourse denotes *reciprocity*, as in giving a gift *in* return. It is not the Derridean sense of the unconditional but of the purity of the gift that feminist theology may have to return, that is, graciously refuse to accept. Here is the rare point where I have agreed with John Milbank against Derrida and Jean-Luc Marion (at one point where they do agree). Against the opposition of all reciprocity to the gift, Milbank insists on an "asymmetrical reciprocity." But then he unwittingly makes reciprocity itself impossible by sacrificing it to *impassibility*, which for him characterizes "the absolute creative power of the Father."[33] And unilateral power bodes far worse for feminists than unilateral gift!

We all might concur, however, that a gift is not a gift if it is *withheld* because of uncertainty as to whether it will be reciprocated. Love takes the risk of *initiating*. It makes the first improbable offering without prescience of outcome. The gospels want us to emulate that amorous gesture without presuming that the recipient will respond in kind. At the same time, we are asked to receive that gift, its treasures, its invitations, its seeds, and, no matter what, to bear fruit. To actualize the possible. And yet in one problematic parable the steward who just saved the money is tossed into the outer darkness: "You ought to have invested my money with the bankers, and on my return I would have received what was my own with interest" (Matt. 25:4). An impure gift indeed, this clumsy parable, all too anachronizable by capitalism. But in its own context it captures something disturbingly unsentimental: The gift may be unconditionally *given*, but its effect depends upon its *active reception*. Not because the Big Boss might fire us, but because to take a gift is to take a constitutive action, formative of the giver and the receiver. So how would a gift-giver, even anonymous, be indifferent to the reception? That would be no gift but a mere giveaway. Attention to the difference of the receiver, and so to the difference that might therefore be made by the gift, makes the gift a gift. But the difference made, in surprise, enjoyment, and use, *is* the return. This love that shines or rains on just and unjust alike—across, in other words, the most radical difference—would not signify *in*difference to whether the unjust remain unjust. It continues to shine, no matter how dense the cloud cover. This counter-apocalyptic care, beyond judgement, beyond resentment, always comes again. What it can offer—which is to say, what can be received— may, however, be sorely diminished. And still the rays come.

Actualizing this radiance we too radiate. In *eros* we rightly *desire* the reciprocity but in *agape* may not *count* on it. The privileging of a desiring eros against the unilateral agape, against any sacrificial economy, had made possible the emergence of feminist theology in the first place.[34] Unilateral grace is just the other edge of the blade of unilateral power. If I give with no interest in receiving your response, I am devoid of vulnerability, I am impassive, unmoved, pure act. The eros, when it is not thrown into opposition to agape, realizes itself not in a passionate demand and not in a pious self-sacrifice but in the fuller embodiment of passion, the com/passion that makes passion possible again even after the loss of its object and the betrayal of its hope.

I am suggesting that feminist theology will not refuse the gift of the infinite giver, of the very notion of such a gift. We will not send theology back to its senders. To simply return God just as S/He/It is making such fetching returns would be for any theology an act not just of theocide but of suicide. But what we offer—in return—is not a unilateral but a relational gift. If we want to deconstruct omnipotence, a desire that most feminist and poststructuralist thinkers share with all process theologians, we might need to accept an *impure* gift *as* a gift. Outside of ancient ritual contexts of purification, the "pure" itself will always echo the unmixed, the One, the Same. And it will perilously suggest a cultured transcendence of those racially marked, tribal potlatches renarrated by Marcel Mauss at the origin of the twentieth-century gift debate.[35]

Might we, for a change, imagine icons of infinite impurity, incarnate in the dust and the dirt of us all? Mingled in the multiplicity of selves, sexes, species, stars, such divinity might find itself endlessly entangled in the matter of the world, endlessly materializing in the reciprocities of and with the world. Down on the ground, at any rate, on a living planet endangered by an imperial denial of all of our living interdependence, the web of creation might not mend without a counter-apocalyptic conversion to grateful interrelation. Elite ingratitude is devouring the life of the planet. It reeks, as ecofeminism demonstrates, of millennia of matricidal disdain of the dirty work of the earth, of all the mothers—and of all the others of class, race, and species who render material and thankless service. Whose ever-returning gifts our species has been taking for granted.

The grant may be running out. Deconstructive undecidability highlights the difficulty, the trade-offs, the local apocalypses of needed decision; it does not excuse any wavering in indecision about, for example, global warming.[36] The collective paralysis, compounded by the habit of ingratitude for the gifts of the earth itself, will just assure the apocalyptic scale of destruction. Not surprisingly, many younger people find hope for the shared future impossible. And then they cannot actualize their possibilities, they cannot give their gifts. What we must convey in the face of unpromising odds may be less *the impossibility of the gift than the gift of the possible*. The possibility, for example, that we earthlings will not only survive into the far future but *better* actualize the promise of our genesis collective.

Life is the ferment of possibility. Actively receiving the gift of our shared life, whether or not the metaphor of a divine giver becomes explicit, releases the effervescence of gratitude. We actualize our possibilities only in enmeshed networks of asymmetrical reciprocity. Our bodies are networks of networks within larger networking fields. This boundless multiplicity of interdependent socialities offers a theological supplement to the singular event of incarnation.

We may call this supplement—the alternative to the repetitions of the *incarnatus interruptus*—the *intercarnation*. It might be narrated as the becoming body of God—but only if the God-metaphor does not defeat the multiplicity.[37] This fluent, fleshy interactivity will not sustain what Laurel Schneider is calling "logic of the One."[38] It supports cooperation by way of mutual differentiation. Forgive me if I preach: But for the difficult relationality that forms the matrix of feminist theology in its specifically Christian heritage, the multitude of the *basileia*, now and coming, amplifies the shared body—returned and returning—of the Christian messiah. Porous solidarity does hope for the gift of a messianic arrival. But for Christians does that boil down to the return of Jesus? Did he not already rather fully give his gifts? He could have lived longer and done more, but do we think of him as having failed to actualize his potential? Quite apart from the question of the competition with the Jewish sense of the messiah who did not come, would not a coming "again," the Christ revenant, partake of the radical novum of Jesus's life? And so be just as unpredictable, as mysteriously linked to but irreducible to its antecedent event? If so then Christians can share Jewish—and Derridean—hope for a coming that is not mere return, a repetition of the same. Like Gilles Deleuze irreligiously intended "repetition as the habitation of difference," repetitions of the way of the Jewish body of God called Jesus would—if partaking of the gift of his lively spirit—offer hospitality, not confinement, to that which is yet "to come." When not clogged by the Christological monopoly, there has poured through the porosity of the body of Christ the messianic energy of the revolutionary movements of much of the world. As those movements recognize in each other an intercarnational potential, what polyamorous politics, spirituality, planetarity might yet come to be?

They would be different but never dissociable from the Christ event. Of course the aporia of "his" impossible representation, an inclusion by exclusivism, is still enshrined in the arguments for the nonordination of women, in the Christian lock on salvation, and in the returning waves, stoked by a revived Islamophobia, of the religious right. An aporia is answered only by *poria*, porosity. And that body, only nameable as Christ if the word opens rather than closes its own boundaries, itself signifies and amplifies the porosity of our every body. And so the body of the intercarnation infinitely exceeds that particular, if infinitely signifying, body. The "flesh of the world," in Merleau-Ponty's promising invocation, exceeds the sum of its bodies. Indeed, bodies subjugated by Christian conquest still exhibit the fluent incarnations of relationality in ways lost to the conquerors. The intercarnate body resembles, for example, Sylvia Marcos's account of the pre-Conquistadoran genders of the Mesoamerican body as "a vortex generated by the dynamic confluence of multiple entities, both material and immaterial and often contradictory."[39] Those entities combine and recombine in endless and vulnerable interplay. Before and beyond Christianity, evolutions of entangled embodiment offer their gifts, lost and found, refused or exploited by the Christian monocarnation, but in no contradiction to the porous Christbody or its polyamorous God.

Uncertain Returns

The love that brings this network of reciprocity to fruition—to intercarnation—may itself be barely possible. Ask Hadewijch, the thirteenth-century beguine poet of *Minne*, the troubadour's name for love, and the poet's name, a grammatically feminine noun, for God. "Where is now the consolation and the peace of Love with which she provided me so splendidly at first?" Hadewijch yearns for the gift of her return. There is no triumphalism in this eschatology:

> At great favors before the time,
> And at great promises before the gift,
> No one can rejoice overmuch.
> Both have largely failed us:
> > False joys
> > That implied the possession of Love's being
> Have swept me far from myself.[40]

What an achingly evolved self, that can write her disappointment so sharply. And return, with ardor, to herself, the self from which she had been swept, and only so to the love of Love . . . this erotic spirituality that tilts toward apophasis communicates the struggle of a woman to find voice, a struggle with the cruelty of men and the queerness of Love. It opens a truth-space beyond the possession of truth, God, or being, beyond the possessable *being* of Love. (Thus Marion's apothegm, "Gxd loves without being.")[41] "I let Love be all that she is; I cannot understand her fierce wonders."[42] Incomprehension, however, does not silence the poetry. "Because I wish to live free," she persists. What it meant eight centuries ago for a woman to "wish to live free," we can barely imagine. She was practicing an amorous austerity—depending on, indeed receiving with immense creativity, a gift that so often seems to fail: "I cannot do without this gift,/I have nothing else: I must live on Love."[43]

If feminist theology is to receive the very gift it gives, it perches close to this amorous apophasis. It cannot flee its epistemological double edge of affirmation and negation. Perhaps, now, perhaps, we are learning to be humbled rather than humiliated by the quandaries and thickets of our discourse of sex, gender, and love—divine or human. The eros of variously affirmed sexualities bubbles into the struggle of love for a sustaining justice. Then we can construct a pluralism of embodied difference rather than another relativism of indifference. And in the theological register of this relational pluralism reverberate the endless multiplicity of divine names for the nameless. Of finite bodies for an infinite intercarnation.

Any divinity I can "get" is unfurling, unfinished, unfolding in our own unpredictable becomings, which come, which fold or crumple back, as her multiplicative body. Under the sheets, perhaps, of the old luminous darkness? Of some new dark energy? Perhaps the double gesture of return will prove more effectual than the double-edged sword. We receive, we embody—we give back to the world some overflow. And we may return—refused—the theologies that do not give back, that come down to final payback. We recognize them by their s/words of final truth; they are betrayed by their defenses against the multitude of bodies of the earth and the manifold ways they have unfolded.

The unfolding of the infinite as the manifold makes manifest an irreducible plurisingularity hinted at in the trinity.[44] It may help us shift now from the feminist logos of the *cutting* edge to something more promising than "postfeminism": a transfeminism that ripples through the multiplicity of movements now giving their gifts—of a queer polychrome species dangerously distinctive among the many talented species of the living earth. These are gifts we receive now in rigorous gratitude. Or waste them and thereby ourselves.

For all the love in the universe cannot evaporate for us the uncertainty of what is coming. Or who. Or not. We cast God on the waters and S/He/It returns manifold, many-faced and faceless. In the gentler mystery of love or apocalyptically shrouded, deadly or just dead. The gift of feminist theology will not have replaced an expiring father with a maternal reassurance. Feminist theology, by whatever name, has always been beginning again, and never from nothing. Not unlike the earth, which awaits the unlikely gift of our still-possible solidarity. "In the beginning there can only be dying, the abyss, the first laugh."[45]

CHAPTER 2

"And Truth—So Manifold!": Transfeminist Entanglements

> We learned the Whole of Love—
> The Alphabet—the Words—
> A Chapter—then the mighty Book—
> Then—Revelation closed—
>
> But in Each Other's eyes
> An Ignorance beheld—
> Diviner than the Childhood's—
> And each to each, a Child—
>
> Attempted to expound
> What Neither—understood—
> Alas, that Wisdom is so large—
> And Truth—so manifold!
>
> —EMILY DICKINSON, "We Learned the Whole of Love" (1862)[1]

I

It is the sense of transit, transition, and translation involved in the non-linear and necessary evolution of feminism that I wish to consider here under the heading of *transfeminism*. It is just an opening word, an experimental neologism for minding the uncertainty and the multiplicity of the situations of women at the beginning—yes, still beginning—of a new and quaking millennium.

Transfeminism, emphatically, does not mean *postfeminism*. That term, advanced already in the '80s, implies that feminism has already delivered on its promises, thank you very much, but the second wave got essentialist, strident, anti-male, orthodox, old, unsexy; now it is time to think of women just as people. At this point, postfeminism—named or unnamed—may

---

A first form of this essay was delivered as keynote at a European gathering on feminist relational theology under the leadership of Professor Lisa Isherwood, Director of the Institute for Theological Partnership, at the University of Winchester, July 2012.

suggest more of a *Sex and the City* mood or a *got*-it-already assumption than a considered antifeminist positionality. And of course, especially in the vicinity of theological symbols (God the Father & Co.), postfeminism reverts quickly to prefeminism.

Transfeminism would grant that feminism has almost from the start been in danger of freezing into its own orthodoxy, even as it challenges various ortho-patriarchies. Any movement that speaks a new truth strongly—and repeats it—risks orthodoxy. And will get old. There have been no stronger truth-openings in the twentieth century than those provoked by the movement of women, within and beyond the churches. And whatever else they are, truths, if they are, are openings, *dis-closures*, no? So to consider feminism in this moment as transfeminism is to consider a discourse and a practice in transition, transversing the andromorphic closures of rule or habit; it is transgression in service of transformation. It is also to admit that I no longer teach a course called "feminist theology" and only sometimes assign a preponderance of texts by women. And I now write shamelessly on for pages at a time with no explicit reference to a woman author, female figure, biblical heroine, or even to the question of gender or sex. I consider this symptomatic not of any feminist exhaustion or postfeminist triumph but of an indelibly feminist transgression of identitarian enclosure. The transformativity of "gender" now comes entangled in the manifold of pressing matters of embodied context, of race and economics and ecology, and most intimately of sex and its LGBTQ alphabet. The trans identities of the "T" reverberate with their fresh disclosiveness in an enfoldingly transfeminist perspective.[2] Let transfeminism then signal the transformation of the identity politics of the so-called second wave into an ocean of waves; and at the same time, a warning against any naïve confidence in our historic achievement.

The ultimate context or ocean of transformation is, of course, the context of the ultimate itself. That is why this text is theological. So this transfeminist version of feminist theology will come into play here with three criteria I am finding indispensable to being a theologian or, for that matter, a woman: *entanglement*, considered as relationality stretched from intimacy to infinity; *unknowing*, considered as apophatic uncertainty stretched from ignorance to wisdom; and *multiplicity*, considered as the teaching of the manifold, stretched from orthodoxy into pluralism. Logos, including that of theology, speaks honestly only when it minds its own contextual relativity. It beholds there its own irreducible uncertainty—and therefore the taunting, tantalizing multiplicity of truth.

2

"Truth so manifold": this poem of Emily Dickinson's has haunted me. Its author was not part of the early suffrage movement or, for that matter, of any movement. Nonetheless, and oddly, it will help to ease open the transfeminist criteria I have just named. It is by the mid-nineteenth-century New England poet whose aura of tragically reclusive Victorian femininity has obscured for most feminists her dark brilliance; one can miss the edgy radicality of what she calls her "compound vision."

> We learned the Whole of Love—
> The Alphabet—the Words—
> A Chapter—then the mighty Book—
> Then—Revelation closed—

Pause there. She is referring to her good Christian education. "We learned the Whole of Love": Dickinson seems to be summing up the orthodox certitudes of biblical Christianity. She lends it the texture of its letters, its literality, its revelatory Book, and then—Revelation closed—*dash*. It takes a moment to realize that she *means* all the layers of her own compressed signifiers. The book of Revelation is the final book of The Book; it closes the canon. And with it, history itself. It seems that revelation itself, as *apokalypsis*, as dis/closure, has closed for her, and with it perhaps salvation history itself. And her private abyss of lost love echoes in this closure. This stanza makes theological trouble: the already-known, already-learned totality of love is by definition closed, in its traditional rendition: This is the word of God, and Christian salvation offers the final closure. Period.

For her that closure was inseparable from the other closures imposed by conventional faith, family, and language. In another poem she writes: "They shut me up in Prose—As when a little Girl/They put me in the Closet—Because they liked me 'still'—." Again, the dash. Again, the prophetic use of language. One need not—tempting as it is—anachronistically sexualize her closet to recognize the proto-feminist force of the image. It is the silencing of her young female voice she protests. And, as for so many women, the violence of the silencing takes the form of the imposition of prose: the poetophobic dominance of the straight—oh very straight—logos.

And note how the closet itself is already resisted by the sign of the dash. The dash is a much discussed syntactical transgressiveness of her writing, where lines, stanzas, and whole poems end in dashes, insistently refusing closure. Closeting. The closure of prose in its syntactical strictures, the closure of the closet. "Psychologically as well as syntactically," writes Robert Weisbuch, "Dickinson's dashes create a pressure, a tension, a nervous breath which tells its own story."[3] At the same time they serve as a transitional "hinge."

> But in Each Other's Eyes
> An Ignorance beheld—

In the intimate gaze of the other—perhaps another with whom one shared the narrative that closed—ignorance has taken the place of all that we had learned, the totality of belief. And in each other's eyes we glimpse that appalling blankness. An abysmal unknowing seems to descend. But she is tricky. What follows immediately performs a startling shift of signification:

> Diviner than the Childhood's—

So no mere lack of knowledge after all, no childish naïveté, no simple void of faith. This ignorance seems itself to be marked as something "diviner." In the open eyes, has the closure been answered by some new dis/closure? Might we associate this divine ignorance with the tradition of negative theology, with the "knowing ignorance"? The *docta ignorantia* was a fifteenth-century alternative to the oblivious ignorance of believers who do not know how much they do not know, the know-it-all ignorance of those who already have the truth.[4] Those who think they have learned "the Whole of Love"? Is Dickinson, in her late Puritan, transcendentalist context, hovering mysteriously close to the sensibility of apophatic mysticism—that negative theology that unsays whatever it first says of divinity? That unsays apodictic prose through apophatic metaphor?

Her next line seems to negate the prior one, intensifying our unknowing even of this ignorance:

> And each to each, a Child—
> Attempted to expound
> What Neither—understood—
> Alas,

It seems that the very relation of each to each now makes possible a new effort to speak. There is insinuated a new beginning: becoming a child, again? The perspectival interplay of this becoming-child seems to be reinforcing our attention to speech out of its element. Incomprehension at once pulls us to explain even as it thwarts our capacities. No grace comes cheap to Dickinson. But when it comes it bursts with revelatory force.

. . . that Wisdom is so large—

In other words, this unknowing encodes not a void, not a *nihil* of knowing, but an excess, not of knowledge but of Wisdom. We will want to consider the size and the spirit of this sophic immensity. One thinks of Luce Irigaray's inflection of the infinite, *infini*, as the unfinished. This incomprehensible Wisdom reveals no dearth of truth but, to the contrary, a perspective then and now impossible for standard models of knowledge or of faith:

And Truth—so manifold!

Mirrored in the eyes of the others, she announces the multiplicity of truth. It is the excess of a wisdom liberated from the closure of revelation that *dis*closes its manifold. Augustine, in his exegesis of the first couple of verses of Genesis, had already come upon that manifold: "an abundance of true meanings."[5] But the thinking of that originative multiplicity did not quite make it past the doctrinal closure of his own subsequent writings. The pluralist potential remained latent. What Laurel Schneider calls the "Logic of the One" has proven formidable in the formation even of a trinitarian orthodoxy.[6] We conspired on the *Polydoxy* project because we find nothing so vital to the spirit, indeed even to its attempts to "speak rightly" its orthodoxies, than attention to our entanglement, each to each, in the abundance of this multiplicity.[7]

So perhaps you sense how this diminutive, reclusive, New England poet hints at a possible transfeminism. Dickinson's transgressive truth manifold—her compound vision, contracting, achingly, so much into such brief poems—lets us expound what we also may not yet quite understand. And, in particular, where feminist revelation threatens in this millennium to shut down, it might convey "the alphabet, the words"—uncertainly, relationally, multiply—of genders, sexes, loves, opening in a manifold Wisdom.

3

What I am trying to expound, what keeps luring me and eluding me, could be called a negatively theological relationalism. But that sounds more negative than negative theology ever is. Perhaps, then, an apophatic entanglement.[8] It attends to how what we most need to know exceeds our capacities to capture it even though we are inseparable from it. It therefore inspires, requires, fresh speech. Even fresh theology, perhaps better called theopoetics. And, for some of us, the history of our feminism, by way of so many paradigms of gender, entangled us in other intimately entangled paradigms—of sexuality, race, ecology, ability, economics, and so on. In truth, we can only unfold in and as a whole manifold of issues: all too many, many too true.

I went through seminary in the mid '70s, just as feminist theology was coming to be as such and as an organ of second-wave feminism. Then subsequently, in a PhD program, I gleefully worked with Rita Nakashima Brock to bring Mary Daly (*GynEcology* just) to campus. I was absorbed in the prophetic intensity of the voices of women, worried and engaged by debates about how you could "be a feminist and a Christian too," and unconcerned to relativize the identity—that of Woman—that was being "heard into our own speech."[9] Of course, I was not oblivious to the fact that my male doctoral advisor was doing some sensitive hearing of me to my own speech, explicitly as feminist. And I had been gripped by the relational cosmology of process theology. For all its anglo-male metaphysics, it helped to articulate the feminist meaning of interdependence, constituted in a sociality that precedes and exceeds any single identity or context, even that of the human. Whitehead in the 1920s had taken a responsive sociality down to the level of the quantum interactions (and also spoke at rallies on behalf of women's suffrage). And by the '80s I was hungry to think the manifold of populations and perspectives in its complication of the feminist voice. I had grown mildly allergic to the unifying feminist certainties, even as I depended upon them. (Social movements come swollen with auto-allergic reactions.) Nonetheless as the wavelets of the second wave swelled and crashed, the conceptual carnage on the US scene was considerable. The tension between a monolithic focus on gender and the needs of lesbians was difficult but often contained within the same Euro-American cadres. And Black women, but then a wide spectrum of women of color, two-thirds-world women as well as the hyphenated -American identities, were talking back, now not just to the pale male but, painfully, to the white Woman. Breaking up a political illusion of growing unity, these voices in their multiplicity made clear that we whitefeminists did not already *know* them, did not speak for them, but must first be still and listen. Not easy for women only just unlearning an imposed stillness.

Yet some of us have sought out—as part of the very unlearning—another stillness. So I have sometimes called upon an "apophasis of gender": As in the ancient mysticism of unknowing, the negation of what we thought we knew opens us to an otherness that we have yet to understand.[10]

Mystery thwarts mastery. It confronts us with our own ignorance, be it imposed or inevitable. So the negation makes possible a new affirmation, something oddly like the *docta ignorantia*, in each other's eyes. Far from an excuse to remain ignorant, such teaching teaches me how much more I have to learn and can learn. One can unwrap this excess only as multiplicity. For example, in terms of the feminist folds: it opens, with no linear necessity, from a genderfold into a colorfold to a queerfold to the manifold itself.[11] The manifold serves as place holder, an infinity of finitudes, for the open sequence of intersecting, entangling, and asymmetrical social contexts (gendersexraceethnicityclassspecies . . .). And surely the ellipsis of the open-ended list of names—what Judith Butler adorably dubbed the "embarrassed etc."—recalls Dickinson's destabilizing dash—. Moreover, it recalls not just namings but unnamings: We were not ladies, we were women—a term then problematized by sexual identity; we were lesbian, then LGBTQIA (though never quite Dickinson's alphabetic "whole of love"), or just queer; no longer negro but Black, then African American, womanist now, but no, some remain Black feminists; and we are Hispanic or Latina/o, or mujerista or—. We always leave some out, and they, or we, negated, roar self-affirmingly back, briefly silencing us/them again. And what about ageism? The differently abled? Religious difference? Animals? Or, pardon, nonhuman animals? And the Earth, planet, Gaia, her/itself?

Of course, this restless tumult of issues, the instability of naming, has provoked not just postfeminist eye-rolling for decades. One may laugh off, or lament, the impossibility of getting a liberating list stabilized in language. But might we instead welcome its excess as the symptom of "Wisdom so large"? Indeed, it echoes the apophatic affirmation of the many names of that which infinitely eludes any name. It demonstrates how our inextricable entanglement in each other's contexts, from the personal through the political to the planetary, makes any notion of a saturated or a separable context delusional. That separability was the problem with identity politics from the start.

We meant to take account of the social nature of the self by insisting on context. A good start. But we named those contexts as though they were divided from each other by evident boundaries; that is how gender and race and class were made knowable. All too knowable, eventually. A kind of essentialist closure, sealed sometimes more by knee-jerk suspicion than by conversation, hardened notions of identity and context. But if social contexts are no more discretely bounded than individuals, they live by intersection and interdependence as surely as do selves. It is no accident that from the start, voices of the most vulnerable within the women's movement were countering the delusion of a monolithic identity context. For instance, the notion of *simultaneity* was articulated already in the 1970s by the Combahee River Collective to express the complexity of the situation of Black women as enmeshed—simultaneously—in race, class, gender, and sexual oppressions. And then the critical race theorist Kimberlé Crenshaw's famous notion of *intersectionality* theorized the same challenge over a decade later.[12] Though one need not infer that womanists were in general less prone to essentialism than others, it was African American women who were from the beginnings of the second wave already pointing beyond the "embarrassed etc." of competing contexts of oppression to a systemic complexification.

Methods poststructuralist, post- and de-colonial, have intensified the work of multiplicity, pitting difference and multiplicity against all simplifying closures, all uniform contextualizations. And all along feminist theology has been branching into ecofeminist theology. Our sociality can no longer be described as merely human. Increasingly we recognize the hideous peril to which our civilization has subjected the context of all our contexts. We begin to understand that we have not understood, alas, the most elemental truth of all—the delicate interdependence composing the living earth. These transfeminist vectors all converge upon a manifold that is not a mere many, not a bunch of single ones, not a set of single identities externally related. Their "mutual immanence," in Whitehead's parlance, is crucial. The wisdom of relationalism invites no relativism of merely many contexts—you in yours and me in mine, competing for scarce resources. It invites, rather, a conspiracy of complexification: the work of a multi*pli*city connected by the *pli*, the fold, between each of its members. Each *plies* the earth as living manifold. All things are unfolding, materializing, in multiplicity, and simultaneously being enfolded in complex unity. This process is open-ended, *infini*, unfinished. And, ultimately, theological.

The cosmological breadth of this embodied relationalism has not gone unnoticed by women far less known than Dickinson. I occasionally get possessed by its ancestral female voices, some of whom wrote theopoetic prose, such as the British viscountess Anne Conway or, more recently, Antoinette Brown Blackwell.[13] In 1914 Blackwell wrote *The Making of the Universe: Evolution the Continuous Process Which Derives the Finite from the Infinite*. "Constitutionally we are at once individual and social," she writes. "All phases of our amazingly complex activities work together in correlation."[14] Besides a handful of naturalist philosophers, few in the still Newtonian world were thinking of such co-relationality. "Creation is a boundless and endless adaptation of coworking methods. Every invention is a new correlation."[15] This cosmos infinite and unfinished in its interactivity is unfolding in our own constituent relationality. Hear also the stunning anticipation of process cosmology. "Process, as a total, is continuous and unending, but it cooperates in the relative as local, temporary pulses or waves of action and reaction, and some of its results move onward in endless threads of changes."[16] I do not, of course, argue that it was Blackwell's gender that opened her to the vision of the self as a cosmic interactivity; but I have long argued (not quite as far back as Blackwell) that there were fewer obstacles in female than in andronormative socialization to the breakthrough of a relational ontology.[17]

To encode the boundless connectivity of all localities, I am in *this* century intrigued by the metaphor of quantum entanglement. It suggests a wave-like "intra-activity"[18] that instantly crisscrosses any distance: It is a cosmic simultaneity. It is as though even a galaxy apart the entangled electrons belong to one immediately interlinked system. One body. Indeed, the physics of entangled nonseparabilities supportively intensifies ecofeminist theological intuitions such as, for instance, Sallie McFague's model of the universe as God's body.[19] In and as this body we glimpse a universe that appears open-ended, a multiverse in whose synergetic fields the tiny Earth comes enmeshed. The members of such a body function not like a bunch of neatly bounded organs, in life-contexts stacked as in Chinese boxes. This is an unfathomably wide and wild body, even in its self-organizing complexities: something like the deterritorialized "body without organs" of Deleuze and Guattari, where bodies live within bodies and cross space-time through virtual networks, in rhizomes that may exchange energies in simultaneities, at "infinite speed."[20]

Entanglement for a transfeminist theology signifies the politics of cosmology itself. Such a cosmos, a Joycian chaosmos, of reciprocal and risky relations evinces less the political theology of "the king's body," the order of hierarchical sovereignty, than the uncertainty of a radical democracy and the assemblage of a multitude.[21] If the cosmos of theology has never been free of politics, here we hope for a cosmopolitanism in which a universe of nonseparable differences becomes perceptible. Indeed, Antoinette Brown Blackwell already recognized in the cosmic scale of cooperative interactions a sociopolitical imperative. It demanded for her an alternative to the standard epistemology of the mind abstracted from its and other bodies: "to educate the intellect too exclusively at the expense of the justice which involves the social sympathies is a growing mistake."[22]

At this point, an intellect that cultivates its own embodiment in the world recognizes that the width of the relations that compose us makes social justice both dauntingly difficult and dauntlessly possible. The actualization of that just sociality now requires a mass consciousness of our ecological interdependence. The width of our nonlocal connections may doom us through its commodification by global capitalism. And at the same time its web and cloud of virtual communication may disclose at its disturbing new speeds "the truth so manifold" that no one can remain innocent of our far-flung entanglements. Note all those ambiguous "co"-words! Con-sciousness, knowing-with, is itself a co-relational concept. And as the mother of the word *womanism*, Alice Walker, writes: "No one is exempt from the possibility of a conscious connection to All That Is. Not the poor. Not the suffering. Not the writer sitting in the open field."[23]

A conscious connection to All That Is: wisdom so large, truth so manifold . . . In this field intersectionality blossoms into a simultaneous density of interrelations not merely crisscrossing but taking part in each others' self-composition.

4

Our transfeminist con-sciousness of such connectivity remains possible for theology—which wraps All That Is in its own ultimacy—only if the three criteria of dis/closure remain in play: a *knowing ignorance* in our *relationality* as it unfolds indefinitely and as it enfolds the *manifold* in polydoxical truth.

Truth talk, however, seems to demand of us a self-questioning that opens us perilously to each other. "In each others' eyes an ignorance" . . . As Judith Butler put the question: "Is the relationality that conditions and blinds this 'self' not, precisely, an indispensable resource for ethics?"[24] That blinding, which she calls opacity or unknowingness, makes us, when we perceive it all, a bit queer to ourselves and more susceptible to the ethical call of the others. This secular feminist *docta ignorantia* finds a theological sister, for instance, in the fierce Christian ethics of Ivone Gebara: "We believe in the dimension of 'not-knowing,' a fundamental dimension of our being, a not-knowing that makes us more humble and at the same time more combative in order to gain respect for differences and the possibility of building an interdependent society."[25] The radical relationalism of such sophic knowing cannot be decoupled from our *conscious* unknowing. Perhaps the future of feminism lives in the interstices of this relatedness, ever embodied in gender, sex, race, wracked by economic and ecological horror and embraced by "our Sacred Body," her paraphrase of the Body of God—that multiversally expansive metaphor.[26]

Truth so manifold—that we can expect our speech to stutter and falter, sometimes to fail and to fall silent. Before it finds some tendril of poetry, some twist of metaphor and tries yet again. Of negative theology, Elliot Wolfson writes: "Silence is not to be set in binary opposition to language, but is rather the margin that demarcates its center."[27] That margin of silence lets us hear voices we had missed. It empowers a speech that had been missing. And so a certain ignorance—"diviner than the Childhood's," nothing like a return to innocence—is part of "overcoming speechlessness." That was the name of the book written by Alice Walker, in response to her time in Rwanda and Gaza.[28] She opens it with an homage to the peaceable Buddha. The transfeminist manifold knows itself, its polydoxy, to be always already interreligious. We find ourselves on this shrinking planet, entangled in a multiplicity of religions, through bodily diasporas, virtual communication, and the postsecular intensification of pluralism. In *Polydoxy*, the comparative theologian John Thatamanil performs not just relation to other religions but a disclosure of relationality itself by another religion: "Relation names the truth that nothing *whatsoever* is what it is apart from its relation. To be is to be in relation . . . . More rigorously still, no being whatsoever has an essence or core that is non-relationally derived, not even God. On this reading, [Buddhist] emptiness is just another way of designating that all of reality is *pratītyasamutpāda*, dependent co-arising."[29]

The divine can be experienced diversely—and often not as God—inasmuch as "God" does not name the object of a Revelation but a revealing perspective. A perspective in language that unsays itself every time the fixity of an exclusive truth begins to kick in. Divinity suggests, then, not an undifferentiated singularity but rather the difference of a plurisingularity. If this multiplicity signifies no mere many, as for instance of three discrete personal entities, or a simple One, it discloses the divine *complicatio*.[30] Polydoxy gladly absorbs an ancient triune logic: "distinct not separate, different not divided."[31] But these folds of complexity in the divine remain abstract apart from entanglement in our own. "The universe is immensely complex," wrote Antoinette Blackwell, adding: "truth itself is complex."[32] That truth may seem obvious; but obviously we are all together still just getting wise to it.

Wisdom does not enclose *a* world, a religion, a gender, a sex, a race, a class, a nation, a species. Rather it dis/closes the truth-opening, mystery, multiplicity and connectivity of each of those manifold bodies. To conclude, here, if not to close: We may all be readable as wrinkles in the body of God, folds of intensified becoming, uncertain agents of an Infinite

Complication. If All That Is appears occasionally again in gynomorphic splendor, let her be.

In a transfeminist moment, much will come unfolded, unsnarled—"diviner than the childhood's"—even as it is all folded together otherwise, exposing yet more knotty webs. No doubt I have attempted to expound here what, alas, I still do not understand.

The wisdom so large, the truth so manifold—

CHAPTER 3

Nuda Veritas: Iconoclash and Incarnation

> Longing for the naked truth is like longing for the purely
> spiritual: they are both dangerously close to nothingness.
> I prefer truth warmly clothed, incarnated and strong.
>
> —BRUNO LATOUR, *Dismantling Truth*

I

Signs everywhere proclaim "The Naked Truth." Banners and billboards are advertising a major exhibition at the Leopold Museum subtitled "Klimt, Schiele, Kokoschka and Other Scandals." I am in Vienna with free hours after a conference. There beckons a stunning assemblage of paintings from around 1900: the "hour of the birth of a new era," in the language of the Vienna Secession, the Austrian avant-garde that waged in painting a revolution for freedom, honesty, modernity. For these artists the modern did not take the form of abstraction, writes Max Hollein in a commentary on the exhibit, but of a "radical form of realism—the demand for an absolute and uncompromising truthfulness."[1] To open the contemporary viewer's eyes to the context of these works, painted "in the interest of achieving a radical revelation of reality," he finds himself hard-pressed to bring home the scandalous impact of this turn of the century art and "how violent was

---

Originally drafted as a chapter in a book on truth, one that would not write itself as such.

the public reaction to such radicalism."[2] The challenge is to break through the tourist images of "the coffee house culture complete with *Sachertorte*" and the refrigerator magnets of Klimt's *The Kiss*, not to mention current Western saturation in images of nudity.[3] For the great weapon and "obsessive preoccupation" of this modernist "truthfulness" had been none other than the unclothed female body.

So there she hung all over contemporary Vienna, the poster girl of the exhibition: the nude with a wild mane of flower-sprinkled ginger hair, standing straight as a tree, full front, confronting the viewer face-to-face. A century earlier, however, it was not her nakedness per se that affronted Viennese society. It was her unabashed posture, the naked body unjustified by allegory and "referring to nothing but itself." Also pubic hair was a public no-no. Differently also from the soporific female of so many Klimts, curled in on her own desire, this one is holding a round looking glass to her viewer. She bounces the gaze back upon itself, at once revealing and short-circuiting the objectification she seems, at first glance, to invite. Who is the subject, who the object, here? Who is actually getting exposed? Her wide eyes, silvery like the mirror, coolly mesmerize; they engage the viewer more with an attentive irony than with invitation or allusion. They do not pierce but neither do they yield. She stands flat against, or within, a design of golden spirals unfurling above a field of watery blue. Framing the scene in poster style are large rectangles of gold leaf, inscribed in the new (to its contemporaries graphically plain) *Jugendkunst* script. A black snake circles her feet, its tail curling down from the shimmering blueness into the lower gold field, where it crosses and highlights the two words: NUDA VERITAS.

The new Eve for a new world, born out of the watery ground? No pretense of innocence: Her gaze is sophic, knowing, grounded in a shameless sexuality. The modern woman. At least as the artist, this new man of modernity, saw her, makes her, *becomes* her. His gaze is fertile, world-creating: He produces her as his truth. A truthfulness of flesh and of eros, a truth of matter in image, of image materializing. The snake of tempting knowledge, wrapped beneath her feet, as in medieval depictions of Mary, Queen of the Universe, seems here less defeated than collegial. It spirals in the shape of a dark question mark precisely iterating the gold spirals above. Surrounded by decorative figurations of a celebratory and sinuous nature, indeed arising from or upon a paradise ground, she worked as a weapon. Against, first of all, a religion for which, according to one contemporary critic, "Nakedness is the inexplicably evil, the demonically evil, in the existence of which man has to believe without qualification."[4]

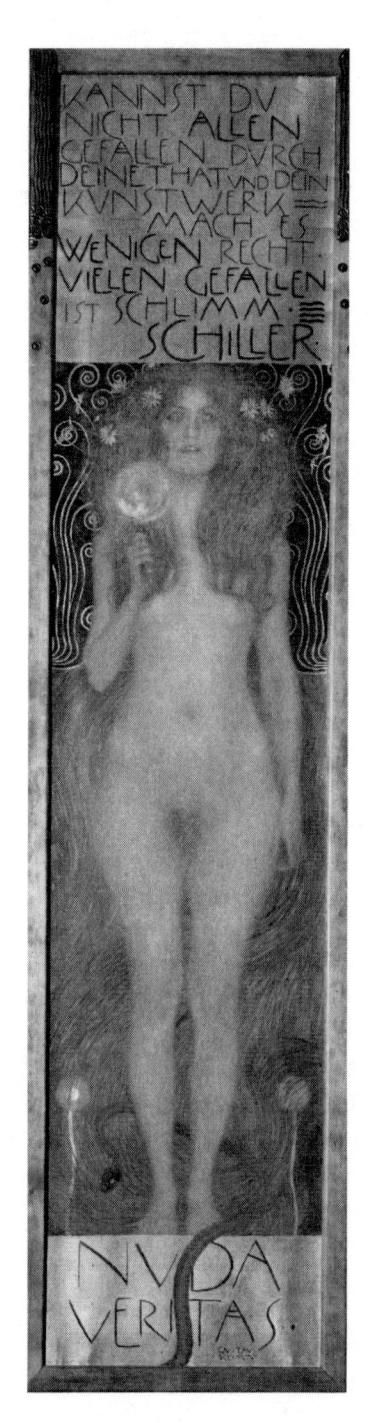

Nuda Veritas (1899), Gustav Klimt.

In answer, the artists of the avant-garde believed "that by drawing attention to the naked body, they would reach a sort of truth that had been concealed by religion." By this means "they thought to overcome not only the power of religion over the human ability to know the truth," writes Christina von Braun, "but also the bourgeois insistence on the status associated with the ownership of property." For bourgeois decency, also modern, capitalized on its own variant of the Christian moralism of concealment. Von Braun meaningfully complicates the artists' truth claim. If bourgeois morality had already, with the onset of the technosciences of sexual reproduction and, indeed, of the Freudian variant, brought sexual morality into a new register, "the avant-garde for its part, became the beneficiary of precisely those achievements that had been brought forth by the new bourgeoisie. In both cases the naked female figure had the same function: it was at one and the same time an object of desire and the manifestation of the potency of this desire. And to both these roles it brought the semblance of 'naked truth.'"[5]

Of course, after generations of critique of any such semblance of bare and representable truth, running concurrently with the systemic exposure of the sexist gaze and its intensively heterosexist presumptions, one cannot directly partake in the scandalous excitement of a now antique avant-garde. Quite apart from the routine commodifications of the nudity of young women, the radicality of this great burst of fleshly visibility, let alone the specificity of its argument, has itself become invisible to presumed postmodern eyes.

Still, I cannot dispel an affect of protective respect for this young woman, with her defiantly steady gaze back at her viewers. She is still holding up that mirror not as a symbol of representational verity but as a challenge to self-recognition. Of course "she" is not separable from her painter. As to the woman painted, I know nothing. I will not explore Klimt's sexual exploits with his models and the series of paternity suits brought upon his death to his estate. Feminism from the start contended with the ambiguity between sexual exploration and exploitation. And of course a transfeminist defense is also possible—for instance by calling upon an "indecent theology" that extends its grace even to heterosexual excesses.[6]

Something about this figure with her mirror-like eyes and her eye-like mirror, this materiality in flagrante, keeps signaling. She sees me seeing her seeing the others seeing themselves seeing her . . .

"Whoever sees it sees himself or herself. Whoever sees it is seen."[7] Thus writes the art historian Marie-José Mondzain of the impossibly different, distant art of the Byzantine icon. Radiant in gold leaf, intimately impersonal intensity emitted by her wide-eyed, silver-plated gaze, body laid with pre-Renaissance two-dimensionality upon its symbolic ground: What, in truth, has Klimt painted but an *icon*? Theology is already curling like the snake around the feet of this modernist Verity.

2

I will not cease from honoring that matter which works my salvation.

JOHN OF DAMASCUS, *In Defense of Icons*

Why would we slow down enough to lock eyes with an icon? We know those ancient Byzantine images and their Russian descendants, great dark eyes upon a haloed face, a Christ or a saint, male or female, painted or mosaiced upon a gilded, hallowed, ground. It takes a disciplined historical effort to pause in a museum and look at them at all, to *see* them. So, well, *iconic*, is their imagery, like that of the scenes they depict, that they lie flat, *plat*, frozen in platitude upon their flattened surface.[8] Yet the movement of *Jugendkunst*, Art Nouveau in Paris, in its reaction against the dominant school of "academic painting," also chose to flatten the visual field into a decorative plane, thus challenging the two-dimensional illusion of the third dimension that had structured Western figurative art since the Renaissance. And sometimes, as in this painting of Klimt's, it evidently cites the direct gaze at the viewer and the flat and symbolic surface, glowing with metallic gold paint, of the Byzantine icon.[9]

Her ironic gaze holds our own even while holding back. With her body at once—to her original viewers—attractive and repulsive (not only too naked and hairy but too thin and boy-like for the public) *Nuda Veritas* pulls and pushes. Her look simultaneously confronts and withdraws. First of all, she confronts a nineteenth-century bourgeois Christian moralism and, in one fell swoop, any religion of spiritual transcendence of the flesh. Her gaze as it withdraws does not let us withdraw from our own materiality.

Does not every Byzantine icon, however, perform its own incarnational liturgy of gilded attraction and cool resistance? "Christ is not in the icon; the icon is toward Christ, who never stops withdrawing," writes Mondzain. "And in his withdrawal, he confounds the gaze by making himself both eye and gaze." The icon, contemplating us, becomes in its turn "God's gaze at the contemplator's flesh, which gets caught in an informational and transformational circuit of relationships."[10] She situates the image upon a nonobjectifiable, nonrepresentational surface. Christian icons are thus to be read in terms of an active relationality, an irreducible reciprocity, in which the invisible cannot be captured in visibility. In the face of two ferocious waves of imperial Byzantine iconoclasm, in which in the eighth and then ninth century "all graven images" were prohibited and icons destroyed, this active reciprocity drove the popular defense of the icon against the charge of idolatry.[11] "The icon attempts to present the grace of an absence within a system of graphic inscription," argues Mondzain.[12] The grace of an absence—a negative theology of sight rather than of speech?—hints at the withdrawal of the pressure, the oppression, of a pure presence that would demand assent or command subjugation.

From the safe distance of a Muslim territory, the Syrian monk John of Damascus opposed the imperial war on icons. Against the charge of idol worship, his treatise *In Defense of Icons* carefully distinguishes between "honoring" (or "reverencing") the materiality of icons and "worshiping" it. "I do not worship matter," John protested. "I worship the God of matter, who became matter for my sake, and deigned to inhabit matter."[13] The theology of the icon thus brings materiality itself to a new pitch of theological attention. Against the pressure of an absolute theocratic power, he developed the argument that the icon does not represent and so risk reifying divinity. On the contrary, the icon "participates" in the very incarnation of God. As God became flesh in one incarnation, an inhabitation in matter, so, he argued, the icon *is* an act of incarnation, and so also a divine inhabitation. Try as we might, we cannot perceive or know the invisible itself. Not long before, another Syrian monk had composed the classic statement of negative theology in terms precisely of the invisibility of a divinity experienced in "brilliant darkness."[14] Dionysius the Areopagite says of the unknowable *as unknown* that it "reveals itself in naked truth."[15] And so for the iconophiles, the icon offers itself, because precisely in the face of the unknowable, the finite matter of the flesh participates—as revealed unquestionably in the incarnation—in the divine; it is *capable*, as Irenaeus had put it even earlier, of the divine. *Finitus capax infinitum*.[16]

So the reciprocity of the viewer and the viewed becomes the incarnational field, the intercarnation, in which the relationship of the body of the image and the body contemplating it activates what we may call a nonseparable difference. If as in Christ the relation of difference joins human flesh to divine infinity, the mattering of all matter becomes visible in the particular body. The iconophiles were materiophiles.

According to Mondzain, "the flesh transfigured by the icon transfigures the gaze turned upon it." In this sense the icon acts: "It is an effective instrument and not the object of a passive fascination."[17] Of course, icons were understood to produce all sorts of supernatural effects—bleeding, healing, even killing—that lent fuel to the iconoclastic reaction. Yet these popular side effects seem to express, to press outward, the specific flesh of the icon as a theological art form predicated on the transfigurability of flesh itself. It was the activity of icons that rendered them at once politically useful and dangerous, when the political climate shifted.

It is then less surprising, from this point of view, that such secular political materialists as Michael Hardt and Antonio Negri express solidarity with John of Damascus and other early medieval defenders of icons. For the icon provided a "way to participate in the sacred and imitate the divine," not as a source of religious belief but of empowerment of the "multitude." "The iconoclastic monarch had to put an end to even this small opportunity of power and salvation. God must be completely separate from the multitude such that the Basileus is the only link between them, the only means of salvation."[18] The exceptional power of the sovereign channels the exceptional incarnation as proving the rule of a dysrelational deity. Do we pick up faint echoes in Klimt's neo-Byzantine *Nuda Veritas* of this revolutionary coding of the original icons?

If active participation in the divine threatens to empower the multitude, the iconic relationality has haunted Christian history, spooking its empires, provoking insurrections. The incarnation has materialized repeatedly in the utopic movements of the spirit, in redistributions of the body of Christ that threaten to transform their world.[19] Theologically we might put it this way: The connectivity of the flesh, once unleashed, stops at no religious, moral, disciplinary, or public borders. Nor at *pubic* boundaries. If—in the flow of recent theological affirmations of the body and its unfolding genders and expressive sexualities—we read *Nuda Veritas* as an honorable icon, it is, in the language of an ancient contemplation, to "honor that matter which works my salvation."[20]

3

It is not, then, theologically irrelevant that Klimt's painting *acted*. As an act of protest it made not just a statement but a social scandal, involving civic and cultural authorities. Just a bit more context, then, for its moment of art history. *Nuda Veritas* was Klimt's succinct "statement" in response to the devastating response to the murals he had painted for the new university buildings of Vienna. These were a state-commissioned project, immense in scale. These murals raised a furor. They unveiled a critique of the disciplinary achievement—that of the faculties of medicine, philosophy, and law—whose progress he had been hired to rhapsodize. It was his failure to monumentalize properly the achievements of modern rationality that got him in trouble. His murals (of which only black-and-white photographs remain) relativized and exposed modernity and its patriarchs, their pettiness and egotism. He had produced a bubbling mystery of bodies, "a throng of humanity in every imaginable form," the subjects and objects of these disciplines embodied and billowing in naked, sometimes sexual, sometimes suffering, bodies of all ages, in all conditions, male as well as female, all together. They are visually reminiscent of the effervescent clouds of angel-beings in El Greco. To one contemporary critic they looked like "a sausage boiler" or a "chaotic tangle of decrepit [i.e., infirm] bodies."[21] The entanglement was read as a betrayal of the proper hierarchy of learning. From all but a few professors the murals provoked charges of "ugliness." The presence in Philosophy of a "seer's visage," in Medicine of a (clothed) noble figure of Hygeia, a glimpse of a learned judge in Jurisprudence, did not offset the misty depiction of the history of the failures of wisdom, of healing, and of justice.

Apparently, however, it was the unpardonable sin of the flesh that provoked the wider public uproar and the definitive rejection of the paintings. For he had began in these murals to depict "nakedness for its own sake." Nudity, again, was not as such a problem; Hans Makart, whom Klimt was expected to succeed in popularity along Vienna's Ringstrasse, had painted endless sexually alluring nudes—but as *symbols* for ideas considered edifying, such as his lasciviously, classically posed, and pubically plucked, clothed in allegory, the sophisticated Viennese public was unperturbed. When, however, Klimt eschewed "the traditional allegorical masking of nakedness, he had painted human bodies as undisguised flesh and blood."[22]

From the Renaissance on, formalized conventions of nudity had overcome the modestly clad figures of medieval art—but ever in the service of allegory. Now emerges this painterly revelation, referred to as realism, that revels in the truth of the flesh itself. Indeed, it was in the midst of these disputes over the *Faculty Paintings* that the Vienna Secession had been organized in 1897 by Klimt and his artist colleagues as a radical act, as "an expression of artistic re-orientation." Art historians consider the work of his followers Schiele, Kokoschka, and Kolig (for whom the bodies are all male, and sensuously so) and Klimt in his watercolors, "even less compromising in their commitment to unveiling the body."[23]

When commentators describe this moment as an "end of allegory," however, they fail to consider how intensively *symbolic* the *Faculty Paintings* remain, how distant from any representational composition. The murals do indeed investigate human embodiment in its carnality and suffering "for its own sake." But these bodies are incarnate upon a surface where in each mural a kind of cosmic personality is portrayed, with the multiple mysterious blurred faces of its immanence. As in one "the gleaming head of Philosophy emerges out of the depths of infinity," wrote the leading Viennese critic, "so here too there rises out of the gloomy abyss the luminous figure of Hygeia."[24] A gold snake—perhaps the same who would soon coil about the feet of *Nuda Veritas*—is here spiraling around her arm and mixing with the decorative spirals of her gown and other curling vectors of embodiment. So if the flesh appears now "for its own sake," it seems as such to participate in an intentionally spiritual force field. And these cloudy figures in their very materialization remain as symbolically supercharged with meaning, as distant from literalism, as any allegory.

In, then, the 1899 *Nuda Veritas*, as precisely as this "natural" woman, is she not posed as an allegory of Truth? It may signify allegory turned against itself but works no less symbolically, even in its withdrawing—in its very materialization—the power of an authorized truth. So charged with significance beyond literal figuration is she that *Nuda Veritas* breaks from painting into text. Above her head is inscribed a quote from Schiller: "If you cannot please everyone through your deeds and your work of art, then please the few. It is not good to please the many." "The many" here should not be read as a democratic or revolutionary multitude so much as the empowered status quo and its overpowered mass. Of course, this is an ambivalence toward the public that plagues every radical movement. The Secession formed itself as an elect of the new truth. They developed the role of the painter as the outcast prophet. Klimt, but especially Schiele and Kokoschka, paint "christological self-portraits in which the modernist artist is to be observed stylizing himself as social victim and martyr."[25]

And my feminist Truth mutters: Well, yes, familiar, this alienation, this creative withdrawal of the (male) individual for the sake of a truth that society cannot abide, a truth inscribed on the bodies of women. Modernism negotiated in female flesh—is this after all what *Nuda* was signaling to me? Where the collapse to the sensuous surface works salvation as the voluntary new fall into Edenic sex, with all the fresh new Eves. Then there remains what Simone de Beauvoir named "the sex," herself trapped forever in the invitation to a sexual bliss that for *her* can only end in exile, in expulsion from the garden of youthful desire. And so an icon of the avant-garde can be well read as an idol of the modernist elite.

4

Jean-Luc Marion's distinction of idol from icon might then apply: "The idol accomplishes the phenomenological reduction of the given visible to the pure seen. It takes back this given to the surface, without withdrawal, emptiness or depth."[26] The idol yields to the gaze so that the gaze stops there, on the surface. Marion takes from Lévinas the notion of the *plat*, the flat, the platitude of the façade, as the very opposite of "the face": "The idea of infinity, the infinitely more contained in the less, is concretely produced in the form of a relation with the face."[27] So the face of the icon performs the negative theology of its own invisible infinity, drawing the gaze in over its depths. Whereas the idol "returns the gaze to itself." Is this not what *Nuda Veritas* does, precisely, with her mirror? Modernist idol after all? Or rather, does the face beside the mirror not make this return its own undoing, precisely by surfacing its platitude?

And to Marion she might signal back this incarnational concern: A body, hers or the Christ's, does not reduce to a face. We might say that the infinity matters just as it materializes in its bodies. And sometimes those bodies make their mattering visible. The transfiguration that illumines the flesh, that figures it intercarnally, for that moment melts or shatters the façade. Even those pubic hairs perform their own spirals of infinity.

Citing the iconic surface of an ancient incarnationalism, Klimt's interplay of gazes will not reduce to platitude, theological or feminist. Its surface trades its third dimension for a more mysteriously mattering depth. The mirror-gaze of the painting continues to precipitate a dimensionality beyond the painterly plane, implicating the viewer—from whom the image withholds herself, indeed withdraws into the nonrepresentational field—in an irreducible relation. As Mondzain says of the religious image, one may say of Klimt: The "contemplative gaze produces the truth of the icon, the truth as an existential relation."[28] But only because no truth happens outside of relation, not because the gaze constructs its object ex nihilo. To contemplate is to look with a certain steadiness, one might even say a faithfulness, practicing a kenotic withdrawal even within the passion of desire. The contemplative gaze is not that of the irritable critic, the ogling voyeur, or the idolized modern artist. The idol-producing patriarchies of culture, art, religion, capitalism will not cease to refreeze and reduce matter to its façade. But the contemplative gaze—in its receptivity and in its creativity—enters the reciprocal motion of the mirror without getting frozen to its surface.

The complex interplay of presence and absence is the dynamism of contemplation—a subtle motion to be sure, a slowing motion. Indeed, for this reason the distinction between idol and icon can never be fixed: The icon necessarily slows, stills, the time of its action into the space of visualization. Thus religious images have so massively turned to kitsch—idols well intended or just good for business. How, indeed, in the postmodern chronotope of what Deleuze calls "infinite speed," where the ultimate sin is stasis and the virtuality of virtue always new and different, can we possibly lock eyes with a painting, an icon, mandala, a living landscape, really any image offering itself to spiritual exercises? How can the visual immobility of the image—even those forming moving images—hold our attention and even ask for honor? How will its flat surface not appear as platitude, as idol of an absolute truth to which one can only and hopelessly seek to conform? Even if truth has been reduced to stereotyped ideals of feminine beauty?

In Jean-Luc Nancy's reflection on painting itself, he seems to be describing a gilded icon and its venerated matter. He could almost be describing *Nuda Veritas*. "For the image is always material: it is the matter of the distinct, its mass and its density, its weight, its edges and its brilliance, its timbre and its specter, its pace and step, its gold." The image of glowing flesh distinct from, or upon, its ground of rhythmic potentialities reveals a "truth of image"—and therefore of distinction, difference, itself—that cannot be left hanging within any epoch's gallery: "If flesh has played an exemplary role in painting, that is because, far beyond the figuration of nudity, flesh is the spirit of painting." *In spiritus et in veritas*? Nancy suggests that in painting, the distinction of the image from its ground enacts a "real presence" in the Christian sense, "participating and participated, communicating and communicated, in the distinction of its intimacy."[29]

In this participatory communion, we may—without investing in Nancy's own theological hierarchy—glimpse in the interchange of viewer and viewed the intimate interplay of the infinite in its bodied universe. The immobility of the image then permits perception of vastly varying spatiotemporal fields, with speeds spiraling between infinite velocity and synchronous stillness. This would be the contemplative truth-practice—erotic, prayerful, questioning.

"The self-coincidence of the image in itself excludes its conformity to a perceived object or to a coded sentiment or well-defined function. On the contrary, the image never stops tightening and condensing into itself. That is why it is immobile, calm and flat in its presence, the coming-together and co-inciding of an event and an eternity."[30] The dynamism drains into dead fabrication when the event-character is lost. Eternity cannot coincide with an event if it means an abstract timelessness or removal from the matter of temporality. The eternity that takes place in the slow time of the image may characterize a timeliness, a time-fulness rather than a timelessness, thus appearing in the visible as a "tightening and condensing" (a sort of stillness full of energy well-known to practitioners of any forms of mental and bodily contemplation).

The contemplative condensation of our vast drifts of experience into images that stay with us, that gaze back, that sustain relationship, does not immobilize us. It may rather be a practice that transfigures and thus mobilizes new forms of coming together. Like the stillness that comes in the Einsteinian synchronizing of speeds; like the "atemporal sequence" of the Whiteheadian "concrescence," the instantaneity of the event of becoming, not *out of time and space but rather within it* and thus constitutive *of* it. To materialize, to become incarnate, means to actualize a possibility. In itself that possibility is the abstract eternity, not actual, not living; in concrescence it takes *place*, it becomes body. Only then does the eternal *matter*. And all of our art, our fabrication, our cultural and linguistic and spiritual constructions, aim to matter, to materialize possibilities, be they of high art or base survival, that would otherwise not have been.

We will be perennially tempted to freeze the event of becoming: to capture it in its own eternity, to nail it to its own truth, to gut its timefulness and so sacrifice its life to its image. Its idol. Its failed modernities, its antique futures, its marketable flesh. The defiant icon of female indecency is captured for mass production, as in Klimt's heterosexy *The Kiss*. The revolutionary event of incarnation hardens into the exception proving the rule of this or that empire.

In truth, I cannot disagree with Bruno Latour: "Longing for the naked truth is like longing for the purely spiritual: they are both dangerously close to nothingness. I prefer truth warmly clothed, incarnated and strong."[31] Latour may not realize how much he sounds like Paul writing to the Corinthians: "We wish not to be unclothed but to be further clothed" (1 Cor. 5). For here too the incarnation signifies not the nude exposure of a spiritual abstraction, not direct access to any eternal truth, but "the image (eikon) of the invisible God" (Col. 1:15). Latour is not referring to Paul or to Klimt. In the spirit of an uncertain, a more contemplative, radicality, he had named a major art exhibit *Iconoclash*: an alternative not just to an unquestioning iconophilia but to standard modernist iconoclasm, in its utter certainty of destruction, its omniscient critique. A multiplicity of images come into play, into mutual contestation, into becoming and passing away.

Latour would ask Moses to revise the second commandment thus: "'Thou shall not freeze-frame any graven image!'"[32] The present perspective dons the robe (embroidered with spirals) of atheological iconoclash. Neither smashing nor freeze-framing its images, it glimpses itself reflecting the mirror in the mirror of the icon itself.

It is not the first time some glowing icon first leaves me cold, then slows me down, draws me in, and demands a complicating solidarity. I would just insist that in her defiant composure, her proud indecency, *Nuda Veritas* does come lushly clothed—in her own flesh. The gold field keeps her warm and radiant. Her name mocks any pretense of purity—spiritual, sexual, revolutionary, or nihilist. The iconic is rescued by the ironic. The clash calms for a moment. Her mirror-plated gaze emits the strength of her honorable matter.

CHAPTER 4

Tingles of Matter, Tangles of Theology: Bodies of the New(ish) Materialism

I believe in one matter-energy, the maker of things seen and unseen.

—JANE BENNETT, *Vibrant Matter*

Matter and meaning are not separable elements.

—KAREN BARAD, *Meeting the Universe Halfway*

In the name of a new materialism, an interdisciplinary conversation of appealing vitality has danced across campuses and screens. It is as though this movement of thought draws its energy from the vibrancy of matter itself. Indeed, thinking about materiality can then only be read as its own complex responsiveness to itself—an "it" that ceases to register as inert, lifeless, and indifferent stuff. It would liberate matter from the frozen format imposed by the epistemic disciplines of both a mechanistic naturalism and a transcendent supernaturalism, from the congealed objectifications of either traditional materialism or traditional theology.

Offered as part of the conversation on the relation of religion to the "new materialism," in dialogue with Karen Barad and Jane Bennett, at Drew's annual Transdisciplinary Theological Colloquium, 2014. The essays from that colloquium are gathered in Mary-Jane Rubenstein and Catherine Keller, eds., *Entangled Worlds: Science, Religion and Materiality* (New York: Fordham University Press, 2017). For more on the conference and the series see https://www.drew.edu/theological/2014/01/13/entangled-worlds-the-thirteenth-transdisciplinary-theological-colloquium/.

So then what kind of *theology* might materialize in conversation with the so-called new materialism? If theology as such is to survive the intra-action, will it have brought to the table a materialism of its own? Is theological materialism, at least of Christian ilk, an oxymoron? What sort of theology might already identify itself as a Christian materialism?

Despite a half century of dialogue with Marxism, liberation theology, for example, has not routinely waved such a banner, though it was naturally dismissed from the start by its conservative opponents precisely *as* materialism. Similarly, a range of ecological and cosmological theologies have for decades been insistent upon nondualist affirmations of materiality, but not in the name of materialism. And though Christian progressives decry the consumer capitalism of the health-and-wealth Prosperity Gospel, its evangelists hardly trumpet their own and Jesus's "materialism" as such. The biblical heritage never escapes a dense and complex relation to a matter always deemed God's creation and "good," later thrust down as the lower partner of a Platonized Christian dualism but still haunting every supernaturalism with the massiness of scriptural materialities, the narrative weight of bodily justice, resurrection, incarnation. But what theology, I wondered, would actually insist upon the term "Christian materialism"?

Imagine my surprise when this answer revealed itself: The Spanish Josemaría Escrivá, canonized in 2002 as a saint, writes that we can "rightfully speak of a Christian materialism, which is boldly opposed to those materialisms which are blind to the spirit." For "authentic Christianity, which professes the resurrection of all flesh, has always quite logically opposed 'dis-incarnation.'"[1] What progressive Christian would not assent to this sentiment? Dis-incarnation signifies the Hellenized idealism we are all against! Escrivá, however, happens to be the founder of Opus Dei. That organization may not be as colorfully sinister as the *Da Vinci Code* version but has from the start been criticized by mainstream Catholics for its alliance with authoritarian regimes, its misogyny, its secretive access to power. As to the movement's widespread and emphatically "materialist" practices of mortification of the flesh, particularly with the use of the cilice, the thigh clamp, or the corded whip, no doubt a queer theorist could offer a creative BDSM counter-reading. Not that this essay's titular tingles intend such flesh-punishing sensations.

Nonetheless, this mortifying Christian materialism participates in an affirmative biblical incarnationalism and, as such, forms part of the complex manifold of the material practices of the world's spiritual traditions. If this whole polyvalent history, with its extreme contradictions and insistent evolutions, is to come into theological self-explication, what could be more important than fresh insight into matter itself? I will, in what follows, highlight a version of the resignification of materiality that produced its own theological movement, that of process theology. To this end I want to pull the physical cosmology of its founder, Alfred North Whitehead, into relation especially to Karen Barad's current philosophical physics. His early-twentieth-century response to the (then very) new physics produced its own theological movement. It is a movement whose current liveliness is linked to its irreducibly ecological commitments. So the comparison of Whitehead's early unfolding of ontological relationalism with Barad's fresh version will allow us to cut to the theological quick. Indeed, the quickened, which is to say enlivened, notion of materiality that emerges from such an exchange may help to reorient our endlessly entangled bodily lives and their spirited practices.

I will, however, want to consider how any honest materialism (however new) will have to admit its own inextricable, if imperceptible, entanglement in the long-contradictory history of religious bodies. Those contradictions congeal particularly around figures of "the body of Christ." So the recognition of the interlinked history of the bodies will not diminish the differences, ethical or ontological, of the schemata of matter or the specificity of bodies; rather, it situates them all within the enlivening intra-actions of Barad's "spacetime mattering." "Intra-acting responsibly as part of the world means taking account of the entangled phenomena that are intrinsic to the world's vitality and being responsive to the possibilities that might help us and it flourish."[2] This cosmological ethics will take on in the present context a theological charge. Or perhaps I should say (not wanting to be out-sexed by Opus Dei) a theo-erotic charge. Whitehead's trope of the "the Eros of the universe" and Whitney Bauman's queerly ecotheological "polyamory of place" become figures of a boundless mattering. In the attempt to foster resonance between the impossibly diverse bodies of our particularly fragile world, I am hoping against hope—against traditional hope for top-down salvation *from* this world—for help from the bottom up: even from the vibrant "energy-matter" of the quantum minimum.

Superstitions and Superpositions

In meditating on mattering bodies, Christian theology confronts, first of all, the dense global mass of "the body of Christ." An amalgam of metaphoric and material entanglements, the history of the body of Christ—as the always redoubled figure of the church itself and of the church's founding figure—includes quite a lively mass of bodies in addition to that ubiquitous, tortured one. The formidable biblical apparatus of the creation and all its good and sinning bodies, its codes for material practice, its prophetic insistence upon material—not ethereal—justice for vulnerable bodies, beyond the first and second testament spectrum of always bodily resurrections, endlessly recirculates all that mattering matter.[3] Then there come all the later practices of "material Christianity."[4] Think, for instance, of the relics, little bits of the flesh, perhaps of bones, tooth, or foreskin, of shroud or cross, of some spiritual ancestor. As the rules for moving, "translating," and then subdividing corpses relaxed, the Second Nicene Council (787 CE) prescribed at least one saintly relic inside every altar. (Someone will no doubt soon interpret the affective efficacy, the requisite physicality, of the reliquary as quantum entanglement channeled for popular piety.) Or consider the contemplation of icons, understood to be materializations, never mere representations, of the holy ones depicted: "The flesh transfigured by the icon transfigures the gaze turned upon it." Contemplation of the body of Christ, according to Marie-José Mondzain's study of Byzantine icons, became participation in his incarnation, transfiguration, resurrection. But depictions of resurrection and its bodiliness seem to shift theologically from participation to resuscitation. In twelfth-century depictions the resurrection of the dead appears as "the regurgitation or reassemblage of exactly the body we possess on earth."[5] They do not, however, lose their materiality. Of the same period, Caroline Walker Bynum describes how in art "those who rise include skeletons still lying prone in their coffins, bodies emerging from sarcophagi entangled in shrouds, and body parts vomited up by birds, bees, and fish."[6]

Of course, these iconographies and these practices arise amid the incense and music, the sacramental rituals performed in multisensory drama, or the homey habits that compose so much of every religion.[7] The particularly Christian bodies multiply them with rosary beads, the founding of hospices and charities, peasant revolts, apocalyptic communes, reactionary counterrevolutions. On and on, Catherine of Siena and Angela of Foligno kiss the lepers' wounds, Saint Francis preaches to the birds. The endless pilgrimages, *milagros*, healing or weeping Guadalupes, the layings-on of hands hardly end with the Middle Ages.[8]

Superstitions or superpositions? At any rate, these holy matters are nothing if not vital. Yet the matter itself—tongue, wound, incense, icon—was not normally understood by theologians to be inherently alive or meaningful so much as enlivened by invisible forces. If explicated, the metaphysics would be more dualistic supernaturalism than, say, Jane Bennett's naturalist version of vitalism as "heterogeneous monism."[9] The enchantment of life is conferred from above. But, first of all, these were practices, not theories. And there would be dense parallels in every spiritual tradition, including all those the church suppressed as idols.

Within Christianity all these numinous materializations thinned out rather dramatically with the Reformation, which marked this density of material practice as works righteousness, Papist superstition, and Catholic idolatry. Of course, Protestantism did not expel the goodness from the creation, salvation from incarnation, or sacramentality from the edible body. But the way was being vigorously and inadvertently cleared for the (then) new materialism of natural science and, therefore, for the whole modern history of the bifurcation of science and religion, of matter and meaning. Religion appeared to back slowly and spasmodically into the private sphere—its social, political, and sacramental bodies ever more immaterial—while science left "meaning" to religion for the *hoi polloi*, to philosophers for the few. It focused instead on the facts of the matter at hand. And as mere matter of fact, matter ceases to matter spiritually or ethically.

The repressed returns, as it often does, in conservative gestures. But the new-old orthodoxy of Christian materialism does not only take the reactionary form of Opus Dei, or of the pro-capitalist prosperity gospel, or of the natalist neo-vitalism of the "culture of life" that Bennett tracks.[10] It has also taken, for example, the canny form of radical orthodoxy, as in John Milbank's argument that "materialist materialism is simply not as materialist as theological materialism."[11] That former tautology would refer to secularized matter. The "alternative Catholic metanarrative" he champions features the human as "eroto-linguistic animal."[12] It seductively celebrates the whole medieval aesthetic sensorium washed out by Protestantism. And it derives its materialism (unseductively for any feminist theology) from the "absolute truth" of the Incarnation of God the Son, which mediates the Father's transcendence and so "enchants" material reality through the "Trinitarian interpenetrations." Milbank's dispute in this instance is with the Hegelianism of Žižek, which he finds "a sad, resigned materialism which appears to suppose that matter is quite as boring as the most extreme of idealists might suppose."[13] Žižek, the self-designated "Christian atheist," loves this debate. He responds, "Yes, if by 'materialism' one understands the assertion of material reality as fully ontologically constituted, 'really existing out there,' which I emphatically do not: the basic axiom of today's materialism is for me the ontological incompleteness of reality."[14]

While I do not love this conversation, Žižek's specific retort is right on target for our present discussion. He celebrates a materialism that undermines the mere (indeed, boring) matter of fact "from within, just as quantum physics, for example, undermines our common notion of external reality: beneath the world of simply existing material objects we discover a different reality of virtual particles, of quantum oscillations, of time-space paradoxes, etc., etc.—a wonderful world which, while remaining thoroughly materialist, is . . . breathtakingly surprising and paradoxical."[15] Žižek's version of the new materialism falls from this angle of his parallax closer, in other words, to the present transdisciplinarily theological conversation than to that of the orthodox Christian materialism he dialectically engages. But I only want to borrow from him here the quantum allusion, as it springs into play against the claim of a Christian materialist theological orthodoxy. The little quantum bristles in Žižek's countering version of Christian materialist discourse also with resistance to a capitalist economy that would master all the matter of the globe, down to the genetic codes. Such a capitalist materialism (not identifiable with Milbank, Žižek, or "new" materialism) indeed reproduces matter as pre-existently "out there," fully determinate or determinable. Of course, Marxist materialism helped to crack open history, to confer subjective vitality on the material bodies of workers, and to collapse the superstructure of supernaturalism; but it did little to challenge the closed determinism of Newtonian matter. And those who can be called new materialists do not align themselves with the matter of any totalizing orthodoxy. They are not, therefore, apolitical or, indeed, opposed to historical materialism but entangle economics in a political multiplicity—ecological, sexual, racial—and so embody resistance to the newer capitalism of neoliberal economics.

In a universe of incompletion, quantum indeterminacy—to begin to build on Karen Barad's reading of Niels Bohr—destabilizes the entire apparatus of substantialist matter and its metaphysics. That metaphysics of substance dominated medieval scholasticism, however complicated or decorated by the myriad material practices of the religious. And it learned to do without any God-essence in modernity. The independent substance of a mastermind, observer, and, finally, owner takes center stage, with the substantial properties that are properly attributed to "men [sic]" of substance. But the transcendently objective posture continues to mimic the Unmoved Mover of all matter, at His ghostly remove, Himself selfsame and impassive, even when He comes as Logos clothed in the flesh of His single and exclusive materialization.

Perhaps, then, the appearance of the innocent little quantum in big debates about science and theology is neither new nor innocent; and among numerous publics, some present readers included, it still tingles with interest.[16] Will it point us—beyond the relics of antique material practices, beyond the orthodox reactions—to the really new, the *right*, materialism? Or rather to an uncertainty, indeed an indeterminacy of discourse, where the very name "matter" seems to mirror and mock the name "God"? In the meantime, the phenomenal quantum arrives interlaced with a theological tradition uninhibited by orthodoxy, one that loops back—*reculer pour mieux sauter*—through work contemporary with and not unrelated to that of Bohr.

The Matter of Simple Location

The mysterious quanta of energy have made their appearance.

ALFRED NORTH WHITEHEAD, *Process and Reality*

It was the enigmatic attraction of the barely beginning quantum mechanics, together with the newly established principles of relativity, that provoked the mathematician Alfred North Whitehead to shift course in the mid-1920s. The math of the quantum delivered him such a dramatic challenge to commonsense substantialism that he began to write a speculative cosmology. He read substance metaphysics as the tacit presupposition of science from Descartes and Newton on. He articulates the challenge at the quantum level, where "mere endurance," which characterizes the "undifferentiated sameness" of substance, collapses into "the vibratory streaming of energy."[17] With this "dissolution of the quanta into vibrations" he zooms in on the common sense that formed the unconscious foundation of modern science, facilitating in the two centuries following Newton its triumphant freedom from questions of value or meaning.[18] To the ancient question "What is nature made of?" Whitehead writes, the modern "answer is couched in terms of stuff, or matter, or material—the particular name chosen is indifferent—which has the property of simple location in space and time.... What I mean by matter or material, is anything which has this property of *simple location*." Matter is present in a simple sense that "does not require for its explanation any reference to other regions of space-time."[19] "Simple location" characterizes for him the Newtonian atom, the massy, impenetrable, separate stuff that is what and where it is independently of its relationships. Such simplification is now read as an act of unrecognized abstraction by a dissociated observer. It is a symptom of the larger presumption that he famously names "the fallacy of misplaced concreteness."[20]

Whitehead could very well have then written the following: "We are not outside observers of the world. Neither are we simply located at particular places in the world." But in fact that happens to be Karen Barad, announcing "we are part of the world in its ongoing intra-activity."[21] However, Barad writes in the name of matter itself and shines as a star in the new galaxy of new materialists. And Whitehead reads "matter" *as* the content of the fallacy and materialism as its inherent reductionism.

In other words, I have got a problem, semantic at the very least. I do not come to the present conversation apart from the Whiteheadian cosmology in its impact upon both a margin of physics and a wider swathe of theology, particularly feminist, ecological, economic. And from his point of view the fantasy of the "quiet extensive stone with its relationships of position and its quality of color" has yielded the metaphysical concept that has "wrecked the various systems of pluralistic realism." So materialism here—in this early Jamesian voice for a cosmic and not only social pluralism—appears as an unconsciously metaphysical anti-pluralism. In the light of quantum physics, he writes, "this materialistic concept has proved to be as mistaken for the atom as it was for the stone." As "these quanta seem to dissolve into the vibrations of light," materialism itself begins to dissipate.[22]

In the interest of a realistic pluralism today, *theologically* if indirectly kin to the "agential realism" unfolding in Karen Barad's mattering matter, I suggest it will be worth bearing with the apparent contradiction. The discursive tension only mounts in the enchanted buzz—so resonant with Whitehead's vibratory universe, of Jane Bennett's "vibrant matter." It forms the other stellar manifestation of the new materialism. Yet Whitehead wrote an entire alternative to materialism and its matter—notions that in his view, ninety years ago, seemed fundamentally frozen into both the dualisms and the monisms of substance. The alternative for him was neither idealism nor theology. He called it the philosophy of organism, in which every creature, or actual entity, including most expressly all those traditionally called inorganic, is an "event" of interrelation. A *live* event: it *is* "an actual occasion of experience"; it "feels" or "prehends"—usually with no consciousness—the world from which it comes, the world of which it becomes. Every quantum of energy is thus metaphorically describable as a "throb of emotion" or a "subject of experience": a "vibratory organism." Such a subject is not describable as an enduring entity unfolding in time, "having" experiences and attributes, but an occasion of becoming in relation:

> Every actual occasion exhibits itself as a process: it is a becomingness. In so disclosing itself, it places itself as one among a multiplicity of other occasions, without which it could not be itself.[23]

Whitehead's actual occasion thus transmutes the enduring substance—*res cogitans* or *extensa*—of separable individuals into the relationally constituted moments of becoming. This "becomingness" instigates a radical shift of ontology. Relation is no longer external. It is a matter, indeed a materialization, of "mutual immanence" or of "internal relations" constituting emergent subjects (superjects) rather than of attributes possessed by substances. For Whitehead, every subject—quantum or queen—experiences, feels, and responds spontaneously to its world. Each process of becoming counts as a responsive materialization of its world. In other words, relation no longer signifies an interaction between beings that exist before the interaction itself.

The resonance with Karen Barad's innovative language of "intra-active becomings" is dramatic. She has also, and no less radically, composed—drawing on a different, later, and largely continental philosophy—a full-fledged "relational ontology" as the basis for her "posthumanist account of material bodies." These bodies do not appear as classical agents, merely *inter*acting with their objects from the outside. "Rather, phenomena are the ontological inseparability/entanglement of intra-acting 'agencies.'" For her the "ontological inseparability" of the agencies of a becoming intra-action is often pictured as the scientist, the apparatus, and the quantum. (She stays much more consistently than Whitehead within the scene of physics.) The point is that the phenomena are "relations without preexisting relata."[24] I find Barad's work to be a great uplift and update of an ontological relationalism that comes already entangled in the phenomena of process, ecological, and feminist theology.

If Whitehead did not anticipate the neologism of intra-action, interactivity for him signifies always the mutual immanence of becoming occasions, which are not what they are in abstraction from one another—except in the mirage of "misplaced concreteness."

Far from simply located, every event in its unique perspective here and now is involved one way or another, significantly or trivially, positively or negatively prehended, in every other. The singular perspective in spacetime is a momentary decision—it does not establish any boundary of mere nonrelation to anything. Meditating on the mysterious quanta, the undoing of simple location registers its spookiest logic. "In a certain sense, everything is everywhere at all times. For every location involves an aspect of itself in every other location."[25] In a "certain sense"—as mainly enfolded in potentialities, most of which will remain forever irrelevant, "negatively prehended." But nonetheless the relativity of every location for the appearance (the phenomenon) of each actualization can fix no final boundary.

No wonder physicists like David Bohm, Henry Stapp, and Shimon Malin, seeking support for a paradigm to help make intuitive sense of quantum entanglement, each found in this early proposal philosophical aid and succor. In *Process and Reality*, Whitehead would formulate this radically nonsimple location as his "ontological principle": "Everything is positively somewhere in actuality and in potency everywhere."[26] This potentiality, suggestive of the quantum potential or vacuum, also anticipates the French quantum physicist Bernard d'Espagnat's snapshot of a stone: "its 'quantum state' is 'entangled' (this is the technical word) with the state of the whole Universe."[27] This is far from the stone we see as so solidly and stolidly there. Such simplification is an abstraction—not wrong at all. Until we mistake the abstraction for the concrete.

Whitehead does not apply to that stone the language of "quantum entanglement," the phrase that Schrödinger only coined a few years later. But for the purposes of the resonance machine building up in the name of the new materiality, it is not insignificant that William Connolly's recent book, *The Fragility of Things*, has a stirring chapter called "Process Philosophy and Planetary Politics." He draws therein from Whitehead a specifically *quantum* account of our vulnerable worldwide entanglements. "If Whitehead were writing today he would doubtless say that the fallacy refers in the first instance to those who still ignore that mysterious process by which two 'particles' separated after having been adjacent, now shift together simultaneously, even when at a great distance from one another."[28]

We witness here the entanglement of quantum theory, by way of Whitehead (with a little help from Nietzsche), in the energized current of a politics intensively sensitized to the matter-energy flows of the planet. There emerges the possibility of a cosmopolitics with *cosmos*.[29] Connolly's illustrations are germane:

> For Whitehead, misplaced concreteness means more broadly the tendency to overlook entanglements between energized, real entities that exceed any atomistic reduction of them, as when a climate pattern and ocean current system intersect and enter into a new spiral of mutual amplification, or when a cultural disposition to spiritual life befuddles

the academic separation between an economic system and religion by flowing into the very fiber of work motivation, consumption profiles, investment priorities and electoral politics.[30]

That "cultural disposition to spiritual life" might signify what he earlier and famously calls the "evangelical-capitalist resonance machine."[31] That would characterize the prosperity gospel and its political collusion with its ecumenically right-wing moral agenda. Or to the contrary, it may engage a theological friendlier spirit of "existential faith"—such as the sort highly developed along the left flanks of theology, where process and liberation theologies have long labored—conducive to the cosmopolitics of a positive resonance machine.

It is in the interest of that planetary resonance machine—machine read now as an intra-active Baradian agency, of course—that transdisciplinary theological engagements such as this volume represents proceed. The very notion of a bounded academic discipline is always already deconstructed by such an agential manifold. It is also for the sake of gathering such an ethico-political, ecotheological materialization—call it *ecosmopolitics* for short—that I foreground here the affinity between projects of becoming relationalism, and particularly between Whitehead and Barad. That Barad does not refer to Whitehead is just as well. The process vocabulary may exact too high a hermeneutical price. And the differences remain significant between these relational ontologies. For instance, while intra-active agency supersedes any individual agents in Barad, Whitehead's actual occasions count as individuals, albeit only as momentary events of relation. These are different strategies, equally committed to undoing individualism at every level.

And such comparison only highlights the power of Barad's creation of a new interpretive apparatus, with current physics and with a timely range of poststructuralist and feminist theory otherwise lacking any explicate ontology. She notes that even Bohr, her primary source, "never spells out his ontological commitments."[32] This she does magnificently and in a way that attributes responsive value to every creature, including a particular starfish-like echinoderm. The brittlestar, a brainless creature with astonishing optic capacities, "may not get full credit for its superior ingenuity, which exceeds the current technological ingenuity of humans."[33] Her point is that in its enfolding parts of its environment and expelling parts of itself to the environment, its apparatus is an active part of the space-time manifold. It does not "have" but "is" an eye.[34] "Brittlestars are living testimony to the inseparability of knowing, being and doing."[35] Her radical redistribution of mindfulness (like Whitehead's "mental pole" at work, usually unconsciously, in every actual occasion) cannot be written off as a romantic vitalism. Not that Bennett's work will any longer permit the dismissal of the ancestral observers of "vital things." This emergent sense of a knowingness entangled in the least conscious of creatures will take ever-new forms. The differential inseparability of knowing, being, and doing yields a rigorous rereading of matter itself.

What I have called elsewhere entangled difference demands an irreducible pluralism: Only so does the space of intra-action resist a monist reading. Indeed, difference here produces a bottomless ethic. For the responsiveness of things cannot be abstracted from its most extensive ethical "diffraction": "We are not merely differently situated in the world; 'each of us' is part of the intra-active ongoing articulation of the world in its differential mattering."[36] Does such matter correspond to that which stands accused of the fallacy of misplaced concreteness? Au contraire, does it not displace the dysrelational abstraction that poses as the concrete matter of (not new) materialism? At any rate the mattering of matter is dismissed—as a pun or a projection—at the peril of everything that really does matter. For humans or brittlestars.

But for God? Developing the emergent conversation on materiality by means of such a Whiteheadian intra-action with Barad might be left to an arcane dissertation, were it not for two developing scholarly publics, one Deleuzian, the other theological. The first consists of the expanding circle of a more Deleuzian-cosmological constructivism, exposing the extent of Whitehead's influence upon Deleuze himself, and being now drawn into the philosophy of science by Bruno Latour and Isabelle Stengers.[37] She especially funnels an unforeseen cone of continental philosophical respect—after the sheer acosmology, the anti-metaphysics, of poststructuralism—toward a process-relational ontology. Of course, this all depends upon the atheist street cred of these interpreters, who can thus dispel Whitehead's theological aura. Also the metamorphosis within poststructuralism toward "divinanimality"—attention to the nonhuman in its animal registers and its theological figurations—has begun, along with developments in phenomenology, to dislodge the continental anthropocentrism. As to the theological public: Especially in its Protestant forms it had remained Word-centered, lacking all interest in material cosmology. In this it paralleled the philosophical preoccupation with language and culture. The marginal but tenacious web of Whiteheadian theologians have, in the meantime, been weaving a startlingly planetary public of process thinkers. Perhaps because of its ecological prescience, it can no longer be successfully silenced as heterodox or unhip in the theological mainstream.

It was in its pluralist redistribution of incarnation that process theology had first captured my interest.[38] Amid its "democracy of fellow creatures" any event of materialization may carry sacramental significance.[39] At the same time its constituent relationalism was key—I found in the 1980s—to articulating a feminist alternative to the separative ego. Of course, I admit that the metaphor of deity as "Eros of the universe," its persuasive lure displacing omnipotence, was the first seduction. It continues to destabilize the truth-power authorized by every religious absolute, including the materialism of radical orthodoxy. Process theology now collaborates across these registers with an expansively embodied relational pluralism.[40] In its avowal of the intra-activity of theology with the multiplicities of discourse, religious and irreligious, that have come entangled in theology itself all along, process theology joins a destabilizing polydoxy.[41] In this, process theology has steadily advanced a pluralist practice of the nonseparability of religious from other, and not least of all from scientific, practices.[42]

Whitehead considered it the primary task of Western philosophy to heal the modern split of science and religion. He considered civilization at peril in its ongoing bifurcation of fact from value, matter from meaning. In other words, recognition of an ongoing entanglement of modern science in premodern theology—not any return to a presecularized worldview—may be called for. Non-European civilizations and, indeed, the Greeks demonstrated mathematical and cosmological genius; but why then, asked Whitehead, did experimental science only develop in the modern West? Empiricism itself betrays "the inexpugnable belief that every detailed occurrence can be correlated with its antecedents in a perfectly definite manner, exemplifying general principles. Without this belief the incredible labours of scientists would be without hope." Their labor, in other words, is motivated by the conviction "that there is a secret, a secret which can be unveiled." Materiality is not just illusion or distraction. This conviction stems, he argues, from "the medieval insistence on the rationality of God," as a kind of hybrid of the "personal energy of Jehovah" with "the rationality of a Greek philosopher." His point was that for good and for ill, the scrutable world of modern science "is an unconscious derivative from medieval theology."[43]

We might add that this trust in the unveiling of the secret derives from the original narrative revelation—"it is good"—with respect to each space and species of the whole intra-active creation. So then an ethico-aesthetic motivation infuses the epistemic trust: matter is good, worthy, engaging. The scrutable thus implies the scrupulous. Its knowability does not entail its transparency so much as its relationality: as "Adam knew Eve." The metaphor of incarnation for a time intensified this trust. Yet the ontological dualism that soon captures Christianity so orders the God-world relation as to keep incarnation the exception that proves the rule of external interaction. Indeed, it proves the dominance of an eternally pre-existing being over a world of substances preceding their relations to each other. That supernatural dualism underlies the Cartesian substances upon which, through Newton's atomic substances, the subjects and objects of pre-quantum science subsist.

In the liminal transition between the medieval and the modern another kind of science, inseparable from an alternative theology, was at least possible. I consider elsewhere the road not taken.[44] Exemplified in the cosmological implications of Nicholas of Cusa's *docta ignorantia*, the "learned ignorance": Here such secrets as the infinite universe, with an earth neither at its center nor fixed, indeed with no fixed center, are revealed a century before Copernicus.[45] God the *complicatio/explicatio* enfolds as infinity the material manifold, which unfolds in free, indeed agential, inseparability: "All is in all and each in each."[46] Whitehead himself makes no reference to Cusa. I am here only suggesting that a dense force field of materiality pushes at once through medieval popular practice and cosmological speculation, not successfully contained by the disciplining dualism. It makes possible the modern science that the church also comes to oppose, in both the Reformation and Counter Reformation repression of cosmological speculation (witnessed in the martyrdom of Cusa's follower Bruno).

If in response to the "secrets which can be unveiled" through relativity and quantum mechanics Whitehead takes up the thread of cosmology, the problem remains: He is arguing that the substantive "matter" signifies the fallaciously simple location. Matter suggests a solid, pre-existent stuff. Actuality is for him actualization, it is embodiment; it is actualized as and in spatiotemporal bodies. Matter remained for him too static and stuffy a notion to capture the vibratory relationalism of any photon, atom, or scientist engaging them. Perhaps, however, nearly a century later, the quanta have given the noun *matter* a new chance.

Be that as it may, we might agree that Whitehead rejects materialism for approximately the same reason that the new materialists espouse it: to enact mindfulness of the live processes of *materialization*, minuscule and far-flung, of which we are a part and for which we are always partially accountable. Process thought shares with the new materialists the sensibility of a vibrant and agential realism, unfolded as a full ontological relationalism. We cannot account for *any* reality apart from giving a scrutable and scrupulous account of ourselves—inclusive of the contextualities, opacities, and indeterminacies that shadow our becoming.[47] Whether you want to tag every vibrantly, queerly, or mindfully embodied relationalism as materialism will depend upon your own shifting context of discursive accountability—on what language may enliven the ecosmopolitics of your context. Of your matter-energy.

Apophatic Matter

For my part, I might experiment with the possibility of an *apophatic materialism*. The ancient mystical apophasis, the "unsaying" that characterizes negative theology, has recently come back into play, as theology recognizes the apparatus of its own inescapable contextualism. But it is never just "God" that comes unsaid. For there seems to be something hard to say, something that constantly comes unsaid, about matter itself—something revealed by the quantum phenomenon. Newton's atom was created in the faith "that God in the Beginning form'd Matter in solid, massy, hard, impenetrable, moveable particles."[48] If it has since morphed into the nuanced materiality of the quantum, matter itself turns woozy, wavy, wayward. Energy remains nonidentifiable with matter: Matter and energy translate in and out of each other, they form matter-energy, they are not the same "thing." And now dark matter is incomprehensibly different and more (almost eight times more) than baryonic matter—what had been understood to be matter; and dark energy differs from both as the sheerly unknown. A new common sense emerges: that "we live not in a cosmic clockwork, but in a cosmic network, a network of forces and fields, of nonlocal quantum connections and nonlinear, creative matter."[49] Scientific challenges to the received meaning of matter—and so to what materialism has meant—cross the spectrum of physics, chaos, complexity, biology, neuroscience.

If I can still rarely hear *matter* the noun, the substantive, without a clunk of reduction, a dissociation from the verbs, from ethical or existential mattering, from the engaging process of materialization, this hardness may be softening. Any supposedly new materialism will have deconstructed the fallacious concreteness of that lifeless, separative stuff. The naming now comes accompanied by fresh and vibrant language—and so always by an *unnaming* of what usually is named "matter." Such materialist apophasis does not make matter any less real (no more than theological apophasis makes God unreal). On the contrary, it is precisely the felt reality, the affect of *mattering*, that causes language to shudder. The very intensity of our *mindful* relation to matter renders received language for it inadequate. And this happens with particular vividness among those hovering close to the phenomenon. In science the quantum phenomenon has provoked great bursts of apophatic incomprehension. And none knew this unknowability more than Bohr, laboring over "*this terrible riddle* which the quantum theory is."[50] Or as Feynman put it: "There was a time when the newspapers said that only twelve men understood the theory of relativity. I do not believe there ever was such a time . . . . On the other hand, I think I can safely say that *nobody understands quantum mechanics.*"[51]

So you see how the problem of naming "matter" has come to rather hilariously mirror the problem of naming "God." *Si comprehendis non est deus* (Augustine). And from the seventh-century Pseudo-Dionysius on, the apophatic margin undid the language of God as any kind of "being." Eckhart captures it famously: "If you love God as he is God, as he is spirit, as he is person and as he is image—all this must go!"[52] But as with the quantum science, the knowledge of this unknowability, the knowing ignorance, does not repress, inhibit, or lose its subject "matter"—it produces new openings, new kinds of knowing.

The mysteriousness of matter has been recently considered under the sign of "apophatic bodies."[53] It enacts one register of the transdisciplinary theological perspective of apophatic entanglement. Drawing on the ancient antecedents of the *docta ignorantia*, a theology that unsays any metaphor or idea of God, the apophatic entanglement unsays any certainty as to the *creatures* as well. For *in their material entanglements*, in their intra-active complexity, they "slip, slide, perish,/Decay with imprecision, will not stay in place,/Will not stay put."[54] They refuse to remain the knowable, predictable, or controllable subjects of each other. Let alone of a knowably controlling Creator who always already knows–it-all before it comes to pass. The language of spirit, being, divinity, God, infinity, *posse ipsum*, possibility itself can, possibly—from this theological perspective—be otherwise and meaningfully activated, even after the death of God, the deaths of so many gods. But when the icons of an unknowable infinity cease to undergo their own iconoclasm, they freeze to idol.[55] And mask the entanglements of their own becoming.

Not just a mirror-game between the apophatic God and the apophatic matter is in play but a chiasmus: The infinite folds in and out of the spontaneously materializing intra-actions. God as *complicatio/explicatio* nicknames that very enfolding and unfolding, is embodied, broken up, multiplied by it. There appears a crossover between negative theology and affirmative materialization in and as a world, which crosses back as the apophasis of matter at its mysterious limits, to all the affirmative bodily God-names of every tradition (mothers, fathers, lovers, daughters, sons, doves, snakes, fire, cloud, planets . . .). The interrelation of God and world in the ancient model swerves in Cusa's early modern experiment into an almost unprecedented formulation of material intra-activity: "Since the universe is contracted in each actually existing thing, it is obvious that God, who is in the universe, is in each thing and each actually existing thing is immediately in God, as is the universe."[56] So then an apophatically entangled theology may be said to diffract the entanglements of matter itself: for example, between earth and its "heaven" of subtle atmosphere of shifting parts per million of CO_2, between Christianity and its Jewish and pagan ancestors, between the apparatuses of science and those of religion, between the apophatic infinity of Cusa's cosmos and the unfathomable infinity of infinities of the current multiverse . . . [57]

In such a God-mattering or matter-divining chiasmus the experimental metaphors of process theology may now benefit from such an apophatic gesture, preventing them from congealing into some ontotheological super-entity. (We do not want God to misplace her concreteness.) At the same time the ancient Neoplatonic lineage of apophasis needs the Whiteheadian figure of divinity as an open process of becoming, not as a simply free agent but rather as, indeed, intra-active energy entangled in, not determining in advance, all the creaturely becomings of the universe. Such a theos would be, inasmuch as it would be, always *materializing*. It was Whitehead's student Hartshorne who offered the trope of "the universe as the body of God."[58] The "most moved mover,"[59] affected by every ripple of matter, here displaces the immaterial changelessness of the Aristotelian Unmoved Mover.

"One matter-energy, maker of all things visible and invisible." Bennett's ironic mimicry of the Nicene Creed lands far from Nicaea but rather close—apophatically speaking—to such a chiasmus as this: "It is as true to say that God creates the world as that the world creates God." In other words, in its transdisciplinary apparatus the *theos* only becomes determinate outside of our constructive relation to it—not unlike the way the phenomenon remains inseparable from Barad's "agencies of observation." Of course, here one is not observing through measuring devices but material practices by which one becomes an *observant* Hindu or Catholic, equipped with whichever apparatus of participation enhances that observance, and at the same time, in the more honest cases, responsibility for the participatory effects (the sun dance, the exodus, the mandala, Torah, gospels, the circumcision, incense, stained glass, the cilice, the relics, the cantatas, the march on Washington, the yoga mat, the pastor performing the same-sex wedding, the televangelist denouncing her, etc. ad infinitum).

But in theologies supplemented by new materializations we discern animation in the materials themselves, even in the invisibility of the photons coming through the live molecules of wine and cup into the colorful display of your sophisticated retina; in the bread, flesh, sex, paper, tongues, community, in the vibrancy released or repressed of the participants. If some ultimate *complicatio* or *anima mundi* comes entangled in all of it, it would not be to confer life upon a world external to it, let alone to create it *ex nihilo*, but rather to partake of the unpredictabilities and creativities and precarities of that shared life as its own.

Polyamorous Panentheism

Okay, so I have talked about God, or whatever s/he/it nicknames. Otherwise I would feel transdisciplinarily disingenuous. But let me make something else clear: The theological metaphors of Whitehead's thought—as, for instance, his "poet of the world"—do not turn up in the work of the quantum physicists he has influenced. Physics retains its distinct disciplinary register, which we may observantly *entangle in* theology but which does not thereby spookily at a distance, by superposition of the Holy Ghost, materialize the deity.

As a physicist Henry Stapp says this much: "Even if we discount the gods of various religions, it seems difficult to imagine how idea-like realities could emerge from a world completely devoid *of any such aspects*, and how physical laws could come to be fixed by a purely physical mindless universe."[60] He says "gods" only in this unsaying way, which does at the same time question any unquestionable atheism, along with the "purely physical mindless universe" that is pretty much the bottom line for any *old* materialism. He is thinking about the observer problem from a fresh point of view. He elsewhere notes that the way all actual occasions in Whitehead might be said to "observe" (nonconsciously but feelingly, and in Stapp's language "mindfully") obviates the absurd solipsism, which would have the moon exist only, as Einstein feared of quantum mechanics, when a human looks at it.[61] Whether in collapsing the wave function into the particle, or perceiving the wave as particle, each particular creature appears only in its observance of the other observant creatures. Stapp infers speculatively a whole "psychosomatic universe."

There is in this line of thinking anachronistically some echo of old vitalist or panpsychist counter-traditions. Yet Whitehead's vocabulary is a bit different, as he reserved "psyche" as well as "consciousness" or "mind" for highly complex animals and considered vitalism still a dualistic compromise. But as noted above, he found not simply life but a nonconscious "mentality" or awareness that prehends or feels in every quantum of matter. His "subjective aim" bears comparison with the "entelechy" that Bennett has found in the vitalism of Hans Driesch.[62] The process theologian David Griffin, who has written on the re-enchantment of nature and of science, suggests the term "pan-experientialism."[63] If some vitalist philosophies more closely approximate a pure immanence, or pantheism, than the pan*en*theism by which process theology sometimes labels itself, these are not mutually exclusive intuitions.[64]

For a theology of apophatic entanglement, God and matter name, indeed materialize, *different* but not *separable* becomings. Difference signifies not separation but relation. So theology cannot properly divide its deity from the matter of the world, or, for precisely that matter, panentheism from pantheism, without violating the entanglement that lends both *pan* and *theos* their flares of meaning. And by the same token, transdisciplinary explorations of natural science, or of "vital materialism," may fruitfully avoid all theistic avowal without thereby severing relations of historic, poetic, and ethical affinity to certain theologies.

This is not just a matter of polite exchange between disciplines but of the creatively inseparable difference that what, for instance, Bennett develops as the political ecology of vital matter will require of us all. The apophatic element I hope contributes at least a theological hospitality to the uncertain reaches of pluralist engagement. It keeps scrutibility scrupulous rather than smug. It may also serve, in the face of a still hopefully indeterminate planetary future, the responsible determinations needed for ecosmopolitan imperative. Thus Whitney Bauman concludes *Religion and Ecology* on this profoundly and becomingly apophatic note: "Built into both science and religion is a sense of the unknown and ever changing process of becoming life: the truth regimes of science and religion are always changing and changing the worlds in which we live. When these truth regimes are taken to be reality *en toto* or as closer to nature *en esse*, then violence is perpetuated on the becoming planetary community."[65] That essentialism, which he deconstructs with the help at once of polydoxical religion and queer theory, perpetrates the fallacy of misplaced concreteness across all the straight-laced regimes of disciplinary power. Those regimes impose the impermeable boundaries of the natural sciences, of Christian orthodoxies, of identitarian politics. Bauman destabilizes the ground they stand on by "queering nature"—in the full ecology of its cosmos. Then, with his sense of the unknown, which apophatically energizes the theological practice of his planetary ethic, Bauman is able to propose, far from the stasis of classical theism or materialism, a "nomadic polyamoury of place."[66] That traces precisely the places of an apophatic materialism.

In other words, an observant panentheism cannot do its work without periodic revitalization of its apophatic matter. That work now insists upon the planetary ethic that locates all of our perspectives at the precise intersection of the microcosm and the macrocosm (where we meet the universe halfway). The quantum infinitesimals and the cosmic infinities entangle each other as the "great work" of our planetary cosmopolis: Opus Earth.[67] And that opus involves sometimes setting forth recognizably Christian alternatives to the unquestionable truth-regimes of the religious right (Opus Dei, Pat Robertson, Michele Bachmann, Senator Jim Inhofe, etc.). This cannot work as a simple opposition. For the certitudes of conservative Christian materialisms seem to arise in compensation-reaction to a certain disembodied liberalism, to the vacant immateriality and fading vitality characteristic of so much mainstream religious and secularized faith. The reactive formations may be perilously misguided, but they do react to a real problem. But they do so within the terms of an ancient supernatural dualism, in which the divine participation in matter matters only by way of the one exceptional incarnation. Which then simply proves the rule of a dualistic transcendence. And in that gap between God and world there grows the standard exclusivism (*nulla salus extra ecclesiam*, Jesus saves, etc.). Whether in the fading mainstream or the empowered right, the christomonism feeds on the sense of the supernatural as what *makes* the natural and alone makes it worthwhile; and which alone makes humans, and humans alone, as Jane Bennett notes, "eligible for eternal salvation"—i.e., rescue *from* the material world. Their supernaturalism can claim the mantle of Christian materialism precisely by intensifying its own binary oppositions—as, quite congruently, the scientific materialism of the West builds upon the Cartesian dualism.

Modeling an entangled relationality, the panentheist alternative withdraws from its theos the status of an independent entity or substance that enters and enlivens from the outside or that is contained within an inside. It can name the spirited oscillation of a sea bird "vibrating" on the waves the *mayim* (Gen. 1:2).[68] And instead of a transcendent being "coming down" and donning external human flesh, there appears the figure of a becoming-body, in an incarnational poetics, or a phenomenology of the flesh of the world.[69] The singular incarnation undergoes radical redistribution. Already experimentation in multiple Christs—Black, Latino, queer, or the female Sophia—has over a couple generations effected what we might call a *superpositional christology*, in which communities in their material-ritual apparatuses diffract Christ differently. Yet in each case there can be no separation between the observant community and the bodily marking of their Christ. This is the one who in Matthew's account cannot be disentangled—to the consternation of the "Lord Lord" sayers—from the hungry, the imprisoned, the "least of these my siblings" (Matt. 25:40). Marcella Althaus-Reid argues that inasmuch as in such liberation theologies "God has been the object of theological de-essentialization processes," fuller and queerer implications have yet to be drawn: There appears the "omnisexual God" of a "body-grounded theology," where God's omnitude "might be able to return the lost presence of the polyamorous body to its theological discourse."[70] That lost presence signifies no metaphysical substance to return to but a multicontextual ecology to create. There the love-body of Christ morphs into something very like Bauman's polyamory of place, the "love of many places as part of a larger, planetary community."[71] Such experiments in bodying God—decolonial, queer, ecological—dissolve the exclusionary body of Christ. In each case a concrete materialization is at stake. And taken together (from the viewpoint perhaps of a queerly planetary body) the intersection and coalitions may apophatically unsay any Christ-talk in order to form a superpositional cloud that—in the relational pluralism of religious and irreligious discourses—makes honest christologies possible.

But if such incarnational intra-activity breaks into an interreligious and transreligious diversity, it does not forfeit theological intensity. One may note indeed some unintended resonance between the theological polyamory and Whitehead's "Eros of the universe" luring all bodied occasions toward greater intensity, togetherness, and satisfaction.[72] For itself, too.

Such theological experiments have practical effects. They let us access the spiritually saturated materiality persisting in the diverse global materializations of spiritual practice. They make sure we do not abandon "Christian materialism" to any religio-political right. In this we do not merely disenchant supernaturalism but offer enticement to ecosmopolitical solidarities.

Not that any queer, Black, female, or green-bodied divinity (let alone Whitehead's primordial and consequent natures of God) will win over religious conservatives. But versatile versions of relational theology that work sympathetically with *spirited* matter or holy flesh, across the ecumenical manifold, will remain indispensable in the attempt to energize diverse local solidarities for planetary revitalization. These apophatically entangled theologies may begin to release, within the cloud of impossible difference, the widening crowd of relations that may sustain a convivial planet. If such will now collude in fresh materializations of race and culture, of gender, sex, and species, no simple transcendence of the old and evolving spiritual ways will be possible. Discernment between them will be.

And really, is it foolish to imagine, even across the surface of dispirited, reactionary, or dying religions, even here and there tangled in tawdry superstitions, the breaking of wave upon wave of dimly felt superpositions? Felt unexpectedly, healingly, prophetically, amorously. And always with a tingle of mystery. For the nonlocal—planetary, cosmic—materializes, it incarnates, locally. Sacramentally.

Tingling Tissue

As to the sacramental—Protestants did not stop performing the ritual of communion. But we certainly abandoned the notion of transubstantiation, with its embarrassingly direct physicality of eating and drinking a body mysteriously incarnate through the priest/believer/Eucharistic apparatus. We might have cut off some access to the materialization of shared flesh, to the future unfolding of the enfolded past in the ritual entanglement of an elemental re-collection. "'Transubstantiation' is a religious term, and yet one that could just as well be applied to quantum phenomenon." So writes Vicki Kirby in *Quantum Anthropologies* (channeling Barad) of the "superposition of differences" of culture and nature, of mind and body.[73] Or as I must ceremonially intone, of God and matter. The separated substances decompose even as, in the indeterminate interval, "naturecultures" (Haraway) and "matter-energy" (Bennett) and "ethico-onto-epistem-ology" (Barad) are composing and recomposing themselves unpredictably.

Each new insight into quantum entanglement has, I admit, caused my flesh to prickle in a way that the Eucharist rarely has. Not because God or anything else is getting proved; but because something about what we all, human and nonhuman, together *are*, what it is we are *part* of, is coming through when we need it. And it comes with the dark luminosity of apophatic mysticism through the antimystical apparatus of a science that had not been looking for it. Maybe that is why it conveys the tingle of novelty, of discovery, so often stifled in traditions that already own the truth. The meaning of quantum entanglement—inseparability of once-linked bodies at unfathomable space-time distances—is spreading with the excitement of cutting-edge science.

So the tingle I have in mind is only fleetingly personal. It is the tingling of matter itself, in its newly revealed apophatic indeterminacy. A tingle—a prickle, sting, buzz, or quiver of excitement—captures something about the particle, the particular phenomenon, and so of any moment of matter. The wave of potentiality materializes qua particle (whether or not there is a "collapse of the wave function") only as a phenomenon of relation, subtle, sentient, vibrant. Each particle appears now less like a hard bit of stuff and more like an event of materialization: a tingle in the flesh of the world. What Mary-Jane Rubenstein calls "strange wonder" insists itself upon us transdisciplinarily.[74] Its recognition may be its own reward, but it is provoking something more.

Here is a passage that fosters that "more," without in any way theologizing it, a text that tingles every time I read it:

> If we hold on to the belief that the world is made of individual entities, it is hard to see how even our best, most well-intentioned calculations for right action can avoid tearing holes in the delicate tissue structure of entanglements that the lifeblood of the world runs through.[75]

The holes are growing. They take the shape of melting glaciers, spreading droughts, dying oceans, desperate and migrating millions. Our civilization's violation of its own materiality is building to its climax. It seems we now ignore the message of that minimum matter at peril of what matters maximally. The point, however, is not to cry doom but to stir an alternative. Prickles of fear are not far from tingles of attraction. If a "delicate tissue of ethicality runs through the marrow of being," no one needs to "believe" in God or materialism.[76] Within the field of an apophatically entangled energy-matter, the transubstantiation of the blood of the world will happen willy-nilly. We can continue to spill it wantonly. No supernature will rescue us.

Or we can attend to the delicate tissue of our entanglements. Such responsiveness might make us more ethically affective and effective, capable of stronger coalitional conversations, collective actualizations, terrestrial communions. If so, we have to do not with the imposition of beliefs but with the superposition of possibilities—and so of more convivial, maybe even ecosmopolitical, materializations.

CHAPTER 5

Confessing Monica: Reading Augustine Reading His Mother

With Virginia Burrus

It is difficult to force Augustine to confess his mother-fixation, partly because he is already so eager to do so. He is, after all, the man who virtually invented the closet, so that he could come out of its hollowed, hallowed interiority again and again, making a subject of his private perversions, flamboyantly exhibiting his stubbornly bent will. Monica is among the guilty pleasures enjoyed by the author of the *Confessions*. Moreover, unlike stolen pears, she is a love that the author cannot possibly renounce, a pleasure he cannot forgo. She emerges as the irrepressible subject of a holy Life in a work that resists hagiography, as an irreducibly carnal figure in a tale that insists on love's sublimation, as Wisdom seductively incarnate in a book that has little to say about Christ. Finally, she erupts, she opens

---

This collaboration with Virginia Burrus, the scholar of antiquity and ancient Christianity, emerged out of our shared interdisciplinary investment in the feminist engagement of certain nondismissable fathers of the faith. It first appeared in *Feminist Interpretations of Augustine*, ed., Judith Chelius Stark (University Park: Pennsylvania State University Press, 2007). Burrus has written the first half primarily, I the second.

up, as an excitingly fertile, disturbingly overdetermined, matrix of meaning, at the very place in the Scripture where Augustine—sitting in silent contemplation—expects to find nothing at all.

This present meditation on the mother in Augustine's *Confessions* is written with two hands, one historical and literary, the other theological and exegetical. The text may, like *Confessions* itself, seem to divide naturally into two parts. Yet thoughts overlap, words interweave: It is finally impossible to say precisely where one subject begins and another ends. We shall see that in writing Monica Augustine is already anticipating the unfurling of Scripture "herself." Likewise, in reading Scripture he is still testifying to his own ambivalence in the face of the maternal depths, re-encountered both in the figure of "tehom" and in the tehomic fecundity of interpretation itself. We may, after all, force Augustine to confess a bit more than he wants to, as he hovers agonizingly at the brink of a theology of "becoming" that is also a "becoming-theology," evading the static doctrinalism to which he elsewhere more wholeheartedly succumbs.

VB

Confessions is a woman's Life. Is that so strange a claim? More paradoxical still, the womb of the Life—cradled in the center of the text—is the account of the woman's *death*. It is in grieving his mother, Monica, that Augustine discovers his point of departure, just when we might have thought he was finished with his account. He departs, he begins again, then, in the middle—*in medias res.* (*Every beginning is also a departure—from something.*) Grieving Monica, remembering his mother, delivering her eulogy to God in the pseudo-privacy of his ancient prayer closet, Augustine learns to read; he begins to write in earnest. *In principio Deus creavit*, runs the text. "In the beginning you made heaven and earth," he addresses the author of both Scripture and cosmos wonderingly (11.3).[1] Augustine creates too—he is also a writer: *he makes his confession* brashly "in this book before the many who will read it" (10.1). But perhaps *we make too much* of his sheer originality, his auto-generativity. We forget—or fail to notice—that it is his mother who provides him the narrative material out of which to conceive time and space, to frame the very cosmos. Monica's Life (centered on her death) gives him his opening, keeps his story of conversion open. Monica is Augustine's eternally unfinished business; she is present in all his beginnings.

A beginning that is in the middle of the thing, an irruptive potentiality that resists narrative closure, Monica plots and is emplotted, simultaneously generates and disrupts storylines. Less an item than a happening, she *takes place* in the argument of Augustine's *Confessions*, and thus we must strive to understand *what that place is*. Present from the beginning (1.11), she meets her end (and in a sense also makes her formal debut) in Book 9, where the narrative portion of the *Confessions* likewise concludes. There is a certain substitutionary logic to the mother's dying the death impossible for the author of an autobiography. The existence of Book 9 nonetheless presents a dilemma, for Book 8 already contains all the makings of another kind of ending, having staged the intense struggle of will that culminates in Augustine's dramatic "conversion" (the liberating death of his formerly enslaved self). For the first-time reader, it must come as something of a surprise when Augustine extends his story into a ninth book that relates, first, his ascetic withdrawal and baptism and, second, his memories of the life of his mother. The centerpiece of these memories is a shared mystical experience occurring shortly before Monica's death and Augustine's oddly unexplained and open-ended departure for Africa at the portentous age of thirty-three. Such a dizzying spiritual encounter, following the dramatic experience of divine intervention in Book 8's scene of conversion, seems excessive—more than the story demands, almost more than it can accommodate.

Yet, perversely, having scripted such a dubious *double climax*, Augustine may seem to add narrative insult to injury by going on to write a distinctly *anticlimactic* tenth tome. Previously swept along on the waves of the author's passionate recounting of the misadventures of his youth and the struggles of his conversion, tossed high by the unexpected thrill of his maternally mediated heavenly ascent, now as readers we find ourselves stalled on the vast, midlife calm of his mental abstraction. We may share Pelagius's outrage that Augustine is killing the tale in more ways than one: when viewed from the sober perspective of the morning after, conversion loses its sharp edge, the bloom of optimism fades, and old habits reassert their sway even in the life of a would-be saint. (Who wants to read about *that*?) But Books 9 and 10 are only the beginning of Augustine's refusal to allow his *Confessions* their proper end: Three more seemingly superfluous books follow, as he makes yet another fresh start, now posing as biblical commentator in locating his account in the beginning, in *Genesis*, in the generation of world and written word. At this late point in the text, Augustine's snail's pace advance through the first slim chapter of the capacious Book of books may seem to make not only a mess but a mockery of the search for an end to the story of his life. Sucked into the ever-receding depths of Scripture's polyvalence, almost parodically prolific in his interpretive reinscriptions, Augustine the reader has, by any strictly linear measure of progress, come to a virtual standstill. Has the text, drained of desire, simply petered out? Or, rather, as Augustine would have us understand it, has his own restless curiosity—tracked over time—been converted into eternal rest in the performative reading of the scriptural Sabbath?

The question is: Why *does* Augustine keep writing so far past his famous conversion? What—if anything—links the autobiographical Books 1–9 of *Confessions*, which the tale of Monica finally *overtakes*, with the exegetical Books 10–13, in turn *overtaken* by silent repose? (A repose that represents not, Augustine would urge, the stasis of death but instead yet another opening door [13.38].)

We can begin by observing that the reader's quest for the structured coherence of *Confessions* is inextricably intertwined with Augustine's narrated quest for Wisdom: "To love Wisdom herself, whoever she might be, and to search for her, pursue her, hold her, and embrace her firmly—these were the words that excited me and set me burning with fire" (3.4). As Danuta Shanzer interprets him, the author of *Confessions* constructs a deliberately enigmatic and suspenseful text by combining a Proverbial "choice motif"—*Folly versus Wisdom*—with a "search motif"—*where is Wisdom to be found?* At least as early as Book 3, when Augustine explicitly represents himself as seduced by Folly (3.6), "we are detectives with a Scriptural clue (Stultitia presupposes her opposite), and a Scriptural description or identikit picture of Sapientia, if we are prepared to use it to find or recognize her," Shanzer suggests.[2] Shanzer's reference to the "Scriptural clue" of Book 3—namely, the allegorical figures of Folly and Wisdom in Proverbs 9—is itself a further clue but one which we, like the Augustine of Book 3, have trouble putting to good use. Searching for the hidden Sapientia, we may not notice that she is there alongside Stultitia from the start: "And behold I saw something—or someone—neither disclosed to the proud nor laid bare to children, but humble in gait, sublime in accomplishment, and veiled in mysteries. And I was not the type who would be able to enter into her or to bend my neck to her guidance" (3.5). It is difficult to say at what point most readers realize that the Holy Scripture—for that is "who" is here described—does not merely offer clues but is also itself (*herself*) the answer to the riddle posed by the work: The Augustine of Books 11–13, lost in silent contemplation of the biblical writings, absorbed in their depths, has indeed reached the end of the quest delineated in Books 1–9. It is difficult to say at what point readers *also* realize that the end is always only beginning: There is no limit to knowing the beloved, to loving Wisdom, to interpreting a text. Perhaps we only recognize that *Scripture is Augustine's*

Lady Wisdom when we too have become her lovers—readers sufficiently skilled as to be able to perceive the unity in a complex and open-ended work. Some of us may have to read the *Confessions* again and again before we see the Lady at all.

Shanzer suggests that "Scripture's many faces, when she is seen as a woman, prefigure her many interpretations, when she is seen as a text."[3] *One face that Shanzer fails to mention is the face of Augustine's mother*. Indeed, Shanzer's framing of the autobiographical allegory of Folly and Wisdom developed in Books 3–7 and culminating in the Herculean "choice" of Book 8 seems to leave the minibiography of Monica in Book 9 awkwardly caught, along with the rest of Book 9 and Book 10, in the liminal zone between the narrative quest and its exegetical consummation. Yet we would suggest that the "Life of Monica" is the crux of the narrativized enigma (*where is Wisdom?*), a riddle that is not so much solved as displaced—repeated and reframed—by the later exegetical performance (*she is [in] Scripture*).

"Behold, moved by your prayers, I come to you, natural mother of all things . . . whose single divinity is venerated over the whole earth under many faces, varying rites, and changing names" (Apuleius, *Golden Ass* 11.5). Thus speaks the goddess in her seaside epiphany in Apuleius's *The Golden Ass*—a text that may be of special importance for understanding the structural significance of the figure of Monica in Augustine's *Confessions*. As John Winkler argues, the eleventh and final book of Apuleius's novel, which contains the solemn manifestation of the many-named and many-faced goddess Isis, comes as a shock to a first-time reader of this witty and sophisticated text. It also dramatically destabilizes the familiar parodic quest tale that is seemingly Apuleius's point of departure—namely Pseudo-Lucian's *Lucius, or the Ass*. "For if the ass-tale is a take-off on 'I went in quest of wisdom' narratives, then Apuleius has translated the parody, with all its ridicule of the quester intact, but has added at the end the very sort of epiphany and revelation that the *parodied* works contained."[4] Winkler emphasizes the uncertainty introduced by the supplemental Isiac book, which reinstates divine revelation in (relatively) "straight" terms at the conclusion, and outside the frame, of an (ambiguously) parodic narrative. The Apuleian novel, he argues, thereby refuses to adjudicate between competing truth claims and thus shifts the burden of decision to the reader, while at the same time making it clear that the decision lies outside the domain of rationally negotiable propositions. "The *Golden Ass* is an evocation of a religious experience bracketed in such a way that the reader must, but cannot, decide the question of its truth," Winkler suggests. "The implicit argument of the novel is that belief in

Isis or in any integrating cosmic hypothesis is a radically individual act that cannot be shared."[5]

Augustine follows Apuleius's example, constructing a quest narrative that begins falsely with carnal curiosity and ends felicitously with divine disclosure. Here—in contrast to his treatment of Virgil's *Aeneid*, for example—he lets a significant literary predecessor go utterly unnamed. This may be a necessary exercise of tact, where allusion so dangerously combines admiration with aggression. The Apuleian novel is quite possibly already making a mockery of Christianity, and if Augustine subtly turns the tables in counter-mimicry he cannot deny that there is also genuine flattery in his imitation. Apuleius seems to have written his novel less to propagandize the Isiac cult than to question the totalizing claims of all such cults, and Augustine arguably replays Apuleius's plot less to unseat a false goddess—Isis—and replace her with a true one—Wisdom—than to undermine an ironic agnosticism so as to assert the authority of divine revelation, not least by sternly imposing his "converted" perspective on the account of his earlier life. But how successful is he? As Winkler describes Augustine's *Confessions*, noting the contrast with Apuleius, "The present narrator invades his past as an enemy territory, using his god as a powerful ally to destroy the lingering vestiges of the pleasure he originally felt."[6] The contrast is real; nonetheless, we should not exaggerate the differences between these two literary works, the one a novel narrated in the first person and frequently read as autobiography (indeed, so read by Augustine himself), the other a novelistic autobiography occasionally labeled (as Augustine labeled Apuleius's work) a lying fiction. Each pivots around a surprise ending that calls upon us to reassess the text retrospectively, thereby thematizing the necessity for artful interpretation—underlining the indispensability, and also the indeterminacy, of exegesis.

Winkler warns readers of Apuleius not to impose monologic and moralizing readings on a fundamentally complex and deliberately ambiguous text. Such a warning would likewise be well heeded by readers of the later North African. *Confessions* is seductive and hermeneutically challenging precisely where it is most powerfully empathetic—and most surprisingly noncommittal—in its replaying of the emotions of the author's earlier selves. Augustine sustains a remarkable level of ambivalence throughout the narrative books of his work—though unlike Apuleius he (narrowly) avoids parody. To cite merely a well-known example: His recollection of a boyhood theft of pears, frequently viewed as evidence of excessive critique of past behavior, skillfully introduces and interlaces moral judgment with vivid evocations of the fundamentally "good" pleasures that motivated the paltry crime—sensory gratification, social esteem, and above all "the delightful bond" of friendship (2.5). Much as Apuleius's narrator delivers a harrowing rendition of a "murder" that turns out to be no more than a slashing of wineskins (*Metam.* 2.32–3.10), here Augustine deliberately makes much ado about almost nothing. His purpose, it seems, is to cut moral transgressions down to their ordinary, nonheroic size while at the same time restoring a sense of their modest complexities. Likewise, Augustine's tender accounts of his various (with the exception of his concubine, homoerotic) "lovers" (e.g., 4.8, 6.15) appear no more regretful than Lucius's enthusiastic recountings of his luscious nights with Fotis (e.g., *Metam.* 2.16–17). (In fact, if we take Lucius's later recriminations of his mistress Fotis seriously, Augustine may be the less regretful.)

Perhaps even more surprising (and even more often repressed) than the relatively forgiving, almost Apuleian eye that Augustine casts on his own past is the negativity that he introduces into the supplementary "book of the mother." As we shall see, he thereby sustains a positive ambivalence where we might expect (indeed, have been led by his interpreters to expect) a more reductively idealizing portrait to emerge. In this respect, Book 9 of *Confessions* is as much a counterpart to the portrait of Venus in Apuleius's centrally embedded tale of Psyche and Cupid (*Metam.* 6) as it is an evocation of the final epiphany of Isis (*Metam.* 11). (Like Monica, Venus's opinion of what—or who—is best for her son initially differs from his own but is subsequently revised.) The "ultimate" surprise ending of *Confessions*— showcasing an unambivalently positive representation of the divine female figure Sapientia/Scriptura that more closely matches Apuleius's Isis—is deferred to the last three books, which thus supplement the supplement. As in Apuleius's novel, the extended revelation—itself taking unexpected form—includes the equally unexpected message that no revelation is conclusive. Texts continue to give rise to interpretation. "For I know that what is understood in one way by the mind can be given multiple material significations; and what is given material signification in one way can be understood in many ways by the mind," muses Augustine. "For behold the simple love of God and neighbor—how it is given material expression in multiple sacraments and innumerable languages and, within each language, in innumerable turns of phrase!" (13.24).

It appears, then, that Augustine's *Confessions* only pretends to imagine itself the one and only, first and unique, thereby slyly challenging us to notice its deep dependency and intricate intertextuality. Augustine writes over the lines of other texts, both biblical and secular, as we have just seen. He has precursors, but we should not forget that he *also* has contemporaries.

Others of the time—other Christians—are writing female biographies, inscribing the Lives of women. They too are writing over the lines of other texts—tales of martyrdom and letters of consolation as well as stories of love. There is a trend, almost a fad. Gregory of Nyssa writes of his sister Macrina barely more than a decade before Augustine writes of his mother; Jerome writes of his longtime companion Paula a decade or so after *Confessions* is penned; nor are they the only ones doing it. Augustine is not sheerly original, then; he inherits from the past and he is also in the thick of something ongoing. Like Gregory and Jerome, he writes from the perspective of a man grieving; like these other authors, he mourns a much-loved woman, mourns a woman known for her grieving, thus grieves like a woman—reluctantly, and also excessively, with ambivalence. "The tears dried in my eyes.... It did not bring me to tears.... I did not weep." So he begins, only to reverse himself quickly. "The tears which I had been holding back streamed down, and I let them flow as freely as they would," Augustine next confesses, pleading that his reader not despise such womanish behavior but rather imitate it. "Let him not mock at me but weep himself, if his charity is great" (9.12).

Like Gregory and still more like Jerome, Augustine writes with tearful ambivalence of a woman, and he inscribes his ambivalence into the Life. He writes with two hands, giving praise with one and taking it away with the other. The Lives of women are not quite hagiographies, no matter who writes them. Monica, Augustine makes painfully clear, was no saint. She had bad habits, perverse desires. "I cannot presume to say that from the time when she was reborn in baptism no word contrary to your commands ever fell from her lips," notes the son in the midst of his mourning. Since he is stating the obvious, why does he say it? "I will lay aside for a while all the good deeds which my mother did. For them I thank you, but now I pray to you for her sins" (9.13).

Indeed, Monica the well-intentioned sinner never quite gets it right, according to her son. Her life is always in need of revision; she is always in need of our prayers. We see this most clearly from the vantage point of her death, where Augustine, who has just promised to "omit not a word that my mind can bring to birth concerning my mother, your servant," now seems to have an oddly selective memory, zeroing in first on an account of childhood alcoholism framed by class conflict, on the one hand, and spousal abuse interlaced with intergenerational conflict, on the other, positioning his mother as a dubious pupil in a school of very hard knocks indeed. "Each day she added a few more drops to her daily sip of wine. 'But little things despise and little by little you shall come to ruin.' It soon became a habit, and she would drink her wine at a draught, almost by the cupful" (9.8).

Peter Brown notes that, in Book 9's portrayal, "Monica, the idealized figure that had haunted Augustine's youth like an oracle of God, is subtly transformed, by Augustine's analysis of his present feelings upon remembering her death, into an ordinary human being, an object of concern, a sinner like himself, equally in need of mercy."[7] There have also, however, been earlier signs of Monica's flawed character in the text—leading little by little toward her "ruin" in Book 9. Remember? As a young mother, she shuns the "better course" of an early baptism for her son and instead defers the rite, preferring that "the great tides of temptation . . . beat upon the as yet unmolded clay rather than upon the finished image which had received the stamp of baptism" (1.12; cf. 5.9). When, after a visit to the public baths, her husband proudly reports "the signs of active virility coming to life" in their son, Monica again responds inadequately, worrying too little about Augustine's desires and too much about his career. "She was afraid that the bonds of marriage might be a hindrance to my hopes for the future, . . . my hopes of success at my studies." (Here Augustine's subsequent attempt to Christianize Monica's motive—because such an overt rationalization—merely calls attention to his mother's queer worldliness: "Both my parents were unduly eager for me to learn," he recalls, "my mother because she thought that the usual course of study would certainly not hinder me, but would even help me, in my approach to you" [2.3].) Having left the tides of temptation to engulf her son, Monica unleashes a flood of her own into the text, worrying and weeping ceaselessly. "It cannot be that the son of those tears should be lost," a weary bishop finally snaps, a statement that she is pleased to accept as prophetic (3.12). If, as a mother, she is now metonymically defined by her tears, her sorrow begins to seem a bit much. A reader can almost imagine why Augustine sneaks away in the night, "leaving her alone to her tears and her prayers," boarding a ship for Rome—like Virgil's Aeneas giving Dido the slip. As Augustine represents it, even God's patience with the woman has grown thin by this point: Monica's excessive grief at Augustine's departure, "her too jealous love for her son," is identified as a divine punishment that fits the female crime of passion. Indeed, her maternal sorrow is itself the mark of sin, "proof that she had inherited the legacy of Eve" (5.8).

Crying is not all that is left to Monica, however. She still has scope to (mis)manage Augustine's life. Astonishingly, she has followed him all the way to Milan (6.1)—no Dido, she, after all. Now, when it is too late, she finds her son a wife (6.13). In preparation for his socially advantageous marriage, Augustine's longtime, devoted lover, with whom he has fathered a son, is "torn from his side" and sent back to Africa. There, grieving like a widow and vowing chastity, *she* now plays Dido to his Aeneas, while his mother stands staunchly at his side, like Adam's rib. Augustine's unnamed concubine *also* plays an unsuccessful Psyche to his Cupid, with Monica in the role of Venus, most difficult of mothers-in-law. In the meantime, bereft of his soulmate, Augustine suddenly finds his own sinfulness nakedly revealed. He cannot imitate the woman—his former lover—for whom his heart still bleeds. He cannot even wait for his new wife, for if the marriage comes too late for Augustine, it comes too soon by at least two years for the prepubescent girl to whom he is engaged. Into the gap, a stopgap mistress steps. The waves of longing for erotic intimacy with a woman beat upon him with the relentless force of an addiction, "an uninterrupted habit" (6.15). Little by little, he has been hooked, like Monica in the cellar with her sips of wine.

Augustine is not original, but he *is* creative. Writing the Life of a woman, he gives birth to his own Life. His *Confessions* is a "great book" but (like the Life of a woman) not quite a hagiography. The Saint's Life is in his field of vision, but it is not his point of departure. When "a book containing the life of Antony" is read by another, Augustine leaves it lying just barely outside the frame of his text, a found object in another man's story of a stranger's conversion (8.6; cf. 8.12). His own Life thereby also escapes the frame of holiness. It is—necessarily—unfinished. It is unfinished business, always beginning again. It is perpetually in the process of revision.

Augustine never quite gets it right. (This theologically weighty self-presentation is, after all, the root of his famous disagreement with Pelagius.) For one thing, he keeps picking the wrong woman. First there was the Folly of Cicero, and then Mani. Now, so close to a proper catholic orthodoxy, in his final nightmarish staging of Proverbs 9, he finds himself of two minds, struggling to decide between the austere beauty of Lady Continence (looking suspiciously like his virtuous African concubine) and the more local comforts of Mistress Habit, who beckons him to do "this thing or that"—"things so sordid and so shameful that I beg you in your mercy to keep the soul of your servant free from them!" the poor man cries (8.11). When Augustine eventually makes his choice for Continence, his mother, he tells us, is "overjoyed." "For she saw that you had granted her far more than she used to ask in her tearful prayers and plaintive lamentations" (8.12).

Is the reader surprised by Monica's spontaneous delight? We should not fail to note that, if the mother's sorrow has been exchanged for joy, it has entailed a complex conversion. Monica's tears have not been rewarded but chastened by gladness, her dream for the son of those tears not fulfilled but, little by little, revised. Augustine *insists* on it: "You 'turned her sadness into rejoicing,' into joy far fuller than her dearest wish, far sweeter and more chaste than any she had hoped to find in children begotten of my flesh," he assures his God (8.12).

"Time never stands still," writes Augustine (4.8). But once, before the end, they get it almost right, once time almost stands still. For a heartbeat —at the text's midpoint—Augustine and his mother rest together in the embrace of God's eternity; their Lives truly coincide. Leaning from a window overlooking a garden, they converse, he recalls. (It is in the days just before Monica's death, but they do not yet know that.) The flame of their love draws them higher and higher. "And while we spoke of the eternal Wisdom, longing for it and straining for it with all the strength of our hearts, for one fleeting instant we reached and touched it." Afterward they imagine what it might be like to encounter God not through the veil of Scripture but directly voiced. "Suppose that we heard him himself, with none of these things between ourselves and him, just as in that brief moment my mother and I had reached out in thought and touched the eternal Wisdom which abides over all things" (9.10).

Augustine continues to long for the moment of naked truth, but the truth is that he has already touched his Bride. However briefly, he has reached out to Lady Wisdom, there in the window with his mother. Augustine is not ready to die, but he is nonetheless happy to be standing on the threshold with Monica. Where Macrina and Paula on their own deathbeds hasten to their heavenly bridegroom with joyous greeting, Monica uses her dying breath to renounce her desire to be buried next to her earthly husband (9.11). Is she saving herself for Christ or merely choosing Continence like her son? Choosing her continent son? Who is the Bride, who the Groom, in this strange woman's Life? Augustine is grooming himself for Wisdom, but it is Monica who has accompanied him this far. It is Monica, the ever-revisable text, who enables him to recognize the woman with many faces. It is also Monica who teaches him how to submit to the chastening blows of divine desire (how to play the Bride). It is Monica who teaches him not only about sin but also about *charity*. One day the Lady will reveal herself to him nakedly (she may even come as his Lord). Now he gazes upon her veiled form, he unfurls her pages, and it is his own naked hunger that is revealed. He sucks, he gulps, he devours the inexhaustible maternal body of text. ("But the very simplicity of the language of Scripture sustains them in their weakness as a mother cradles an infant in her lap" [12.27].) He consumes Wisdom's material feast of words. ("I had learned that Wisdom and Folly are like different kinds of food" [5.6].) He makes something new of the ancient writing. He makes something new of himself. Writing, he reads. Sucking, he feeds. He feeds us. We eat him. We are eating him, reading him now. We are eating, reading *her* now.

Monica is already there at the beginning, and she is still present in the many-faced and many-named scriptural Wisdom in whom Augustine rests at the end—sign of constant love, figure of ongoing metamorphosis, creature of both excess and deficiency. Beyond that, it is hard to say: She is elusive, adaptive, mobile, and multiple, a trickster skilled at evading domination, disguising desire, guiding by misdirection. She offers no easy solutions. *She demands a strong reading.*

CK

She demands, she wills, by weeping. But it is the tears and cries of her son that lubricate our passage into the second half of his book (and of this essay). Upon emerging from Book 10's labyrinth of time puzzles, in which temporality itself plays trickster, we find ourselves in the metaphysico-hermeneutical convolutions of the last three books. Here, in the interest of a theology of creation, narrative dries to a mere stream, to barely more than the first verses of the Bible. By the waters irrupts again the exhausting wrestling match with those first two verses of Genesis, as Augustine tries from every angle to guide and squeeze them into the established metanarrative of the *creatio ex nihilo*. That would be the driest dogma of them all, indeed the ultimate medium of theological dehydration: the doctrine that rids us of the dark, chaotic waters, the tehom that flows in Genesis 1.2. No wonder the torrents of sex, anguish, and ecstasy seem suddenly to have evaporated along with Monica herself. But not without a trace. The hungry mouth and watering mouth morphs into the mouth of the primal waters. Mysteriously, by way of Sapientia herself, the *Confessions*' trail of iterative tears will open like an estuary into an evanescent ocean: a desert mirage? the mother herself? the matrix of a becoming-theology?

To pick up the trail, let us sneak back to the funeral. The waters of that transitional text will churn up an unexpected net of connections, almost indeed of metonymic equivalences, between the tears and the tehom itself—and so will push us forward into the last triad of books, in which the iconic continuum of the *Confessions* will manifest itself: between tehom and a heaven with the face of Monica, her tears forever dried.

> I closed her eyes, and a mighty sorrow welled up from the depths of my heart and overflowed into tears. At the same time, by a powerful command of my mind, my eyes drank up their source until it was dry. (9.12)

The depth surges up irrepressibly: transmitted by touch from mother's eyes to son's, from death to life. A flood defies his self-control. The tears condense in themselves the salt water of the primal deep. Luckily he masters the waters before anyone notices: As Moses parted the sea with his rod, so Augustine commands the waters with his mind. He deciphers this paradigmatic act of manhood with phenomenological precision. The organs are not puppets. Eyes and heart have wills of their own. The body can collude with the disorderly deep, it rebels against the mind's authority. Only with pain can he suppress the conspiracy of body and tehom: "Most ill was it with me in such an agony!" When his son, Adeodatus, "burst out in lamentation," he is immediately silenced. The pain is passed to the next generation. To mourn the dead is unbecoming in a man, all the more in a Christian. Suppression of grief testifies to faith in eternal life. He resents the vulnerability but glories in suppressing it then and narrating it now:

> But in your ears, where none of them could hear, I upbraided the weakness of my affection, and I held back the flood of sorrow. It gave way a little before me, but I was again swept away by its violence, although not as far as to burst into tears, nor to any change of expression. (9.12)

The private turbulence of this interior tehom is successfully kept locked behind the floodgates of his self-control. This Paulinized Stoicism absorbs the metaphysics of Being into the deep of a newly self-divided soul. Unchanged is the classical presumption that to be affected, to be *moved*, is to *be changed*—and so to occupy the passive/passionate feminine posture. He who surrenders to the fluid and the mutable fails to imitate the divinely unmoved, the impassionable One. Weeping eyes cannot host visions of immutability. Luce Irigaray draws the post-Freudian/pre-oedipal (or just: maternal) inference:

> So the mother's child is engaged in stripping away the membranes, the inheritances that he finds too material. Subject to fading and death. And if this enlightened gaze was already rising above baser and darker attractions, it must also be purified of overly terrestrial sights, and equally he must give up his trust in so finite an organ as the eyes.[8]

What renders the eyes more organic, material, membranous, than their own flash floods? As Augustine resists the materiality of his maternal bond, the torrent pounds within his body. The oceanic imaginary nearly engulfs the text: "I fought against the wave of sorrow and for a while it receded but then it swept upon me again with full force." Yet his introspective analysis exceeds, or is deficient in, Stoic terms: "But I knew well enough what I was stifling in my heart. It was misery to feel myself so weak a victim of these human emotions, although we cannot escape them . . . and so I had the added sorrow of being grieved by my own feelings." With psychological fidelity he captures his entrapment in this "two-fold agony" (9.12). "Human emotions" of grief belong to the same continuum as lust: tehomic revolt—of himself against himself and against the divine order. Yet his stance is not that of simple judgment but of a knowing ambivalence. These tears thus iterate the lachrymose cascades that conclude the prior book, in which the conflict of his divided will was triumphantly resolved by conversion.

After all, tears, microcosms of the deep, were appropriate for his mother to shed—and for him, in his conversion, when he "probed the hidden depths" of his soul and "wrung its pitiful secrets from it." Having then aggressively deciphered the interior flux, "a great storm broke within me, bringing with it a great deluge of tears." The psychic tehom repeatedly challenges his command—but in the case of his conversion, the challenge is divine. These secretions of conversion were "the sacrifice that is acceptable to you" (8.12). Does a tehomic ambivalence persistently shadow his maternal ambivalence? If the unacceptable waters are those that flow from feelings of attachment to a creature—especially to a woman—rather than to the Creator, it happens nonetheless that these tears wash out the obstacle to intimacy with his creaturely mother.

When, later on the night of her funeral, alone, he gives vent to his grief, he acknowledges that he grieves for his own loss, thinking "about her sweet and holy care for us, of which I was suddenly deprived." In a stunningly unstoic moment of compassion for himself, he writes that now he "took comfort in weeping in your sight over her and for her, over myself and for myself."

> I gave way to the tears that I had held back, so that they poured forth as much as they wished. I spread them beneath my heart, and it rested upon them, for at my heart were placed your ears, not the ears of a mere man, who would interpret with scorn my weeping. (9.12)

Now he confesses: He could not face the scorn of other males. But this God does not suppress Augustine's feelings as Augustine suppressed his son's. The divine ear sprouts in the moist, visceral deep "beneath my heart."

It performs here as good therapist. By listening to the sorrow—all the way down—it supports the grief process. In the prehension of the heart floating restfully upon a tehomic waterbed, the scene of mourning prefigures the heart's rest in God. When the deep floods through the armor of the *apatheia* of elite Christian masculinity, Augustine momentarily defies the totalizing male scorn. But does this exception—this sensitive male—prove the rule of patriarchy? Not the crude patriarchy of his abusive father but the spiritual patriarchy exalted by his mother? After all, Christian women have always had recourse, if not to a female-identified divinity, at least to the kindly "father in heaven" who relieves us of the dominance of the more in-our-face patriarchs.

We pick up the trail in Book 11: "Hear me as I cry out of the depths." In the guise of the psalmist, Augustine again reveals himself struggling within the dark waters. He supplements Psalm 130 thus: "For unless your ears are present with us in the depths, where shall we go?" (11.2). Those divine ears again, those gynomorphic organs, open, liquid. I hear Nelle Morton, a mother of feminist theology, writing of the "great Ear at the heart of the cosmos" "hearing us to our own speech"[9]—as women; Augustine's Ear attends him in his struggles. They are rather more textual: He is not struggling with colonizing armies or patriarchs. He is mustering courage to originate his theology, which means for him to start from "The Creation" by solving the problem of origin itself. The doctrine of creation, however, was already a hard shell to crack: When does the starting really start? And when did evil get into a good creation? Is it in the chaos? But surely anything that exists is the good creation of an omnipotent Creator? He had been worrying about this doctrine way back in Book 8, struggling since his conversion to believe in the *ex nihilo* (8.5). He reassures us here that he has now arrived.

If death let the deep gush through his eyes, let us now examine how it wells up in the ducts of his hermeneutics. When Augustine turns to the creation narrative, we should not be surprised that his real concern is not the materialization of the finite creation but rather: How can I be sure of my own immortality? Most riveting, then, is not so much what he wants the text to guarantee, or how he brings it valiantly into line with the Christian metanarrative, but the hermeneutical resonances released in the struggle, in the *distentio* and *intentio*, of his signifying practice. "The lowliness of my tongue confesses to your highness that you have made heaven and earth, this heaven which I see, this earth on which I tread and from which comes this earth I bear about with myself" (12.2). Yes, yes, the matter of creation and of himself. But: "Compared to you they are neither good nor beautiful nor real" (11.4). Even the prelapsarian sky and earth feel burdensome, external. He asks impatiently "But where is that *heaven of heaven*, O lord. Where is the heaven that we do *not* see . . . ?" (12.2).

His desire is not now for life but for life after death. The universe, however pretty, only interests him if it contains the immaterial heaven that God has—surely—made to house us beyond death: the goal of our earthly pilgrimage. But this yearning poses an exegetical dilemma: He must find this "heaven of heaven" within the Genesis narrative of origins. "Heaven" in the biblical languages means "sky." He therefore must find a way of installing his heaven of heaven *above* that shining but, after all, merely corporeal sky. The Bible, however, remains parsimonious in its allusions to an immaterial heaven or afterlife. What kind of hermeneutical depth can he plumb in order to locate the higher "heaven" within this most original of texts?

He presumes that God created not from any pre-existing other, as in the *Timaeus*, nor out of any aspect of the divine selfsame, as with Plotinian emanations. *Non de Deo sed ex nihilo*. Therefore "heaven" must be understood as created. But more. "Doubtless that heaven of heaven, which you made in the beginning, is some kind of intellectual creature" (12.9). This is a problem. Genesis 1.1, which contains the crucial "heaven," functions as an introduction to the rest of the chapter; but the only subsequent reference to "heaven" is the definitely material "firmament" of the second day—"God called the firmament heaven" (Gen. 1.2). Augustine zestfully takes up the challenge. He will need to argue that the "heaven" of the first verse is something altogether different from the "heaven" of the second day. So he suggests that the phrase "heaven and earth" in verse 1 signifies a still-undifferentiated mix of both corporeal and spiritual potentiality. Then he can argue that the materially formed stuff of the sky (firmament) derives from this "heaven and earth"; but so does the invisible, incorporeally formed stuff of the "heaven of heaven." In order to pull off this exegesis, he will make an intriguing use of the tehom of verse 2.

> Lord, have you not taught me that before you formed this unformed matter and fashioned it into kinds, there was no separate being, no color, no shape, no body, no spirit? Yet there was *not absolutely nothing*: there was a *certain formlessness* devoid of any specific character. (12.3)

Almost the hypothesis of *formation from* primal matter (rather than *creation of* all matter) recurs. It is Augustine's preoccupation with the "certain formlessness," his pluralist meditation upon the complexity of this tiny text, that distinguishes his exegesis. Between the absence of the classical *nihil* and the presence of a finished creation, he spots it "in the transition from form to form." First he had been repelled: "My mind turned over forms foul and horrid in confused array, but still forms." These monstrous forms struck him "as by something strange and improper" (12.6). But he realized that these were still forms. Only when he fixed his thought "*on the bodies themselves, and peered more deeply into their mutability*" did he find the knots untied. "If it could be said, '*a nothing-something*,' or '*an is-is-not*,' I would say that it is such." After tantalizing us with this *tohuvabohu* of text, however, he leaves us in the dark. Is this nothing-something too weird to write? His "heart" retreats into a "hymn of praise for those things which it cannot dictate." He will not share his queer pleasure with us. He tells us he is sparing us "all the knots which you [God] have untied for me concerning this question" (12.6). Knotty secrets. Mum's the word?

Augustine's "heart" now dictates another unique hermeneutical strategy: to sketch his knotty filial love upon the face of tehom. The Heaven of Heaven, we learn, "is yet a partaker of your eternity, and because of its most sweet and happy contemplation of you, it firmly checks its own mutability" (12.9). That is, because this incorporeal creature "checks" its instability by "clinging fast" to the eternal God, it "partakes" of eternity. Thus it can offer Augustine's soul an eternal abode. The Heaven of Heaven therefore derives directly from the chaos of verse 2—the tehom. The instant it was created, this Heaven of Heaven grabbed hold of God and clung for dear eternity. Thus it never became subject to mutability. In its state of formlessness, he avers, there can be no change—change is a contrast of forms. Therefore, its formlessness allows him to argue cunningly for its immutability—an attribute otherwise reserved for God, as the eternal Being of form and order itself ("for in you there is no change, of form or motion" [12.11]).

It is as though the ancient assumption of the co-eternal chaos has appeared, and the doctrine of *creatio ex nihilo*—which always caused Augustine such "nagging cares" (7.5)—has temporarily dissipated. Augustine can thus argue that the "heaven" of verse 1 is "the first heaven, the heaven of heaven." Becoming almost unreadable, he then supplies five alternative interpretations of the verse pair. He refutes none of them. In these choppy waters, he realizes that even among Catholic Christians, reasonable objections to his interpretation will obtain. It is here, while considering how to deploy the verse—"the earth was without form and invisible, and darkness upon the face of the deep"—that he bursts into delight rather than frustration at the tehom of the text itself: "Wondrous is the depth of your words...." Heaven, partaking in immutable eternity, while yet created as the chaotic, the aboriginal potentiality, echoes his joy. "Oh happy creature, if there be such, for cleaving to your happiness" (12.14).

This "certain sublime creature that cleaves with so chaste a love to the true and truly eternal God" now shows her face. It is here where she—if there be such—appears as the Wisdom of Proverbs 8: "A certain created wisdom was created before all things, the rational and intellectual mind of your chaste city, our mother, which is above, and is free and eternal in the heavens" (12.14). So the female Wisdom *is* the "heaven of heaven"—or, metonymically, its *mind*. An iconography of incorporeal femininity bursts momentarily into view, variously intellectual, erotic, and filial in its absorption of Augustine's ecstatic hope. "I will enter into my chamber and there I will sing songs of love to you, groaning with unspeakable groanings on my pilgrimage, and remembering Jerusalem, with heart lifted up towards it." He merges its female subject with the feminine New Jerusalem.

> Jerusalem my country, Jerusalem my mother, and you who over her are ruler, enlightener, father guardian, spouse, pure and strong delight, solid joy, all good things ineffable, all possessed at once ... I will not be turned away until out of this scattered and disordered state you gather all that I am into the peace of her, the *mother most dear*.... (12.16)

What is distinctive—indeed, as far as we know, unique—in this conflation of Lady Wisdom with the bridal/maternal New Jerusalem is their manifestation as the upper waters. By personifying heaven, he is able to project onto this unfading face of the deep the unmistakable traits of his own most dear mother.

Monica is not just revised but raised. From her death at the middle of the book—read her and weep—he opens her as the very corpus, the site, the matrix of all resurrection. Monica's best traits—her intelligence, fidelity, and "sweet and holy care"—are iterated and amplified in the medium of the deep. She who adhered to a base husband now clings joyously to the ultimate husband. If Augustine had blessed his own mother to heaven, her traits are now metonymically exalted as those of heaven itself. This poignant sublimation of the mother as "sublime creature" comes wrapped in the obscure correlation of the Christian heaven with the tehom. End things are swaddled in maternal sweetness, cradled in the waters of origin.

Yet this identification of tehom with heaven remains unstable: The waters still also signify the shame of "our dark and fluid inner being." Fluidity, as mutability itself, denotes the very opposite of the eternal stability Augustine seeks. This *deeply* maternal ambivalence answers his need for immortality. In order to move from first to second verse in such a way as to save heaven and his soul from materiality, he needs the waters to signify "incorporeal" or "spiritual matter." So he leaves the "earth without form and invisible" to signify the "corporeal matter" from which the earth and the firmament were produced.

> "The earth invisible and without order" would be understood as corporeal matter before being qualified by any form, and "darkness above the deep" as spiritual matter before any restraint was put upon its almost unbounded fluidity and any enlightenment from wisdom. (12.17)

How does the "unbounded fluidity" of the primal sea become the eternally bounded and bonded stability of Mother Most Dear? His emphasis upon her light and stability, as participating in her High Husband's eternity, seems to belie her chaotic origin. But the following passage confirms our reading:

> I have had much to say of the Heaven of Heavens, of the earth invisible and without form, and of the deep, showing how its darkness was in keeping with the spiritual creation, which in its formlessness, had no cohesion or stability. Such it would have remained unless, by being turned to God, . . . it had received beauty as well as life by the reflection of his glory. In this way the Heaven of Heavens came into being. (13.5)

So then: The upper waters, at the moment of the dividing, become the heaven of heaven, the mother, while the lower waters beneath the firmament become the earth's seas. The "heaven of heaven" as mother/spouse or upper waters is thus distinguished from the sky, "which was later created between the waters above and the waters below" (13.5). The "unbounded fluidity" is thus precariously congealed, its darkness radiated with divine light. Heaven awaits the restless soul, which like a child snuggles up to Mom, who has *her* arms around Dad. A cozy trinity. (What room could there be for Christ, except as intersexually camouflaged in the "principium" of the beginning itself, as Sophia?) She abides forever the same, clinging to her husband, mirroring in her beauty his omnipotence, and thus wraps our finitude in immutable immortality. The most stable of families.

From the violent fountain of tears for Monica has cascaded an epiphany of the upper waters. But how can the signifier of the waters oxymoronically forfeit its fluidity? What are nonfluid waters but ice? *La mère de glace*. Her "almost unconstrained fluidity" gets immobilized, frozen in glory, before it can destabilize the subject of Western theology. Sophia, refashioned as the

New Jerusalem, would become a politely feminine figure of speech for the City of God—a supernatural heaven, not a transformed earth. Eschatology checks its "edge of social criticism" at her door. Sublime, subjected, sublimated, and female: This hope, as he admits—thus enabling a pluralist hermeneutic that allows divergence from his own theory—treads on thin ice. Separated from her wilder materializations, from the something-nothing of a watery "down there," from the filth of bodily femininity, she cleaves to the higher masculinity. She offers embrace, comfort, home. And at the same time she embodies the supernal apathy of the unmoved, the unresponsive, Mover. Frozen, her fluidity denied, she reroutes desire itself. This ice queen–mother attracts the subject to himself—to himself as one defined by an immutable masculine ideal.

In her discussion of Plato's cave, Luce Irigaray tracks the antecedent of what she marks as a frozen femininity. "In other words, man does not get out of the maternal waters here but, by freezing the path that would lead back to her, he gazes at himself, re-producing himself in that paraphragm [parapet, outer raised bank]."[10] So the very path by which he flees from the mother (i.e., from his own fleeting creatureliness) is the frozen form of "her." He cannot simply annihilate her without destroying himself. His speculations, the abstracted vision of his immaterial and tearless eyes, require the mirror of her unmoving surface: the concave mirror, the speculum. He does not see her face, her *panim*. He sees his own. Yet even as this freezing act repeats itself in the *Confessions*, unlike the *Republic*, indeed not quite like the *Timaeus*, the waters actually appear in their cosmogonic dignity and are celebrated—under strictly patriarchal conditions—as feminine. In his passion for the Father—"I glow and shudder"—he almost melts down the ideal of the unchanging Same only to freeze it in the heavenly embrace of the Mother.

At such points of rhetorical liquefaction, where the ice thins into a precarious path upon the face of the deep, one could almost retrace one's steps to an alternative Christianity. The fantasy of the path not taken will not, however, lead to the next step: for instance, provide a constructive theology of becoming, in which the platonic privilege of changeless being would thaw into a sustainable commitment to the creatures of the earth. Yet possibilities may survive in frozen form, like embryos, that would otherwise, in a more straightforward *ex nihilo*, have been simply eliminated. The divine Wisdom we seek would not discard her antique visage, captured in the brilliant mirror of the upper waters. It would, however, reroute the desire for the new, the creativity of the *initium*, dissolving the power of a *creatio ex nihilo* into the energy of persisting becoming. Philosophies of becoming enable the theoretical reconstitution of the constitutive Platonism of theology. For theology this originary shift from the homogeneity of origin enables a *creatio ex profundis*.[11]

For now, how might we *begin* to thaw out the theological potentialities of the Augustinian Wisdom Mother? Is it a matter of *beginning* itself? Hannah Arendt credits Augustine's doctrine of creation with her revolutionary notion of "natality" (and "plurality") in public life. *Natality* as a concept allows her to challenge the Western, and especially the Heideggerian, privilege of death or *mortality* as the source of both anxiety and action. Instead she lifts up "the fact of having become." The self-multiplication of the human species becomes a trope for the shared condition.

> Beginning, before it becomes a historical event, is the supreme capacity of man; politically, it is identical with man's freedom. *Initium ut esset homo creatus est*, "that a beginning be made, man was created," said Augustine. This beginning is guaranteed by each new birth.[12]

In this Augustinian "beginning"—not origin—Arendt locates human freedom and thus the political will with which to resist totalitarianism. "This very capacity for beginning is rooted in natality."[13] The definition of our creaturely finitude through the beginning, the *initium* and thus the *novum*, sheds a new light on the motivation of the *ex nihilo* doctrine. Against Plato, in whom the lack of a strong beginning tended to serve politically conservative ends, she reads Augustine's beginning as a new beginning for thought. Might we glean from her the possibility of an Augustinian freedom to resist domination: after all a certain edge of social critique? This possibility comes sorely barnacled by both the nostalgia for origins and the passion for ultimate stasis.

Yet a tehomic theology, or a chaosophy, would recycle the creativity of the *Confessions* in order to deconstruct that abstract eternity and its omnipotent Origin. It would reroute the desire for the new, the energy of the initium. It may hear echoes of its beginning-freedom, this birthright of resistance to totality, in the prolific flux of the Augustinian text. We natals need the nourishment. As the deafening (Augustinian) master narrative of creation, fall, and redemption itself falls away, we might hear unfamiliar voices amid the waves of his language. Within the sea of his own nothing-something, the improper, multiplying matrix of another birth, a wilder wisdom chaotically reappears. Not just the lachrymose mother or the frigid Sapientia—but *la mère qui jouit*. She of many languages, names, and sacraments, overflowing the division of history and theology—she may begin to satisfy a present hunger.

Might we join Augustine in his praying, if not in his closet?

In you we oscillate like the tide. In us you flow like tears.
In you we beat restlessly against the freeze-dried truth.
In us your parad/ice could melt without apocalyptic flood.
Your laughter wells warm and wild
Yes cracking open again.

CHAPTER 6

The Becoming of Theopoetics: A Brief, Incongruent History

Thinkers across and beyond disciplines today want to create vibrant nodes in new forms of alliance, of ecopolitical assemblage. We who work theologically, that is, with some avowedly religious or spiritual discourse, want to tune the liveliest language of our own fields to the situation of the planet. And in the language of theology we have long dredged up our ancient traditions of world-care, tuning them, amplifying through them, "the cry of the poor, the cry of the earth." But isn't the *theo* of these theologies—liberation, feminist, womanist, Black, pluralist, ecological, radical—the stumbling block to the alliance? No matter how gracefully we transcribe, defer, mask, diversify, or humble our God-talk, does not "God" obstruct the interdisciplinary, indeed transdisciplinary, coalescence

---

In its initial form, this essay was presented as a lecture at Wayne State University on September 23, 2015. The audience consisted of scholars in the liberal arts, mostly the English department. A previous draft was published in Roland Faber and Jeremy Frankenthal, eds., *Theopoetic Folds: Philosophizing Multifariousness* (New York: Fordham University Press, 2013).

we need? Even if that coalescence needs us, with our access to vast God-identifying populations?

I do not propose to solve the God-problem. That has been brilliantly done already, over and over, old theism certifying or old materialism disproving God and "His" existence. The solutions simply do not not matter much; they do not work outside their own circles. Those of us in search of planetary alliance, inclusive of more than the elite metropolitan cultures of the left, want a more multiply mattering approach. It would neither ban nor impose God but keep in play between all our discourses the poetics, the *poiesis*—the ancient Greek term for creating, making—by which meaning materializes. Might we then reconsider, at some distance from the *ology* of theology or of any other circles of insider logic, the notion of theopoetics? In particular, in the present context, might we experiment with a theopoetics of material solidarity?

Theopoetics as a discursive strategy carries some surprisingly layered, if marginalized, history, ancient and recent. Of course, humanists might immediately be suspicious—I would be—that theopoetics is a rhetorical sleight of hand: a way to disguise good-old God with an aesthetic aura, and sneak him—yes Him—back in under the disarming guise of metaphor. Or is it the opposite ploy, which is what some colleagues in theology suspect: atheism mascarading as theos? I may be guilty of failing at both magic tricks at the same time. But at the very least notice that the term *theopoetics* occupies the God-boundary itself. It turns the boundary into a node. And for a few networks that node has a growing vibrancy.

Yet most recent uses of theopoetics remain oblivious to their ancient root. They arise, as we shall see, from another boundary-discourse, that of mid-twentieth-century US radical theology and its foundational drama: the death of God. As metaphor and rhetorical device, the death of God helps in the crossover to secular discourses, to ethical atheisms or radical politics. It links up in complicating ways with recent interdisciplinary discourses of the postsecular, of political theology, and of religious diversity. It morphs, for example, with Richard Kearney into "anatheism"—meaning not the uttering of anathemas by or at theism but a theology "after the death of God" for which theism and atheism count as conjoined twins.[1]

Theopoetics is, in other words, one informal name—just one of many names—for a currently vibrant node of radical theology. It resonates with the transdisciplinary conversations of the new materialism, of affect theory, of deconstructive theology, and of a speculative *aesthesis* in its Deleuzian and Whiteheadian circulation. I want to consider with you how theopoetics may hook up with nontheistic networks of material solidarity in ways that will be intensified by minding its deeper theological history. So I will trace a theopoetic genealogy through an ancient theopoiesis to a modernist and then a current theopoetics. Those three historical moments sound like premodern, modern, postmodern. But they do not constitute discrete periods so much as mutually iterative periodicities: They each come to matter, to materialize, in the present project by way of a negative theology rooted in the ancient theopoiesis, a deconstruction working through modernist radical theology, and then an ecological solidarity hosted by a theopoetics of process.

Theopoiesis: Becoming Divine in Eastern Antiquity

The term *theopoetics* finds its ancestor in the ancient Greek *theopoiesis*. As *poiesis* means making or creation, so *theopoiesis* gets rendered as "God-making" or "becoming divine." *Theopoiesis* appears in the first centuries of Hellenistic Christianity, often and then later consistently in its contracted form *theosis*, normally translated as "deification." The term *theopoiesis* retains the fuller sense of "making divine," "making God." It roots in Christian mid- and Neoplatonic mergers of the Hebrew "image of God" with Plato's "likeness to God so far as possible." Clement in the third century defines *theopoiesis* as "assimilation to God as far as possible."[2] Theosis can only be read in the context of ancient spiritual practices, ascetic and ecstatic simultaneously. Basil of Caesarea's fourth-century version lends theopoiesis particular luminosity:

> When a sunbeam falls on a transparent substance, the substance itself becomes brilliant, and radiates light from itself. So too Spirit-bearing souls, illumined by Him, finally become spiritual themselves, and their grace is sent forth to others. From this comes knowledge of the future, understanding of mysteries . . . distribution of wonderful gifts . . . endless joy in the presence of God, becoming like God, and, the highest of all desires, *becoming God*.[3]

A mysticism of participation is here in play, whereby a reflective brilliance does not merely bounce back or ascend but spreads laterally and relationally. The theologian-poet Ephrem of Syria highlights a startling reciprocity: "He gave us divinity/we gave Him humanity." This is a pretty sassy version of the incarnation.[4] It crystallized already in Athanasius's fourth-century Christological formula: "For he [the Logos] became human that we might be made God."[5] Not just the one exceptional human. In other words, the high Christology behind the Council of Nicaea was originally accompanied by a high anthropology. The glory of the Creator does not yet play the zero-sum game with the dignity of the creature. *Gloria dei homo vivens*: "the glory of God is the human fully alive" (Irenaeus).[6]

I hope the reader hears even now the shocking boldness of this old claim to be making-divine. It was so muffled by later receptions of the orthodox lineage, above all in Protestantism, that it sounds like heresy. Yet there were hints of a more participatory mysticism in the Reformation heritage.[7] And the ancient theopoiesis also whispered its influence upon the Methodist theory of "entire sanctification" or "perfection." Charles Wesley "as a poet-theologian in the tradition of St. Ephrem," flashes this sensibility in his eighteenth-century hymnody. For example:

> He deigns in flesh to appear,
> Widest extreme to join,
> To bring our vileness near,
> And make us all divine;[8]

This is far from the standard exclusive focus on the becoming man of God. Incarnation itself gets radically redistributed as the becoming divine of us all.

This participatory theopoetic potential rests upon a certain strand of scriptural poetics, above all the phrase of 2 Peter 1:4, "partakers of the divine nature," but also Psalm 82:6: "I declare, 'You are gods; you are all sons of the Most High.'" Moreover, when Jesus cites that verse in response to the accusation that "he, being a man, made himself to be God" (John 10:34), he disarms the charge by redistributing the divinity. The gospel of the incarnation deconstructs in advance the theology of Christ as God come down just this once from heaven garbed in human flesh, of the incarnation as sovereign exception to the human condition.

My point is not to idealize any ancestral schematisms but to amplify counterpoint resonances working within a received tradition. Perfection had, for instance, within the mystical theopoiesis, the meaning of fullness rather than of closure. Indeed, theosis is linked to Gregory of Nyssa's third-century formulation of a process of growth that must be infinite, because it is growth toward and in the divine infinite. That infinity, a "brilliant darkness" in his writing of the encounter of Moses with YHWH at Sinai in the dark cloud, became the basis of so-called negative or apophatic theology. From the start there takes place an interplay of theopoiesis and apophasis.[9] The in-finite (a pure negation) was in direct contradiction to the platonic identification of anything divine or perfect with *form* and precisely not with the chaotic, formless *apeiron* signified by infinity. But of course as theology, Christian thought clothed itself in classical substance metaphysics. It thereby broke into a dualism drawing the individual soul toward a changeless immateriality. But the older sense of divinization or perfection as unfinished—infinite—process did not altogether vanish.

For a more recent and more radically nonsubstantialist resonance, I recall being startled by this word from a continental philosopher who perhaps more than anyone in the last millennium shaped the emphatic feminist discourse of the body: "The religious aspect of our becoming has not been considered enough as a way to achieve a greater perfection of our humanity. Human identity and divine identity have been artificially separated. And we generally fail to recognize that *becoming divine corresponds to becoming perfectly human*."[10] Luce Irigaray, who called full human becoming "becoming divine," had swerved through her Nietzscheanism into a surprising rereading of Mary's son and the incarnation he instantiates. Yet she comes to her vocabulary of mystical perfection without reference to the ancient theosis tradition it so precisely echoes.[11] It was for me an early clue.

I am not claiming that this body of resonances is itself perfect, only that from within a Christian imaginary it breaks through a certain boundary, a God-wall that dams up the force of becoming within a Christomonist exceptionalism. That competitive Christ can only be answered by an autodeconstruction. Not Christianity's undoing of itself but of its exceptionalism, it is facilitated not only by the liberative theologies and by continental critique but, on another front, by Whiteheadian cosmology. Process thought is preoccupied with the material interrelations that constitute the world, which are reconfigured in every momentary instance of becoming—the becoming that replaces the being of substance metaphysics. As process *theology* it has, with certain exceptions, had little to do with old forms of mysticism—except perhaps Buddhist. Nonetheless Whitehead, who at one point during his career as a mathematician read several volumes of patristic theology before returning them to the bookseller, calls God "the mirror which discloses to every creature its own greatness."[12] The image of God is the image of the creature magnified. God appears not just as reflection but as desire: as "the Eros of the Universe" and later as the "poet of the world, with tender patience leading it by his vision of truth, beauty, and goodness."[13] Roland Faber, naming a major book after that poet, developed the theopoetic implications in relation to "a negative theology of God's alterity—albeit a God who in God's orientation toward the world" does not disappear "into speechlessness (and irrelevance)" but "instead through God's own transcendence possesses poetic character in creating the world in a reconciled light."[14] Faber thus surfaces—preparing the way of a third-millennium theopoetics—the apophatic poiesis precisely as it intensifies a Whiteheadian cosmology.

Process thought indeed continues to fund emergent interdisciplinary movements as, for example, the new materialism and affect theory. For "amidst a democracy of fellow creatures" we recognize the matter of this world as alive and feeling, a matter not of solidity but of solidarity. And that material solidarity is in process theology provoked, inspired, and consequently embraced by the divine poet—in a process that we might call a cosmic theopoiesis. At the end of *Process and Reality* appears a series of chiasmic statements. One is this: It is "as true that God creates the world as that the world creates God."[15] Cosmic God-making. So then theopoiesis takes on a new and risky double meaning: We are at once making ourselves God and making God. Is such God-creating really only code for making God up? By a certain reading of theopoetics, the answer would be sure—what else is new?

Theopoetics in Mid-Century New Jersey

Early in this millennium I still thought I coined the term "theopoetics." So imagine my surprise when I learned, after already teaching a couple decades at Drew, that theopoetics had sprung into play, in English, in the 1960s—at Drew! In his little 1976 *Theopoetic*, the poet and theologian Amos Wilder writes: "I believe that I had picked up the term 'theopoetic' and 'theopoiesis' from Stanley Hopper and his students, no doubt in one or another of the remarkable consultations on hermeneutics and language which he had organized at Drew University."[16] These conferences occurred in 1962, 1964, and 1966 and were methodologically situated "at the intersection," as Hopper's student at the Theological School at that time, David Miller, has explained, "of left-wing Bultmannian biblical interpretation, the thought of the late period of Heidegger's existential phenomenology, and the Religion and Literature movement."[17] Yet by the time I arrived, long after a crisis in '69 had driven most of that faculty elsewhere, there lingered no echoes of the term. An altogether different wave of progressive theology had kicked in. We had little interest in that old white male radicalism.

This definition of Hopper's, however, merits a new hearing: "What theo-poiesis does is to effect disclosure through the crucial nexus of event, thereby making the crux of knowing, both morally and aesthetically, radically decisive in time."[18] Through intensive readings of religious texts as literature, and of literary texts as religiously meaningful, the poetics of theology was disclosing itself as inseparable from poetry. Hopper loved citing Wallace Stevens:

> It was when I said:
> "There is no such thing as the truth,"
> That the grapes seemed fatter.
> The fox ran out of his hole.[19]

The theopoetic effort to explode any prosaic -ology, any objectivization, of the Christian referents was linked early with a pre-Derridean engagement of Heidegger.[20] And a psychological depth dimension sometimes translated into the "mythopoetic."

David Miller has offered the distinction between *theopoetry* and theopoetics. The former would be the assertion that all theological language is really already poetic, already metaphor: This is "the poeticizing of an extant religious faith or theological knowledge."[21] This allows the "re-inscription of objectivization and of the onto-metaphysical tradition in which Being is viewed as a being or God as an idol." But in the sense of theopoetics, the poetic is not made up of metaphors, which he assimilates to similes, similarities, but of difference, fragmentation, and multiplicity. Theopoetics, in other words, is not reducible to a literary style. It does not camouflage the tawdry sanctuaries of dying belief with bouquets of language. Indeed, the theologian of the death of God, Thomas J. J. Altizer, was deeply involved in the Drew symposia. Theopoetics, in Miller's characterization, does its work "after the death of God": "It involves a poetics and not a poetry, i.e., a reflection on poiesis, a formal thinking about the nature of the making of meaning, which subverts the -ology, the nature of the logic, of theology."[22]

Theopoetics vs. Theology?

For Miller, then, it follows that "theopoetics begins when theology ends."[23] Theopoetics is thus distinguished from mere theopoetry, for which theos lives on in refreshed metaphoric outfits. The end of theology is then the only honest response to the death of God. Hard indeed to see how that would not follow. So is the work of the progressive theologies—often less than purely academic, to be sure, often caught up in the struggles of communities, churches, social movements, global networks—at best theopoetry? All well-intended but still deluded by our own fictions?

Of course, as feminist theology matured we knew ourselves to be performing a subversion of every established logos of theos. We have lived upon the death of a certain God—Blake's Old Nobodaddy, who shored himself up with the logoi of identity, essence, noncontradiction, supernatural transcendence, exclusionary truth. But we always thought there was an excess, a not-one, to the word *God*, in all its convulsive semantic exhaustion. It is true, however, that in wildly varying ways, often at variance with each other and intersecting across such diverse contexts, we did as much reconstructing as deconstructing.

This is not just some lingering gender tension between waves of radical theology. For frankly, the Euromodernism of the mere death of God and its posttheology still seems to evince dubious world-changing potential—*if* the world includes the poor and the dark-skinned publics of the Americas, the populations of Latin America, Africa, and much of Asia. In our politics we have experimented all along in a new poiesis of the divine itself—making God Black, female, poor, queer, animal, and so on—risking the idolatry of slogans yet insisting that such language is language. Image. Icon. Figuration. Metaphor. As not similitude but difference. We may not have engaged the term *theopoetics* one way or another. But in its this-millennium renewal (even with a primer by Callid Keefe-Perry) it might seem hospitable enough to ongoing experimentation. Until we realize its closure—not disclosure after all?—of theology itself, indeed of theos.

Might we however ask how the "theos" of *theopoetics* gets exempted? How does theopoetics get to keep theos? As some kind of mummy? Is it that theopoetics, because it knows that it is making its gods up, does not die with God? And with the whole fading mainline apparatus of His worship? Of course, only fresh warnings against the worship of our own creations can keep theological creativities honest. The critique of the idols of our own making—*that* is familiar to the Abrahamisms. And to the Sarah-and-Hagarisms. Feminist theology was born as a practice of deliteralizing the He-God and working God, or Goddess, as iconoclastic metaphor (emphatically *not* simile). This politicization of metaphor was initiated by Nelle Morton, the marginalized feminist voice in that same Drew of mid-century, who taught there the first course on gender and language in a theological context in the country. And of course radical theologies are nothing if not contextual and, therefore, subject to the particular idolatries and self-deceptions and false hopes that come with a living context. But does it follow that theology itself is delusional—or rather that any use of theos, poetic or logical, calls us to responsibility for the poiesis, the materializations, of language itself?

Caputo has taken up theopoetics as the fresh title of radical theology, as the "becoming radical of confessional theology."[24] As he puts it game-

The Becoming of Theopoetics

changingly to his *Insistence of God*, "God does not exist but insists." Does this mean, then, that Caputo wants to have it both ways: theos and its death? Yet the radical aura of the divine inexistence here surrounds his munificent engagement of theological texts, often biblical. And this inexistence means to land beyond any atheist void: "The insistence of God is the chance that God can happen anywhere."[25] So the insistence signifies a divine event rather than an essence or substance of divinity. This inessential eventiveness sets off resonances with process panentheism. But he severely distinguishes his model from that of a God who "exists in us, and us in God," insisting again that "God does not exist," and that it is left to us to "bring about something that exists."[26]

On the same page, we read, however: "The existence of God is liable to break out anytime, in great and world historical events, like Paul on the road to Damascus, and in the smallest things, like the rose that blossoms unseen."[27] I cannot see how existence does not mean, well, existence—merely a mode of it radically diverging from the classical substantialisms, existential rather than essential. Or elsewhere: "The insistence of God means that God insists upon existing."[28] Yes? A panentheist could not say it better: Through us and in us—and no mere human "us"—the divine possibility finds whatever actualization it will find. Whiteheadian thought about existence, divine or otherwise, has always been rigorously anti-essentialist, precisely as a metaphysics. But more importantly, Caputo's hyperbolic poiesis does surely nurture Eckhartian blossoms. And crucially, his "theology of perhaps" calls us to take responsibility for what we together—theopoetically, cosmopoetically—are bringing into existence.

So I would not insist on God's existence but on a *more* insistent poiesis. Not only "God" but "existence" become eventive, not just in the occasional happening that blossoms visibly but all the way up and down, in a bottomless becomingness. The eventiveness of becoming demands resistance to the very binary of substantial existence and eventive insistence. We access this insubstantial becoming only as poiesis, creativity. Here we may have recourse to a Whiteheadian argument for insistence itself: Borrowing the term from Deleuze, Faber offers "the mystery of God's insistence." It is articulated precisely as a "primordial process of 'in/differentiation,'" in which the "all-relational" folds in and out of the God of a Cusan negative theology as the "nothing beyond all differences." For Faber "insistence comes to express theopoetics itself."[29]

In its incessant process, God mirrors us back to ourselves darkly. Actually what Paul said, in the Greek, is not "in a glass darkly" but "in a mirror, enigmatically." Theology is *riddled* with uncertainty. In other words, theology that takes responsibility for its own constructions—its poiesis of logos, of theos—does not close its eyes to the glowing darkness of a puzzling unknowability. In its theopoetic condition, modern or post, when it does "God," it can no more do without God than it can do God in. Theos—the word and so whatever it signifies—remains a cloudy mirror, an enigma of what we have become and what we might yet materialize.

Theopoetics of Material Entanglement

Poiesis means materialization. We find ourselves in a chaosmic infinity clumsily making our worlds, making them matter, making them together even when apart. Never from words alone. Never without words. Sometimes we make them work better than others. The enigma does not get solved. It gets endless. There remains, in other words, an interplay of pragmatism and mysticism churning up the dark waters of this God-creation.

In the actual, fragile communities I inhabit, the old, existent God is known to disappoint; and the dead or the inexistent God does not help for long. The theopoetic insistence might. And it requires for its work a persistent iconoclasm, resistant to our idols tawdry or hip. But we should call this an *idoloclasm* to distinguish it from the ancient imperial iconoclasms and so to allow for the icon in its incarnational poiesis. Image of the visibly invisible, word of the audibly incomprehensible, matter of an ultimate mattering: No wonder the apophatic and the theopoiestic unfold in antiquity together, in proximity to the nonverbally mattering flesh of the icon. But the point that this essay may have made by the time it is over is this: The ancient theopoiesis plied in its negative theology its own affirmatively autodeconstructive strategy. By soliciting its resonance with the current theopoetics, a more fluid reach of solidarity becomes possible. For the constructivity of our language, about God and everything else, applies to the whole breadth of our materiality. In the ancient theopoiesis, the trope of the incarnation indicated this becoming-matter of the divine, in chiasmic exchange with human matter becoming divine. The cosmic logos translates into human materiality and only as such then back into God. If the chiasm itself is called Christ, it empties itself, and so its name, into the world. A christomonism of the incarnational exception is the enemy of that logos.

Because the logos of this poiesis is cosmic, we may also say that the theologos of this theopoiesis is cosmopoetic: world-creating. But then the creation names not the absolute singularity of an original exception but a bottomless creative process inseparable from incarnation. *Ex profundis sed non ex nihilo*.³⁰ From its chiasmic oscillation it follows that we no longer privilege one incarnation, an exception that proves the rule of a sovereign singularity—and with it the sovereign Man. We may speak instead of the *intercarnation*. (That word *really* may not have existed for long.) The making divine is a way, one way, of darkly mirroring the enigmatically interconnected cosmos. It is a universe in which my materialization—my existence at this moment—is influenced by and influences yours: The creation is not a one-time event but the beginningless and endless process of our interactivity. Or of what Karen Barad calls, working through quantum entanglement, intra-activity. For the agents do not pre-exist their relationships.³¹ They, we, human and other, become together, make each other even as we come unmade. These matterings cocreate our common world. In this the new materialism sounds more than it might expect like not only process theology but like *Laudato Si'*: "Nothing in this world is indifferent to us." "Our common home" is turning currently into a "garbage dump," an "immense pile of filth."³²

Let us back up for a moment to an older Catholic perspective, one just as marginalized as that of the Pope's namesake, Saint Francis: "God is in all and all is in God because all is in all and each is in each."³³ So wrote Nicholas of Cusa in the fifteenth century. That all and that each signifies the matter of the infinite universe that he is the first Christian to articulate cosmologically. And so the world-body expresses and distributes the divine infinite—infinitely. For him it is not just the human but the universe as a whole that images the divine infinite, which enfolds—*complicans*—everything. In this infinite material solidarity of divinity and cosmos, Cusa is working the medieval riddle of the sphere "whose center is everywhere and boundary nowhere."³⁴ For him it signifies the apophatic infinite of negative theology: a God not represented by the language of Father, or Son, or Light, or Being. This God is not Father, not Son, not Spirit, not light or dark, not existent, not this or that, not God. That is the language that flows from the seventh-century Pseudo-Dionysius into Eckhart's famous prayer that "God rid me of God," into the long heritage of negative theology. In Cusa's early Renaissance cosmo-theology, however, the old theopoiesis and its mystical unknowing produced some stunning new material knowledge. For instance, that the earth is not the center of the universe, which, as without circumference, can have no center (this a century before Copernicus); or, that no single body can be the center or immobile. The omnicentric divinity unfolds "in and as" the material multiplicity of the simultaneously enfolded universe. So though he could not directly name that *explicans* as a becoming of God, a cosmological God-making, it can hardly be read otherwise.[35] This conjunction of cosmological relationalism and negative theology stirred up my *Cloud of the Impossible*—a phrase that appears in his meditation on an "icon of God."

The *Cloud* follows what I call apophatic entanglement through multiple transdisciplinary registers. To be knowingly and materially entangled in each other is to *mind* the acute and shifting limits of our knowing. And so to enhance the solidarity of those entanglements. Such a theology of entanglement would then braid together the shifting strands of theopoetics I have discussed: the negative theology of the mystical theopoiesis, a theopoetics negating theology itself, yet becoming radical theology, a certain postsecular negation of the negation, enveloping the gender/sex/race/class/ecotheologies of half a century's struggle for planetary solidarity. And in the density of this cloud of witnesses, I track no telic dialectic but rather an umbrageous complexity, a *complicatio*, a folding together of ineradicable differences.

In this world of folds, of creatures enfolding and unfolding each other, each fold is an affect, a feeling of its universe, what Whitehead calls a prehension. And Deleuze, dubbing Whitehead the third great thinker of "the event," interprets the Leibnizian "fold" as Whiteheadian "prehension," whereby "bifurcations, divergences, incompossibilities and discord belong to the same motley world."[36] It can only "be made or undone"—in poiesis or its deterritorialization—"according to prehensive units." Here Deleuze identifies the process cosmos with the Joycean chaosmos, finding in it the scene of an infinite material unfolding. A theopoetics of material solidarity arises amid the disorderly conduct of incipient orders of this endless creativity. Such poiesis cannot be reduced to a construction of a world and a God in thought or in language. It retains the realistic edge of perpetual materialization. And so amid the self-organizing and collapsing complexities of the world, it does not let us escape responsibility for its creations and its destructions. As Steven Shaviro writes of Whitehead's speculative realism, "he finds an immanent place for transcendence and an aesthetic place for ethics."[37]

The poet of the world, the world of endlessly entangled cocreativity, comes here into play as one figure, an iconoclastic icon of an ultimate becomingness. The creativity—and the createdness—of God loops interdependently through the creativity of the world. Its deity emits not an impassible indifference but something close to Faber's "in/difference," the theopoetic multiplicity, indeed the "theoplicity," *in* which all difference insists.[38] So our construction of the divine, our God-making, signifies at once a conceptual construction and an effect on that cosmic life we are calling

God. It loses all life and meaning if it operates in transcendent abstraction from all the other constructions, actions, doings, makings.

As to God, then, it is a matter not of believing but of making, materializing God. Doing God. Do the truth, it will set you free. To become God as doing God—doing the prophetic justice, the love thing. It is a theos that ricochets back into the world by way of the golden rule, rendered by the pope before Congress: If you want opportunity, give opportunity; if you want security, give security. "The yardstick we use for others will be the yardstick time uses for us."[39] Time, not God: an apt contextual secularization. The things in the world of space-time at any rate insist upon an indeterminacy so radically entangling that what matters theologically is nothing apart from what we materialize in the world. Amid the intercarnations of our fragile complexity.

The ecology of the planet now reveals through every new climatological report—measure of the melting glaciers, rising seas, expanding droughts, devastating wildfires—that time is running out. Our cocreation of our world, our poiesis, may all too soon cease to unfold; it is threatening to fold down. Our unfolding as a species has proceeded for too long a time in a dream of separation from the beauty that we cannot own. We deadened the poetics in order to maximize the profits. We cut what Roland Faber calls the "theopoetic folds" that link us each to each and all to all. Affect did not get repressed so much as commodified.

No poetics, let alone any theos, will save us. We will have to salvage our collective selves; and we may not. If we do, it will be by opening new nodes of communication for more planetary alliance. But novelties will crash like a computer without the reopening of old, even ancient lines, folds, forces of vibrant relation. To create wider networks of mindful entanglement means moving at least a bit beyond the urban elites of the north and our snarkier secularisms. And the pope from the Global South has made a difference. There is in the encyclical a call to "convert to the earth"—not to any religion. The earth not as under us and outside of us but as what we are made of and what we are in each moment together continuing to become and to make. It is a planetary poetics in process—a *terrapoiesis*.

In honor of the radical Catholicism of the Global South, let me end with poetry. Lured out of literary studies at Columbia by Thomas Merton, Ernesto Cardenal became a priest and returned home to become a leading force in the resistance movements of Nicaragua since the late '50s, founded of one of the first base Christian communities, a revolutionary band of peasants and artists on the island of Solentiname. Later he was minister of culture, repudiated by Pope John Paul II for his political work for the

Sandinistas, though he was a leading critic of Ortega's betrayal of the revolution. All along he continued to write his poetic epic, *Cosmic Canticle*. If his life embodies the theopoetics of material solidarity, hear how *poiesis* itself comes into the theology of his poetry:

> Cosmos like a dark record that spins and sings
> > in the dead of the night
> > or romantic radio borne to us on the wind.
>
> Each thing sings.
> Things, not created by calculus
> > but by poetry.
>
> By the Poet ("Creator" = POIÊTÊS)
> Creator of the POIEMA.[40]

The dead of the night, the Beatles mixed with the cosmic darkness and its communicative unsaying of our words. Each thing sings: an incalculable mattering of the world, an infinite prehensive chorale. And in another poem, "Verses of the Multiverse," he repeats his Pauline theopoetics:

> Creation is a poem.
> > Poem, which is "creation" in Greek and thus
>
> St Paul calls God's Creation, POIEMA,
> Like a poem by Homer Padre Angel used to say.
> Each thing is like a "like."
> > Like a "like" in a Huidobro poem.
>
> The entire cosmos copulation. . . .
> Listen to the murmur of things . . .
> > They say it, but say it in secret.[41]

Can this "like" be disregarded as the mere simile of theopoetry, falling short of modernist radicality? It may indeed recall the ancient definition of theosis as "similitude to God." The likeness insists on its own difference. These bonds of cosmic solidarity do not menace but rather intensify multiplicity. Here the Eros of the universe—*poietes* indeed—voluptuously materializes: The cosmos *is* copulation, resistant to every heteronormative reproductivity or capitalist productivity, insistent in its dark beauty. It is murmuring in secret, *mue*, mystery: an apophatically entangled *poiema*. The call of the earth, the call of the poor, reverberate in the whispered song of the universe, itself repeated, amplified, in the multiplying verses of the multiverse.

CHAPTER 7

Derridapocalypse

With Stephen D. Moore

CATHERINE KELLER. As neither philosopher nor biblical scholar but something like a theologian, I perch at this table with fear and trembling. But then theology is always trembling. It oscillates between bible and philosophy, between a ghostly apocalypse of conjurations and a discipline of the reasonable doubt. Between life and death. Theologians have been embarrassed by the oscillations; we have (unlike biblical scholars) tended to disavow the apocalypse and the disbelief. So no wonder some of us are grateful for the mysterious resonances of deconstruction with our own lost irony, with our haunting uncertainty, and even with our politico-messianic hopes. But beyond this table, among most theologians, such appreciation of Derrida sounds like gratitude for crumbs—droppings from the banquet

---

This interdisciplinary duet with my colleague in New Testament was delivered at the Society of Biblical Literature, with Jacques Derrida modestly seated in the front row. Previously published as "Derridapocalypse," with Stephen Moore, in *Derrida and Religion: Other Testaments*, ed. Yvonne Sherwood and Kevin Hart (New York: Routledge, 2005). Reprinted in Moore's *Untold Tales from the Book of Revelation: Sex and Gender, Empire and Ecology* (Atlanta: SBL Press, 2014).

of high theory for the hungry dogs of doubt. (Not that there is any shame in the intervention of the Syrophoenician woman, the grief-stricken mother who with that image healed Jesus of his Abrahamic chauvinism [Mark 7:24–30].)

In the light of Derrida's coming, hospitality requires admitting this gratitude. But the risk is double-edged, like the Messiah's tongue. Gratitude in the present context may *be* the inhospitable. As it has been said: "When a gift is given, first of all, no gratitude can be proportionate to it . . . . As soon as I say 'thank you' for a gift, I start cancelling the gift, I start destroying the gift, by proposing an equivalence, that is, a circle which encircles the gift in a movement of reappropriation."[1] So without saying thank you, without fantasizing equality or proportionality, without preaching a Sunday-school poststructuralism—shall we take the chance of an appropriation in order to avert a destruction? Shall we risk apocalypse in order to defer it? Doesn't *he*?

STEPHEN MOORE. As it *is* a Sunday,[2] and as "poststructuralism" (however we define the term or be ourselves defined by it) is, let's face it, the only thing, other than "religion" (no more amenable to definition, no less amenable to deformation), that brings us together around this table, the notion of a Sunday-school poststructuralism might not, after all, be such a fanciful conceit. What we preach on Sunday, indeed (those of us who do), we practice throughout the week—or so Jacques Derrida has recently been teaching us.

Derrida, who has confessed, indeed circumfessed, that he "quite rightly pass[es] for an atheist,"[3] has, paradoxically, also declared himself *for faith*, albeit a faith that is "not religious" per se but is instead "absolutely universal."[4] Faith is what enables any and every address to the other, for to address the other, any other, is always to ask to be believed. This request, this *demand*, for faith—utterly quotidian and ordinarily implicit—is, as such, the structural a priori of any address whatsoever. (The elucidation *of* Derrida *to* Derrida, in the *presence* of Derrida—whatever that expression might mean *after* Derrida—is a somewhat bizarre public ritual, a ritual of torture at times, no doubt, to which Derrida has repeatedly been subjected over the years. And it is not without a certain dismay—but, if I may say so, also not without a certain pleasure—that I now find myself charged with turning the screws.)

If the demand for faith is to be regarded as the structural a priori of any address whatsoever, what then are we to say about the extended epistolary address that is the Apocalypse of John? Several decades ago, Derrida, in the course of a dual analysis of the Apocalypse and an antiapocalyptic essay by Kant, argued that the former reveals, in exemplary fashion, "a transcendental condition of all discourse, of all experience even."[5] It seems to me, however, that Derrida has succeeded in making a better case for that contention in his more recent work on faith—even though the Apocalypse is not, so far as I can see, mentioned by name in that work. (Derrida's most incisive commentary on biblical texts, however, often occurs when his attention is directed elsewhere.) "In testimony, truth is promised beyond all proof," Derrida contends near the end of his extended meditation on faith and knowledge. And again: "The act of faith demanded in bearing witness exceeds, through its structure, all intuition and all proof."[6]

On the one hand (to employ a formulation long familiar to readers of Derrida, the corresponding "on the other hand" characteristically being deferred so long as to lull the reader into forgetting that there ever was an "on the one hand" in the first place), the Apocalypse promises, indeed provides, "proof" of the truth to which it testifies, announcing: "These words are trustworthy and true [houtoi hoi logoi pistoi kai alēthinoi], for the Lord . . . has sent his angel to show his servants what must soon take place" (Rev. 22:6; cf. 1:1–2). Is this *visible* proof? Faith, for Derrida, is inextricably bound up with blindness and, as such, with an eclipsing of the ordinarily privileged sense of sight and the entire attendant epistemology of vision.[7] Indeed, "faith, in the moment proper to it, *is* blind. It sacrifices sight, even if it does so with an eye to seeing at last."[8] The Apocalypse is faithless in this sense. It does not sacrifice sight. It is an affair, not even so much of seeing at last, but of seeing from first to last ("John, who testified . . . to all that he saw" [Rev. 1:2]; "I, John, am the one who . . . saw these things" [Rev. 22:8]). It testifies not to the unseen but to the seen. Being "blind" in the Apocalypse, in consequence, is equated with being "wretched," "pitiable," "poor," and "naked" (Rev. 3:17).[9]

On the other hand, the Apocalypse cannot show, cannot make present the revelatory radiance that is its theme. It can only bear witness to that luminescence. The Apocalypse testifies to what it claims to have seen in order to elicit faith from the other. And yet the Apocalypse is no ordinary demand for faith. The testamentary structure of everyday speech acts amounts, Derrida suggests, to declaring: "Believe what I say as one believes in a miracle."[10] But the testamentary structure of the Apocalypse amounts to a still more audacious declaration (and demand): "Believe what I say as one believes in a miracle—precisely because I am testifying to the truly invisible as that which I have truly seen." As such, the Apocalypse might indeed be said to exemplify the quasi-transcendental structure of any and every speech act: It makes manifest (or *reveals*, to use the Apocalypse's own idiom) the structural conditions of the speech act as such (even while chafing at the operational restrictions of those conditions, as we have seen). The Apocalypse, any apocalypse, would thus be a privileged instance of what Derrida has termed "pure attestation" ("if there is such a thing"),[11] which is precisely attestation to the unseen as seen, demanding a response of blind faith. "I am telling you this truth, believe me, believe what I believe, there, where you will never be able to see nor know the irreplaceable yet universalizable, exemplary place from which I speak to you."[12]

Now, faith, in the Derridean sense (or, perhaps, in any sense), bears a privileged relationship to *the secret*. The secret subtends my address to the other insofar as that address, as testimony and appeal for blind faith, ordinarily gestures to that which is veiled from the other. The secret that most preoccupies Derrida, however—what he has termed *the absolute secret*[13]—is not something subject to provisional concealment and that could, in consequence and in principle, be made manifest under different conditions. The absolute secret—which, extrapolating a little from Derrida's own reflections on it, might be said to be the structural prerequisite of faith itself, and, hence, by extension, of each and every address to any and every other—does not admit of manifestation, revelation, apocalyptic uncovering, unveiling, or denuding. The absolute secret is absolutely closed, absolutely clothed, but as such infinitely open because undecidable.

Can an apocalypse contain an absolute secret, or does the apocalyptic genre necessarily make open secrets of all secrets? Is the apocalyptic gesture always and only one of unveiling? Certainly, Revelation's Son of Man seems to have trouble keeping a secret ("As for the secret [to mystērion] of the seven stars that you saw in my right hand, and the seven golden lampstands: the seven stars are the angels of the seven churches, and the seven lampstands are the seven churches" [Rev. 1:20]), and so do Revelation's *angeles interpres* ("I will tell you the secret [to mystērion] of the woman, and of the beast with seven heads and ten horns that carries her" [Rev. 17:7]). But let us begin at the beginning. A secret is evoked in the Apocalypse's opening words; whether or not it is the *absolute* secret remains to be seen. "The unsealed secret of Jesus Messiah, God's gift to him," begins the text (in my admittedly customized rendering of it: "Apokalypsis Iēsou Christou, hēn edōken autō ho theos"). God's gift, then; but given when, given where? In answer, the text enjoins us to gaze, to gawk, to gawp through the gaping door of heaven itself, seductively left ajar by the divine doorkeeper (Rev. 4:1)—the same one, no doubt, who earlier identified himself as he "who opens and no one shuts, who shuts and no one opens" (Rev. 3:7; cf.

3:8). Thus it is that we become openly covert witnesses to the gift of the sealed scroll, the secret scroll—or perhaps it suffices to say: the secret. "Then I saw in the right hand of the one seated on the throne a scroll [biblion]," John testifies, "written on the inside and on the back, sealed with seven seals" (Rev. 5:1). The only anthropomorphic physical trait attributed to "the one seated on the throne" (other than the implied backside doing the sitting—the same derriere formerly paraded before Moses in response to his plea for a vision of the divine glory [Exod. 33:17–23]) is this hand, and the only purpose attributed to the hand is the clutching of the scroll. Thus encircled by the divine fingers, this mystified cylindrical object looks and acts suspiciously like a phallus, and not just any phallus, but the Lacanian phallus that, as "the signifier that has no signified,"[14] can only perform its function when veiled.[15] For it appears that the sealed scroll, the secret scroll—again, it will suffice simply to say: the secret—is indeed absolute at first, indecipherable because inaccessible, and hence unpossessable and impossible: "No one in heaven or on earth or under the earth was able to open the scroll or look into it" (Rev. 5:4). That is, until the mortally wounded Lamb, who, up until this moment, has been bleeding quietly and unnoticed nearby (Rev. 5:6), working earnestly but unsuccessfully, it seems, at accepting his own castration,[16] precipitously steps forward to claim the scroll as his own, with all the phantasmatic power and pomp that possession of it apparently confers: "Worthy is the cut Lamb [to arnion to esphagmenon] to receive power and wealth and wisdom and might and honor and glory and blessing!" (Rev. 5:12). But enough of this Lacanian digression, or regression.[17]

When the Lamb unzips the very first seal (Rev. 6:2), the secret threatens to leap whole and entire out of the scroll—or so it seemed, at any rate, to certain patristic expositors in particular, beginning with Irenaeus, who, taking their cue from the messianic cut of the rider on the white horse thereby let loose (cf. Rev. 19:11), imagined that the Parousia was already underway.[18] But the denuding of the secret has barely begun. And even when the seventh seal has been broken, and heaven itself has been plunged into suspenseful silence ("When the Lamb opened the seventh seal, there was silence in heaven for about half an hour" [Rev. 8:1]), all that ensues is another series of seven—seven further deferrals of climactic disclosure. Seven trumpets are distributed to seven angels, who proceed to blow them in turn. When the sixth trumpet is blown, a further angel—anxious, perhaps, at the prospect of yet another nail-biting half hour of heavenly silence, issuing in yet another stupendous anti-climax—blusters that "There will be no further delay, but in the days when the seventh angel is to blow his trumpet, God's secret [to mystērion tou theou] will be fulfilled" (Rev. 10:6–7).

Immediately before this portentous announcement, however, the "seven thunders" (hai hepta brontai) have sounded—or spoken (elalēsan), rather—and John, pen poised as always to spill every secret, is unexpectedly instructed instead to "Seal up what the seven thunders have said, and do not commit it to writing" (Rev. 10:4). All of which raises the question: What if the real secret, the absolute secret, in the Apocalypse, were the secret revealed, unveiled, uncovered by the seven thunders—and then immediately reveiled, covered over, closed up again; in which case the absolute secret would, once again, have slipped surreptitiously through our grasp? The secret announced by the seven thunders remains secret in the Apocalypse even after all else has been laid bare. It is not covered (nor is it uncovered) by the closing injunction to the seer, "Do not seal up [mē sphragisēs] the words of the prophecy of this book" (Rev. 22:10). But does the text dismiss the absolute secret even as it demarcates it? As if in refusal of the very concept of an unspillable secret, the Apocalypse, following the sounding of the seven thunders, conjures up an impatient angel, as we have seen, who, raising his right hand to heaven for dramatic effect, swears that "in the days when the seventh angel is to blow his trumpet, God's secret will be fulfilled" (Rev. 10:5–7).

So what *is* the secret that is fulfilled, or rather leaked, when the seventh angel finally blows his trumpet? First and foremost, it is *a secret empire*: "Then the seventh angel blew his trumpet, and there were loud voices in heaven, saying, 'The empire [hē basileia] of this world has become the empire of our Lord and his Messiah, and he will reign forever and ever'" (Rev. 11:15). A secret empire, then, that is also a global empire, and as such always already an open secret, administered from a heavenly throne room that, the more we peer through the door left ajar for our edification and instruction, seems to resemble an oval office—except when it resembles a CIA debriefing room instead, or a Pentagon war room.[19] But if this is the secret intelligence that the Apocalypse is only too eager to leak, indeed to flaunt, what might be the secret that it would prefer to keep under wraps, first and foremost from itself? Here is where Derrida's earlier reading of the Apocalypse, aided and abetted by his more recent reflections on justice, proves especially illuminating, enabling us to read the Apocalypse against the Apocalypse and thereby decrypt its internal communications.

The testimony of the Apocalypse, of any apocalypse, to a secret conceived, not as a closed body of content but an open space of possibility,

Derridapocalypse

is, for Derrida, encapsulated in the apocalyptic injunction, "Come!" (as in Rev. 20:17: "The Spirit and the bride say, 'Come [erchou].' And let everyone who hears say, 'Come.' And let everyone who is thirsty come"; and again in Rev. 20:20: "The one who testifies to these things says, 'Surely I am coming soon.' Amen. Come, Lord Jesus!"). By the time Derrida has finished with it, indeed, the apocalyptic "Come" shows all the signs of having become yet another nonsynonymous synonym for *différance*: "'Come' . . . could not become an object, a theme, a representation."[20] But "Come" also beckons us beyond *différance*. As a radical, irruptive opening to and for the other, otherness, the future, "Come" is also inextricably intertwined with certain later Derridean themes or nonthemes, not least *justice beyond the law*; *hospitality beyond reciprocity*; *the gift beyond debt* (up to and including the gift of death); *democracy without sovereignty* (which is to say, the democracy to come); but most of all *the messianic* (more precisely, the messianic without messianism).[21]

Derrida is enamored of a particular anecdote about the Messiah that Maurice Blanchot relates,[22] in which the Messiah appears one day at the gates of Rome, but disguised as a beggar or leper—a dissimulation designed to *defer* his advent, as it turns out. One of those who lays eyes on this ragged Messiah does see through his disguise—but tellingly elects to reveil rather than reveal him, putting the denegating question to him: "When will you come?" For the Messiah, in order to be the Messiah, can never actually be present, can never actually have arrived, any more than justice—justice beyond the law, that is—or hospitality—hospitality beyond reciprocity—can ever simply be assumed to be present, to have arrived. To assume their arrival would be to evade their demands. Derrida's "messianicity *without* messianism" would be "a waiting *without* waiting," which is to say "a waiting for an event, for someone or something that, in order to happen or 'arrive,' must exceed and surprise every determinant anticipation. No future, no time-to-come [à-venir], no other, otherwise; no event worthy of the name, no revolution. And no justice."[23]

Appropriately enough, therefore, when the Messiah does finally show up in the Apocalypse (Rev. 19:11ff.)—and at the shattered gates of Rome, no less (Rev. 18:1–24)—the indiscretion, the inappropriateness, the scandal of the event is duly, if obliquely, marked in the text that announces his advent. His name is secret: "He has a name inscribed that no one knows but himself [exōn onoma gegrammenon ho oudeis oiden ei mē autos]" (Rev. 19:12). He is incognito, then, in disguise. But it is a pitifully thin disguise. It is not as a beggar or a leper that he comes, although it might well have been (cf. Matt. 25:35–45: "I was hungry and you fed me . . . . I was naked and you clothed me, I was sick . . . and in prison and you visited me"). And that, perhaps, is the problem. We dread his appearance, appropriately enough, but for all the wrong reasons.

First, the dread. The Messiah, in order to be the Messiah, is, and must be, a figure of foreboding, as Derrida compellingly argues:

> Who has ever been sure that the expectation of the Messiah is not, from the start, by destination and invincibly, a fear, an unbearable terror—hence the hatred of what is thus awaited? And whose coming one would wish both to quicken and infinitely to retard, as the end of the future? . . . How could I desire [the] coming without simultaneously fearing it, without going to all ends to prevent it from taking place? Without going to all ends to skip such a meeting? . . . The messianic sentence carries within it an irresistible disavowal. In the sentence, a structural contradiction converts a priori the called into the repressed, the desired into the undesired, the friend into the enemy.[24]

The Messiah of the Apocalypse, too, is a figure of dread no less than desire—but less because his Parousia marks the impossible arrival of an altogether unanticipatable future, oriented to justice beyond the law and hospitality beyond reciprocity, than because the Apocalypse's "Come," which impatiently holds the door open for the imminent advent of the Messiah ("I am coming soon!" [Rev. 3:11]; cf. 16:15; 22:7, 12, 20), is an implementation of justice as slaughter on a horrific scale[25] and an implementation of hospitality as a horrid invitation to feast upon the mangled mountain of the slain. The invitation to the dreadful banquet also opens with "Come,"[26] as it happens: "Come, assemble for God's great banquet, to devour the flesh of kings, of captains, of the mighty, of horses and of riders—the flesh of all, whether free or slave, small or great" (Rev. 19:17–18). That which the Messiah establishes through the cataclysm of his coming (in a word, empire: "the empire [basileia] of our Lord and his Messiah" [Rev. 11:15]) is also that which the Messiah has come to destroy (in a word, empire: "I rule as an empress [basilissa]; . . . I will never see grief" [Rev. 18:7]). Because its Messiah can build only by destroying—and by destroying on a stupendous scale—the Apocalypse converts the desired into the undesired, the friend into the foe, the Christ into the Antichrist. We have long been conditioned to regard the Antichrist as a *monster*: "And I saw a beast [thērion] rising out of the sea, with ten horns and seven heads" (Rev. 13:1). But what if the Messiah, the Christ, were the true apocalyptic monster, the emblem and revealer of a monstrous truth? Do we dread the coming of the Messiah precisely because he *is* a monster, *the* monster, the very form of monstrosity itself?

The future, when it is absolutely unanticipated and unanticipatable, assumes monstrous form, Derrida insists (indeed, it is one of his oldest themes).[27] To embrace such a future—one not simply reducible to "a predictable, calculable, and programmable tomorrow"—would be "to welcome the monstrous *arrivant*, to accord hospitality to that which is absolutely foreign or strange."[28] The future is always a monster at the door. Is this the monster—the monster Messiah—that we have begun to identify in the Apocalypse? ("Behold, I stand at the door and knock" [Rev. 3:20].) Yes and no.

The future that the Apocalypse, whipped on by its God and his Messiah, so frenziedly rushes forward to embrace—a war-ridden, famine-ridden, utterly ecocidal, altogether cataclysmic future—is far from unfamiliar. This insufficiently unfamiliar, inadequately unanticipatable future can always, and all too easily, be regarded simultaneously as our present (which, of course, is how the Apocalypse has managed to live on—to live an improbably long life—impossibly surviving the demise of Rome that, on its own account, should have ushered in the end of history). But might not the intolerability, the unacceptability, of an all too familiar present, or an all too easily anticipated future, be far more *monstrous*, in the end—more unsettlingly strange in its absolute familiarity, more disturbingly alien in its absolute intimacy—than a wholly unanticipatable future? Why pretend to cage the monster in the secret structurally destined to remain forever sealed—the absolute secret that the seven thunders have sounded—when it is an open secret that the monster is, and was, and is still to come (Rev. 1:4, 8; 17:8)—and then to come yet again?

CATHERINE KELLER. Really, I would prefer not to know what is coming. All those all too predictable processes seem so vulgarly empirical in their apocalypse. Like the United States' push toward war and more war in the neighborhood of Israel—when as Derrida said already in 1992 "the war for the appropriation of Jerusalem is today the world war."[29] Like the boundless reach of this millennium's oily American Empire, like the boundless blowback of terrorism, like the boundless filling and polluting of the globe. Like the exhaustion of the gift of the bounded earth. The finite future of the infinite drive to profit requires no prophet. Where I come from, the four horsemen star in movies, they have fans on every street. You can rap, dance, or tap your fingers to their familiar hoofbeats. It is, as Stephen Moore suggests, the *anticipatable* future that sends us back into the hard embrace of John of Patmos. And as Derrida insists, it is in the *unknown* coming, the *avenir* in uncertainty, where hope would lie. So we turn (again) to the Derrida of what Gayatri Spivak first labeled his "ethical turn."[30] Turning, of course, is already apocalypse: "then I turned to see whose voice . . . " (Rev. 1:12).

So how would we read, with Derrida's help, the open secrets of apocalypse? How would we see its voices?[31] With eyes wide shut? "And I began to weep bitterly because no one in heaven or on earth or under the earth was able to open the scroll or to look into it" (Rev. 5:4). But it is the messiah with seven eyes, the gory lamb, the First and the Last, whom John (in his "prayers and tears") inscribes as the ultimate reader. The One worthy to read the scroll of seven seals. Or might we mistake Derrida for that hyper-reader. Just count the letters of his first and then his last name! John's coming lamb displays monstrosity from the start—with "seven horns and seven eyes, which are the seven spirits of God." So each eye *is* a spirit, an optical specter. The seven-lensed spectacles fit the lamb-messiah to read the spectacular predictions hidden behind the seven seals. No blind faith, this—but *super* vision.

Read under the supervision of this unsheepish ghost of a lamb, what is the Book of Revelation but a book of specters? Its angels of terror, its ghosts under the altar, its ghost riders—not to mention John as the ultimate ghost-writer for God, or is it for the spooky messiah, head and hair "white as white wool, white as snow," with red burning eyes . . . . In this it dimly anticipates *Specters of Marx*, where Derrida invokes the dread trace of an undead Marxism haunting the triumph of capitalism (that great whore), along with the host of ghosts that haunted Marx himself. But Derrida argues that Marx failed to develop patience for ghosts—including the specters of the Jewish messianism that has energized all political eschatology, religious or secular, since. So Derrida proposes his eerily hospitable spectropoetics. In the interest not of exorcising but of discerning these spirits he writes some of his most theologically important prose:

> If there is a spirit of Marxism I will never be able to renounce, it is not only the critical idea or questioning stance . . . . It is even more a certain emancipatory and messianic affirmation, a certain experience of the promise that one can try to liberate from any dogmatics, from any metaphysico-religious determination, from any messianism.[32]

Is it also the Messiah of the Apocalypse from whom a messianic deconstruction would liberate us? Is Derrida's democracy to come, promise, gift—that which in its vulnerability must be protected from the apocalyptic Coming? The *avenir* from the *futur*? But if we "look into it," isn't such a binary too oppositional, indeed too apocalyptic, for deconstruction? It would make the messiah into the antichrist and Derrida's messianicity into the *true* Coming.

Yet once one reads the scroll with the spectral lenses of deconstruction, one recognizes how closely the monster and the messiah mimic and mock one another—right down to their display of wounds, their surplus of horns and of eyes, their coupling with an urban femininity: New Jerusalem as the Bride in one instance, the Whore of Babylon, as Rome, in the other. A macro-politically charged mimicry: for the messiah has always signified the anti-empire and the whore-beast empire itself.[33] But, as it turns out, they both stand under the banner of the "coming": the lamb-messiah is "the one who is and who was and who is coming"—*ho erchomenon*. It is not just the messianic which comes! People "will be amazed when they see the beast, because it was, and is not, and is to come." Amazed, perhaps, because the beast iterates, it parodies, the temporal structure of the messianic hope—but with its *différance*: one recognizes that the difference between the Messiah and the Monster comes, indeed comes down, to the copula. Both were, both will come. But only the Messiah IS.

This is the infinitesimal but infinite gap: the beast is only as an is-not, as a present of absence, whereas the messiah is the subject of a tense presence, the present tense of a "to be" that conjugates the whole alpha-to-omega of salvation history. But the copulating beast-whore couple mocks the copula itself, it haunts the linear order of "is" with monstrous writing; the beast is "full of blasphemous names." We will have been alerted (by a certain critique of the metaphysics of presence) to the triumphalist potential of such a revelation of a pure present. But how would this messianic wisp of minimally Hellenized ontology, in this abysmally nonphilosophical text (far from even Paul), written in an inelegantly Hebrewized Greek, have caught the ousia virus? Does this "is" rather carry just the precondition for the subsequent ontotheologizing of Christianity—that which Derrida evokes, in distinction from and as the ghostly precondition of ontology, as "hauntology"? Might this precondition lie in the hope, all too human among subjects of imperial injustice then and now, for the cessation of brutality? But of course, for John of Patmos, also for the reciprocation of the torment, and finally—oh surely, so deservedly—for the gift of a life without suffering, without death?

The Apocalypse wants an end to mourning (at least for its own people). Yet Derrida is teaching, if I am not mistaken, that any politics that would eschew brutality, that would not replicate empire even as it revolts against empire, can never be done with all work of mourning.[34] John's ekklesia, with its ghost-martyrs crying for vengeance, its (str)angels bringing justice by way of global terror and mass death, wants "no more tears." "No more death." "No more sea." For tears condense out of the chaos of the primal saltwaters. Not coincidentally did the Bush administration immediately after 9/11 parlay mourning for the three thousand into violence. At the same time, one hundred times that many children die daily from avoidable causes, and, as Derrida has noted, we *let* them.[35] And we can hardly begin to grieve all whom the peoples of the book daily make into ghosts.

No wonder: at the end of the *biblos*, itself an entire *bibliotheque* of texts rich with grief, mourning got shut down once and for all. Along with messianic comfort, the apocalypse offers a merciless pre-emption, indeed a pre-emptying, of history: dis/closure as closure. A closing of the very space of disclosure: *final* revelation. Among us who dwell in the land of pre-emptive strikes and of *Ghostbusters*, a white warrior of they-are-evil-we-are-good-have-a-nice-day comes hybridized with the Babylon/Rome who said "I will never see grief" (Rev. 18:7). How else can we read the peculiar production of a born-again Christian (who says his favorite philosopher is Jesus) as world emperor? Not that the fusion of messianism and imperialism is new. But now this hybrid Messiah-Caesar complex metabolizes in the high-speed global media of what Hardt and Negri have dubbed the "postmodern Empire."

Yet the medium of John's Apocalypse already seems spectropoetic. In its scrolling bombardment of images, blunt bits of the poetry of prophets kaleidoscope at an oneiric speed.[36] It prefigures what Derrida calls "techno-tele-iconicity": the medium of the media, the "techno-tele-discursivity," he says "determines the spacing of public space, the very possibility of the *res publica* and the phenomenality of the political . . . . This element itself is neither living nor dead, present nor absent: it spectralizes."[37] Indeed the *res publica* is now *res privata*—so notes Nestor Miguez, who like most liberation theologians (all knowingly haunted by the ghost of Marx) loves John's Apocalypse for its exposure of the world-destructive power of globalized greed then and now.[38] "Public things" are being privatized for profit, while what was private appears in the public of televised spectacles and internet immediacy. Indeed, Derrida's "Faith and Knowledge" tracks the alliance of religion with "tele-technoscience," which he calls globalization itself. But "on the other hand," it declares war against this power that dislodges religion from "all its proper places, *in truth from place itself*, from the *taking-place* of its truth"—hence the "auto-immune reaction" within religion: "the auto-immunitary haunts the community . . . like the hyperbole of its own possibility."[39] Intriguingly, it is this ghostly global info-technology, which is so effectively deployed among the apocalyptic hyperboles of Abrahamism (the so-called fundamentalisms), that in *Specters of Marx* specifically provokes the formulation of hauntology.

Might we suggest that this exposed global spatiality (and apocalypse is nothing if not global) where the public and private dissolve into each other sheds light on Derrida's "taste for the secret"? Instead of reading this as a symptom of a crypto-bourgeois-individualism, we could recognize its protection of a space of alterity, of nonbelonging: "the demand," he writes, "that everything be paraded in the public square . . . is a glaring sign of the totalitarianization of democracy." (We who mourn the possibility of US democracy will be needing this phrase.) "In terms of political ethics: if a right to the secret is not maintained, we are in a totalitarian space."[40] In the space of the apocalyptic utopia all is exposed to view; the variations of human embodiment, the diversities of personality, disappear along with the darkness, ocean, and death. "God is the light" of the New Jerusalem, "and its lamp is the Lamb" (Rev. 21:23). A ghost-white transparency of goodness and security rules: a neon panopticon, shining through the lamb-lamp. The seven spectral eyes do not just see but shine.

On the other hand, these city streets "transparent as glass" are lined with trees leafing "for the healing of the nations." They heal the effects of the oppression of all then and now living in the filth of slum streets. Those masses will no longer yearn for "water of life as a gift" though now the desert spreads, water wars loom, and the empire privatizes water and every other public good.

The book concludes with an entire riff on *coming*: "See I am coming soon . . . The spirit and the bride say come; everyone who hears, say 'Come' . . . let everyone who is thirsty, come" (Rev. 22:12a; 17). To this water, always at least literal, every other is invited along with the coming of the ultimate Other. "Tout autre est tout autre."

Does John's Apocalypse dis/close—or only close—what Derrida has here and there referred to as the chaos of the gaping mouth, of thirst and hunger as well as speech? No matter how long I peer and glare and wince at it, I still see no closure of this undecidable scroll with the End always already in its sight. Its empire and anti-empire continue to conjugate history, separated only by the negation of a presence too pure to recognize its own irony: its own *is/is not*. No end in sight of apocalypse, empire, or of the autoimmune violence of our bloody legacy. Nor of its capacity for autodeconstruction. Which perhaps, after all, Professor Moore and I perform here and now.

If this text won't close, don't we need an opening within the space of its haunted iconicity? But—within the terms of the sibling rivals of the family of Abraham—how would that space open, except into more desert? Derrida finds a promising chaos in that very desert, a deconstructive kenosis. But what of the rivalrous women, Sarah and Hagar, unsisterly, divided but never quite conquered? Would their ghosts settle now, after so much movement of women, for these desert patrimonies—for the messianic masculinities? For their crumbs? Unexpectedly, Hagar survived in the desert, as did the anonymous goddess of the apocalypse chased there by the first beast.[41] Then the earth opened its mouth: the very maw of chaos nonviolently swallows the vomit of the dragon, the effluvium with which he had sought to drown her. But now—would these desert women, practiced in a wide variety of open mouths, not also open again the watery chaos, Thalassa, the mythic sea, the salty birthwaters—the bottomless flux or *tehom* that apocalypse nihilates along with death, night, and tears?

Not a pure femininity (goddess forbid), not a feminist apocalypse, and certainly not a pure origin, a patristic *ex nihilo*—might *tehom* (in some dream of a divine woman) lend another "nonsynonymous substitution" to what Derrida calls, in a chaosmically clarifying paradox, the "heterogeneity of origin"? "Heterogeneity opens things up," he says.[42] Is this the opening, the dis/closure that opens up the apocalypse itself, precisely there where it would shut everything down, the counter-apocalypse that is no mere pro-, retro-, or anti-apocalypse?

Here my question becomes confessedly theological. If the "heterogeneity of origin" deconstructs (as I believe it must) the *ex nihilo* of an orthodox origin, doesn't it also call for a heterogeneity of the eschaton? But wouldn't such a heterogeneous future upset the purity, the absoluteness, the unilateral gift, of the coming? At times, Derrida's messianicity seems to invoke such a purity: when he calls for the "absolutely undetermined messianic hope"[43] or with Kierkegaard the "absolute secret," *ab-solutum*, absolved from any bond, detached, out of joint.[44] Then it is as though any moment of joining, any connectivity, would deny the time-out-of-joint; as though one is either detached or fused, as though attachment entails determination, confinement, closure; as though we might disavow the chaosmic fluidities of our interrelations for the sake of a deconstructive absolute, purified even of the possible. I realize that Derrida—at these present-transcendent moments—means to save the undetermined future from any (theological) foreclosure: "As soon as a determinate outline is given to the future, to the promise, even to the Messiah, the messianic loses its purity, and the same is true of the eschatological."[45]

Still, is a new messianic "purity" the only alternative to an old determinism? This question is posed within a tradition in which the omnipotent One, Himself the essence of origin and end, routinely determines outcomes. In disclosing the transcendent future, He closes down history. Derrida proposes, therefore, a "messianic eschatology so desertic that no religion and no ontology could identify themselves with it."[46] This is an intriguing tactic: to dry the ontotheology out of eschatology, to bake the religious out of the messianic. I admire its negation of dogma itself, and ipso facto of all the dogmatisms that keep women in the role of God-dogs, licking the leavings of the religious Masters. This desert eschatology answers to his "faith without religion." But here is my worry (and let me state it without the least frisson of feminist fury, without for the moment the distraction of symbolic sex, without apocalyptic ambush): Might this very strategy not be echoing—so inadvertently, indeed with such gentle intent—the foundation of orthodox theology?

For "in the beginning"—not of Genesis but of Christian orthodoxy —the *ex nihilo* had evaporated the *tehom*, the watery abyss or precreation *khora* whose traces remain in scripture until they are vaporized in the apocalypse. The absolute desert becomes then the condition of creation as well as its end. The *ex nihilo* purged the Jewish and mythic residues of chaos and at the same time established a divine sovereignty of pure power—which determines through grace the purity of faith. After all, wasn't Protestant neo-orthodoxy founded on such an opposition between the purity of faith and the heterogeneity of religion—Karl Barth's "Christian faith" vs. any, including Christian, "religion"? Naturally enough perhaps, for a Frenchman, Derrida's Christian interlocutors are often Roman Catholic: Caputo, Hart, Marion, even Tracy—so I am aware that a certain problematic within Protestantism, involving the totalizing effects of transcendence *sola scriptura*, *sola gratia*, *sola fide*s, may for Derrida lack comparable mediation, except by way of Kierkegaard. Nonetheless, some of us within and between the religions have come to depend upon Derrida for help in releasing the infinite indeterminacy—khoric and tehomic—from the anxious grip of every orthodoxy, even the most progressive. Indeed, for this bottomless indeterminism, in its democratically cosmopolitan justice as well as its meditative apophasis, some of us have come to depend upon his mysterious overflow into theology —a divinely Derridean surplus. So then one does not want some spectral afterimage, some theological ghost, of Derrida to be reinforcing the kind of paternalist dichotomy invested in even the socially responsible messianisms of theology.

It is the mirror play of the purity of a desert nothingness of origin and the purity of a drily différant coming that worries me. It worries me also in the most sympathetic, socially responsible form of orthodox Protestantism. The leading eschatological thinker of twentieth-century Christianity, Jürgen Moltmann, early posited the "coming"—rather than any immanent becoming—as the distinguishing mark of the Jewish and Christian Messiah. Moltmann's translation of eschatology into "hope" rather than "end things," hope as the *Zukunft*, the to-come of *adventus* rather than the calculable linearity of *futurum*, needfully intensifies a worldly responsibility that end things trump.[47] Derrida's assertion of the pure coming, the *avenir*, over against the determinate *futur* structurally neatly parallels Moltmann's binary of a pure and promised *Zukunft* vs. the emergent future. Again this coming not only opposes mere ending but also the immanence of becoming. (The to-come in its pure form has no truck with any Nietzschean or Whiteheadian philosophy of open-ended becoming.) Moltmann criticizes the Parmenidean eternal presence, offering instead a *theologia gloriae* of "lasting being in the coming presence of God." The Parousia yields total ousia, in the end—after death and transience have been overcome.[48] The One who comes arrives in His [sic] glory, never again to suffer the *zimtzum* of nonbeing.[49] While the eschatological narrative of the new heaven and earth refuses an otherworldly or supernatural eternity, it remains doubtless as alien to deconstruction as is the pure presence.

Of course, even if it comes dangerously close to mirroring the two-kingdom structure of law and grace, Derrida's own binary of determinate history and absolute promise heralds no total or final coming. *Au contraire*. He presumes—with *theologically* crucial insight—that it is the hardening of the messianic into the messiah that produces such totalizing effects. Revolutionary or reactionary. But if the only alternatives remain a determinist appropriation, on the one hand, and the différance of a pure novum, on the other, does not Derrida's own "gift" harmonize, hauntingly, with the triumphant chorale of God's absolutely free and transcendent gift? The *charis*, grace, *sola gratia*—a unilateral, pure omnipotence, whether coming from above or from the future?

This would be a spooky surplus indeed, no doubt helpful for a certain Protestant poststructuralism. But for those theologies, including most feminist and ecological varieties, which for the sake of a sustainable justice and a credible faith resist the imaginary of omnipotence, indeed for those heterodoxies in which the divine morphs into the *ruach*, *Geist*, spirit of infinite indeterminacy, the desert purity of the gift will remain troublesome. Derrida's "messianic performative" can work within Christianity to gird the loins of a *deus absconditus* who absconds once again with all agency, leaving humanity enough rope to hang itself. But mainly it surely works to provoke spirited and hospitable actualizations of what might not otherwise have been possible.

Instead of re-establishing the dry abyss—between the future that will come predictably from our efforts and *ho erchomenos*, that which comes despite all effort—can we not admit the Derridean heterogeneity into the gap itself? Doesn't it show its own becoming wildness, a chaosmic wilderness characteristic of material deserts? I find a hint of this alternative flow of agencies enacted in Derrida's notion of the "I": "There is no 'I' that ethically makes room for the other, but rather an 'I' that I structured by the alterity within it, an 'I' that is itself in a state of self-deconstruction, of dislocation." And so "the other is there in any case, it will arrive if it wants, but before me, before I could have foreseen it."[50] If the other is already there, then the coming is never pure, already what comes has been entangled in a prior becoming. The messianic Other—*tout autre*—as arriving before "I am" upends the linear determinism of any closed system. It counters apocalypse with dis/closure. At the same time, it suggests a momentary "I" always already heterogeneous with—indeed co-constituted by—the future coming. This "I" comes-to-be as event only through its prehensions of the others that precede it. Indeed, that haunt it!

This impure "I" can never be absolved of its Other. So why impose purity onto the Other itself? Why not let the *tout autre*, whatever or whoever it will come-to-be, also appear as impure, heterogeneous, already taking account of *its* others as it comes? Then *ruach* is emptied of the dominological structure of *sola gratia*—though perhaps not of her wild tehomic grace. As to Derrida's so-graceful gift to theology: He will not offer us an apocalyptic feast, *dieu merci*, but healing crumbs. In the shared spirit of an indeconstructible justice—"as indeconstructible as deconstruction itself"—he will not cease to haunt scripture and its interpreters, even its theologians. As we have come to haunt him.

CHAPTER 8

Messianic Indeterminacy: A Comparative Study

I am about to do a new thing. Now it
springs forth: do you not perceive it?

(ISA. 43:19)

Messianic moments have been multiple. None have achieved an ultimate success, let alone an end of history. So did the messiah not quite arrive? Or rather fail to come again? Perhaps she simply does not linger? But the moments that can be called messianic have delivered some stunning shifts of history. There have been great springings forth. "He has brought down the powerful from their thrones and lifted up the lowly" (Luke 1:52). Now and then. Here and there. The novum may—and thankfully—get normalized as the new norm—the end of slavery, women's rights, civil rights, the end of the nuclear arms race, the legalization of same-sex marriage. No steady progress has achieved it, no full quality is delivered, no future progress is guaranteed by it. But the breakthrough remains irreducible. It was unpredictable in advance. Afterward it carries its register of justice into some practice, law, or structure of relative predictability, some historic fidelity, that teaches us that hope is not in vain. But the implications

---

A version of this essay was presented at a panel at the American Academy of Religion 2012 on "Comparative Messianisms," as a specifically inter-Abrahamic exploration of the wider discourse of comparative theology.

and the applications of the justice achieved remain in their own moments indeterminate as to coming outcomes.

In other words, messianic moments come and go, even as their effects persist. They happen once in a while. They do not wait for the determination as to whether or not a messiah has, or will in the future, come once and for all. Perhaps in this they carry Derrida's gift to intra-Abrahamic discourse: a "messianicity without the messiah." It defers any determinate answer without quite silencing the question of whether there was, is, this is, or there will be a messiah. The messianic moments come and go, but they leave their trace, their specter: determinate residues enriching the potentiality of the indeterminate future.

So I find myself hovering today—in a conversation created by the question of "comparative messianisms"—in something like a *messianic indeterminacy*. This can only sound like an oxymoron. For despite the unknowability of a future, the past of messianism has been charged with perhaps the most ferocious and unifying, the most *determined*—indeed, in their excess of motivation, overdetermined—forces of human history. In their Abrahamic family of origin, they have been directed often and with apocalyptic determination, which is to say, a great force of will, against each other. Yet then the sibling contradictions and oedipal competitions only expose the indeterminacy at the "root of Jesse." From a perspective of comparison, which works to abstain from the rivalry, the episteme of certainty dissolves back into the relation of difference.

Note that the very word *compare*—*com-pare*, "with equals"—witnesses at its root a possible egalitarianism. Leveling hierarchy, not difference, comparison is already to hint at the messianic hope. The equality of the entities under comparison, of course, can be presumed but not predetermined: For the actual content of each "equal," in this case each messianism, each Abrahamism, can only be determined through the comparison itself. For no religion has any meaning apart from its relations of contrast to another. And the comparison will have by its very nature relativized—brought into relation—claims that may be in competition with each other, even politely understated claims to be *primus inter pares*. So comparison, indispensable to any determination of the truth claims of a religion, may itself render final truth indeterminate if not indeterminable.

Perhaps, one might argue, that the notion of comparative messianism itself requires such an indeterminacy—inasmuch as that indeterminacy enfolds the determinate differences of the political history of the messianic. That indeterminacy limits the certainty of the truth claims that it at the same time makes possible. In other words, just where the messianisms break into apocalyptic prediction, does an apophatic darkness open in their midst?

Such an indeterminacy, when it takes here specifically Christian form, springs forth from the overdeterminations of a theological trajectory that seeks even now to deploy the Anointed One *against* Christian legitimations of any messianic supremacism. That anointment itself, according to all four gospels, performs a tender irony: If the gesture of anointing cites the ritual of Davidic kingship, it was the gift of a woman, massaging some fragrant balm onto a loved and vulnerable body. Tradition amplified her powerless and sexually suspect status, identifying Mary of Bethany with the Magdalene. The perfume precipitates a heated discussion of poverty and anticipates a dark outcome. At this moment, a theology of messianic indeterminacy would inhale that fragrance in appreciation of the fragility of flesh in its christological force field. The darkness of the anointment now reads not only as a message of death but as the whiff of the unknown that accompanies any messianic moment yet to come. And the uncertainty of the messianic future then permits, indeed requires, the multiple possibilities of an actually—not just epistemically—indeterminate messianic history that continues even now. In other words, the dark anointment of messianic indeterminacy requires the work of comparative theology.

To *compare* is to draw differences into explicit relation, that is, into disclosure of the relation difference itself already constitutes. Therefore, comparison at once explicates and complicates—that is, enfolds together, co-implicates—the difference that provokes the comparison in the first place. In this way comparative theology invites a plural religious belonging, or what John Thatamanil calls more actively "multiple religious participation."[1] The perspective of comparison, which in this sense puts the lie to any simply bounded identity, cannot then ascend to any neutral outside for itself. I do not separate myself, in other words, from the pathos and potential of a certain messianized ecofeminist Christianity. Such nonseparability does not mark a homogenization but (in the technical Whiteheadian sense) a "contrast": It does not reduce difference but incompatibility.[2] Incompatibility in the zone of the messianisms, whether we are speaking of the interreligious or the—just as conflictual—*intra*-religious differences (as between the right and left wings of Christianity), is rarely a matter of mere contradiction, to be solved by reasoning or preference. We have to do here with a couple thousand years of the wars of what my mentor in seminary, Alan Miller, called "the sibling rivals of the family of Abraham."[3] And it is not as though the earlier ancestral history witnesses to a peaceable origin. In its convulsive continuity we must diagnose, with Derrida's help, an autoimmune condition. "It makes violence of itself, does violence to itself and keeps itself from the other. The autoimmunity of religion can only indemnify itself without assignable end."[4] But the indeterminacy of the end carries with it always also, beyond the failed fraternal reconciliations, the insecure promise of a peaceable kingdom, a religio-political anointment of a multiplicity not enclosed in any known religion or politics.

In other words, with the topic of comparative messianism we have inextricably to do with two currently crucial discourses: of comparative theology and of political theology. Indeed, might political theology provisionally be read as a subset of comparative theology and, in particular, of comparative messianism? Yet of course comparative and political theologies have in practice almost nothing to do with each other.[5] I am wondering the following: Political theology, as the frame of a range of liberation and progressive theologies, has been at key moments engaged with a twentieth-century lineage located outside of theology or religious studies that has recently come to the fore in political philosophy. Political theorists from Agamben to Žižek appropriate Carl Schmitt's definition of modern politics as secularized theology to reinforce not its conservatism but their own postsecular attention to theology. They may be atheists, but they wish to reconsider rather than to repress the religious patterns left and right persisting in the supposedly secularized modern West.

What I am suggesting is that these political thinkers are ipso facto implicated in comparative theology, but then specifically as comparative messianism. This does not mean that they practice Francis Clooney's rigorous "cross-reading" of texts across religious traditions, from a distinct location in one such tradition. But, really, what goes under the heading of political theology now that does *not* dig up the rhizome of Jewish-Christian-Muslim theologies of the political and therefore of their heterogeneous messianisms? Thus Paul is these days extolled as a politically radical (i.e., messianic) Jew. "Paul," declares Agamben, "is no longer the founder of a new religion, but the most demanding representative of Jewish messianism."[6] Enmeshed in readings of Benjamin and Rosenzweig, this recent Paulinism—Judaically well-supported first by Schmitt's prewar Jewish student Jacob Taubes[7]—leads Eric Santner to quip that "Saint Paul was the first great German-Jewish thinker!"[8]

In other words, the Jewish/Christian linkage of comparative messianism—as an acutely nonseparable difference—lies close to the heart of political theology. This relation glows with conflictual intensity in the light of the function of Judaism as the internal scapegoat of Christian Europe, not to mention Schmitt's political allegiance to National Socialism. To affirm the shared legacy of the messianic is one way of turning the redemptive intensity of the Jewish/Christian therapeutic in relation to its internal violence. And yet this particular messianic rapprochement does not happen without certain disturbing edges.

To move beyond fratricide, its fraternal Abrahamism apparently sometimes requires, as its excluded Other, the "Oriental." For instance, Žižek colorfully characterizes his own (faithfully Leninist atheist) "Christian stance" as more or less that of the messiah of Luke 14, costumed as Che Guevara.[9] The revolutionary Jesus is no one new to the heritage of liberation theology that goes largely unnoticed by Žižek. He then proceeds to characterize his favored messianism as "the opposite of the Oriental attitude of nonviolence, which—as we know from the long history of Buddhist rulers and warriors—can legitimize the worst violence."[10] The worst? Who knows this? Certainly Buddhism as a successful world religion enabled its share of atrocities. But worse than which epoch of Christian history? By which global tally? Žižek's Eurocentric version of the comparative history of violence is offered casually, a mere side effect of his messianic universalism. So are his sarcastic orientalist equations of Buddhism itself with a business-class New-Age spirituality. So much for multiple religious belonging. The Muslim remains, differently, the invisible little brother in such moments of Jewish-Christian fusion—over against the East. But as the Muslim was the original "Oriental," formative of the "West" in opposition, it does not need Žižek's help to play the role of galvanizing Other. Note that Schmitt's version of political theology is based on the "friend/foe" binary. In the meantime, Žižek awaits with undisguised glee the return of "the cruel God of vengeful blind justice." Is not such forthright evidence of the force of patriarchal theology beyond theism illumining? "And it is when one is faced with this violent return that one should assert the ultimate speculative identity of Judaism and Christianity: the 'infinite judgment' is here 'Christianity *is* Judaism.'"[11] Thus is the comparative trumped by a messianic copula! Difference flushes into the violence of unity.

Of course, Jesus was a rabbi with no concept of Christianity; Boyarin has taught us that Paul was a radical Jew; and yes Christianity was a Jewish heresy. But to blithely identify the two religions is to send the painstaking development of a religious pluralism—a discipline of comparison that does not confuse respect with sameness—right down the drain. (Levinasian, Derridean, all too Jewish ethics of difference be damned.) If pluralism in religion means a pluralism of separate religions, wan for purposes of comparison and helpless before the needs of political coalition. But mere relativism has not prevailed in the comparativist conversation. I wonder, for instance, if those engaged in political theology might hold Žižek's version responsible to a comparative theology of a relationalist pluralism, characterized by what John Thatamanil calls "interreligious receptivity"? The latter's complex reading of the reception of Jesus by Gandhi and Gandhi by King would trouble the parallactic chic of political theology of divine violence.[12] It would help us to articulate a political theology of nonviolent resistance—inspired not by the Che but the MLK Christ!

Political theology is not one. Other forms expressive of a prophetic resistance to oppression lack all enthusiasm for revolutionary or theocratic violence. Then political theology persists in *messianically* exposing the Christian history of messianic imperialism.[13] That history began in earnest with the political eschatology of Byzantium and its enthroned messiah as represented on earth by the *basileus*. In *Orthodoxy and Political Theology*, Pantelis Kalaitzidis has recently analyzed the affiliation between the theology of empire worked out by the fourth-century Eusebius of Caesarea and that of Schmitt's "affinity for monarchical/authoritarian regimes." Kalaitzidis shows how the pro-Arian bishop and the political philosopher both reject the notion of a trinity that "introduces difference and dialogue among the three divine persons, which are not conducive to a pro-royalist perspective."[14] (The homonymy of Arian and Aryan is pure coincidence.) Schmitt's theocratic vision of realized eschatology was contested in specifically eschatological terms by Johannes Metz, Jürgen Moltmann, and Dorothee Sölle in their reclamation of the term "political theology" already in the 1970s.[15] They stirred the "dangerous memory" of the promise of a justice that opens history—and for Moltmann the earth itself, in a new "cosmic spirituality"—to the solidarity of hope.[16] A messianism of liberation redefines political theology as resistance to the determinism of either otherworldly or worldly power. In such a sense, as Agamben shows, Schmitt's political theology of the counterrevolution is developed "according to an explicitly anti-messianic constellation."[17]

Indeed, the identification of the subversive with the messianic may be said to define Western liberation movements. Thus Marcella Althaus-Reid reminds us that under the Argentinian military dictatorship "the official political discourse was centered on a theological concept: *mesianismo* (messianism) was considered to be subversive. Any political or religious challenge of the fascist government of the times (such as political graffiti) was denounced as 'messianic,' that is, politically subversive of the institutional order."[18] The opening of history was recognized, even by those who would keep it closed, to be *mesianismo*.

This difference of the closed and the dis/closive—*apokalypto*—brings on its own mess of messianic ambiguities, however. That promissory opening within history may itself be read as a providentially assured rather than indeterminate, *actually* open future. But promise is not guarantee. Of course no liberative political eschatology resembles any fundamentalist End. To the latter, the on–the-ground response always more biblical: "No one knows the day or the hour."

No one knows. An apophatic temporality—twisted toward the future. If the timing is unknowable, it is also unknown if history will ever be *fully realized*—knowably done, closed. The *apocalyptic finis* of the messianic— with its reactionary or revolutionary certainties—may in this way be exposed to an *apophatic infinity*. But then one cannot speak of the relation of *apophasis* to *apokalypsis* except as a manifestation of the relation of mysticism to messianism.[19]

Let me make the case for that relationship with reference, oddly enough, to the political philosophy of Judith Butler. She would affirm the messianic within Judaism as "nonrealizability." In this she reads the messianic redemption, by way of Walter Benjamin, not as the final realization of history but as the redemption *from* a teleology of history. She is in this thinking preoccupied with the problem of Zionism and the Israeli-Palestinian conflict: a particularly intense knot of asymmetrical difference. She diagnoses a messianism of teleological return in a troubling symptom of Levinas's words: He warned of the "rise of the countless masses of Asiatic peoples and underdeveloped peoples." Under their "greedy eyes," "we, the Jews and Christians are pushed to the margins of history." According to Butler, Levinas "calls for a new kinship between Christians and Jews" to combat this rise "in what can only be called barbarism."[20] As with Žižek, and with little resonance otherwise between projects, the Asian, the Oriental, here consolidates a new Jewish-Christian fraternity. A comparison conducive to cohabitation is replaced by a unity of defense against the barbaric masses, the Others without faces, of the East.[21] To this Butler juxtaposes the ethics of the face-to-face encounter advanced by the *other* Levinas—the one who avers that "all persons are the Messiah."[22] By noting this dramatic tension between these differently indispensable Jewish thinkers, I do not mean to play a Christian game of *divide et impere* but to point to a problem in the messianism that Jews and Christians do indeed, heterogeneously, share.

It is as an alternative to the politics of return that Judith Butler offers the messianism of nonrealizability: that is, of a nonteleological temporality. For this she turns to Hannah Arendt's insistence on a universal right of "cohabitation on the earth." Arendt had considered the relation of the messianic and the mystical key to "establishing the notion of God as 'impersonal' and 'infinite.'" From that deanthropomorphized theology she gleans the "notion that humans participate in the powers that shape the 'drama of the world,' Arendt here makes a swerve into the mystical, citing the 16th century Israeli kabbalist Isaac Luria: 'Formerly [the diaspora] had been regarded either as a punishment for Israel's sins or as a test of Israel's faith. Now it . . . [is also] a mission.'"[23] Butler then suggests that "redemption itself is to be rethought as the exilic, without return, a disruption of teleological history and an opening [sic] to a convergent and interruptive set of temporalities. This is a messianism, perhaps secularized, that affirms the scattering of light, the exilic condition, as the nonteleological form that redemption now takes."[24] In this way nonrealizability hosts a diasporic cohabitation: Those countless masses have a right to cohabit the earth. The kabalistic infinite thus unfolds in the multiplicities of the finite earth. With the secularization that can also be read as the postsecular in the working of any political theology, this diasporic messianism expresses a profoundly promising convergence of mystical and political Judaism. It carries a universalism that, if eschatological in its hope, interrupts the straight time of teleological triumphalism.

Butler briefly links such universalization to William Connolly's concept of "pluralization" as differentiation. She does not discuss how Connolly's political philosophy unfolds a concept of time as itself a distributive pluralization. He also frames history as nonteleological. Yet he finds it at the same time "teleodynamically" charged, with intensities of becoming circulating often unpredictably between the human and the nonhuman estates. His radical pluralism, derived especially from William James's *A Pluralistic Universe*, develops a cosmologically extended ecopolitics. As with Butler, the invitation is to an indeterminate, dangerously open future. But while he prepares a fresh way of pluralist alliance across religious and irreligious differences, his emphasis on *becoming* sounds a different keynote than the messianic *coming*. In Connolly the becoming explicitly solicits a Whiteheadian spatiotemporality: "What if time is becoming, and the future of the universe—and the multiple, interacting, and partially open temporal systems through which it is composed—is really open to an uncertain degree? What if it is really open to metamorphosis?"[25]

The unrealizable, the apophatically open, the diaspora without final return: Does the messianic undergo its own metamorphosis, where the to-come may already be coming to be and yet may fail to come, where the time of the messianic hope is not the end time but the time of becoming? What happens when we read the mystical infinite darkly, as *in-fini*, unfinished by definition, as therefore the site of a becoming without boundary and without end? Does it then support the diasporic redistribution of messianic energies, in their resistance to both temporal and cognitive closure?

If so, it may be the apophatic that keeps the messianic *comparative*: that is, *relative* to the differences that at once perform and condition the indeterminate dis/closures—the unveilings, reveilings, revealings. This is a semantic field Elliot Wolfson works deeply. In reflecting on the kabbalistic Habad masters, he finds the Messiah linked "to the state of mindfulness designated as . . . the negation of thought, the (un) knowing of the 'naught that is a greater abnegation than the nothing.'"[26] Clearly such Abrahamic "mindfulness" does not here lack its echo of a Buddhist *sunyata*. So how might a mindful unknowing, without which I cannot now think theology at all, perform the pluralizing differentiation that a comparative theology requires? What is the relation of comparative messianism to the unfolding of religious multiplicity more universally?

I wonder if it might, for instance, be illumined by the pluralization of disclosure in the hermeneutics of the twelfth-century Ibn Arabi, commenting upon "the path of Allah." "This path is that concerning which the Folk of Allah have said, 'The paths to God are as numerous as the breaths of the creatures.' . . . When someone believes that Allah is such and such— whatever that might be—[Allah] will disclose himself to him in the form of his belief."[27] The comparativist implications of this mystical pluralization are bottomless. As to the messiah, the *al-mahdi*, the "rightly guided one" does not appear here as a single figure embodying the end or the fulfillment of history. The messiah is whoever, by actualizing that divine guidance, actually becomes the *imam al-waqt*, the "guide-of-the-present instant."[28] I cannot help but think in this sense of Benjamin's *Jetztzeit*—the now-moment, when "truth is charged to the bursting point with time."[29] Does a mystical infinite such as Arabi's give breathing room to an endless multiplicity of pathways, theological and political?

Does mysticism then describe the breathing room within the messianic, the space of emergence within the particular emergency? Rather than coming from a pre-established and thus returning future, its time would then always and fleetingly be now: but only if "rightly guided." Then the messianic possibility would seem to open out of the naught within the now, the no-thing that is the indeterminacy enfolding everything. Is the Coming actually a Becoming? If with Connolly "time is becoming," it is not accidental that he invites theological resonances with the temporality of his eco-egalitarian politics—as long as the theology is not "providential teleology." His radical pluralism extends becomingness to religious multiplicity. It thus contributes to the politics of any comparative theology that takes its own egalitarianism seriously, that resists the sovereignty of any monolithic power. Yet for Jürgen Moltmann, as embodying the European Protestant alternative to Schmitt's political theology, the *coming* interrupts and transcends all becoming. Becoming for him designates a merely immanent process, which is therefore not open to the novum that comes from outside our systems, beyond our ken. These systems close in on themselves unless interrupted by a transcendent future. In this there is an intriguing parallel between Derrida's deconstructive and Moltmann's confessional "to come."

Indeed, any enclosure of the human within our own constructions may require deconstruction by the gift of messianicity, the democracy-to-come, the possibility of the impossible. However, if we will cease to mistake *becoming* for a predictable roll into *futurum*, then what is to come may be the indeterminate edge and possibility of becoming, not its adversary. Becoming is itself the interruption of being: of the status quo of beings and the ontotheology of the sovereign Being. So then it is a world of being, not a "world of becoming," the messianic *adventus* overcomes. And it does it in becoming—in the incarnations, the materializations, of that which has not yet come to be. In unsaying the predictable futurum, we might say instead that the to-come uncorks the coming-to-be that would be becoming among us this very day. Becoming neither trumps nor smooths the path of the *to come*—it enfolds and pluralizes it, it diasporizes it, it prepares its ways and follows in them.

Perhaps then a comparative messianism that steers its own political theology will affirm—with pragmatic force, indeed with prophetic determination—the indeterminate chances of our collective becoming. Then perhaps our messianic teachings can guide our publics, religious, secular, or postsecular, to face whatever comes. With the adaptivity of hope and the lessons of justice. For example, a new diaspora of climate migrants seems likely to hit nine times the present rate of immigration by mid-century.[30] This eventuality will be chaotically mixed and massified by other causes of migration, such as the ongoing cycles of Muslim extremism and Islamophobia characteristic of Abrahamic auto-allergy. There will come to be new meanings to cohabitation on the earth—and no mommy, no daddy God comes to rescue us from our insanity or our inanity. But I do not come to announce any apocalypse. Only to prepare the way for its possibility. Apocalypse is messianism *in extremis*. But even there, in its biblical locus and for all its determinism—that which is to come is never marked as the end of the world. Only of the world as it had been known.

The dark anointment of a messianic indeterminacy may just only entangle us in each others' failed hopes. Alternatively, it hovers, it falters, at the *Falte*, fault line or fold, of an apophatic incertitude that displaces the finalities of return, revenge, or realization. In this the negation, which is the in/finite, disallows any sameness between finitudes: The oneness of a single religion, let alone of the Abrahamic rhizome, breaks boundlessly into the multiplicities that already compose it and that will recompose it in its worlds to come. In this the negation of an apophatic messianism resembles "messianic nullification in the form of the *as not*." Jeffrey Robbins, reading Agamben, thus finds messianic time to be a democratizing, Pauline time of the now and a "thoroughly human project. It is not something that happens to us . . . but, as Agamben writes, 'the time that we ourselves are . . . the only real time, the only time we have left.'"[31]

In the time we have left, what will come? What will we ourselves, we together, become? Messianic indeterminacy darkens into a nullification that renders as-not each finite expectation: In the nonknowing of a not-ending no-one, the naught of our now entangles us indirectly in everyone—without untangling us from the direct demands of some one tradition. For the same negation that allows comparison disallows homogenization of religions (this way is not that one); and at the same time demands a with-ness of equals (*com-pare*). Possibly impossible in the time we have left. Dark anointment indeed. The togetherness that is possible does not settle for itself. It catches the fragrance of a greater embrace and so does not flinch from the chaos of its mutually contesting multiples. In the comparative messiness of our political *mesianismo*, the guides of the present moment have an earthly chance.

CHAPTER 9

"The Place of Multiple Meanings": The Dragon Daughter Rereads the *Lotus Sutra*

> For countless age in the past
> Innumerable buddhas have passed into extinction,
> Hundreds of thousands of billions of kinds of buddhas,
> Their number beyond calculation.
>
> —LOTUS SUTRA

> Am I immersed in this multiple, am I, or am I not a part of it?
>
> —MICHEL SERRES, *Genesis*

Multiplying Lotus

As I write, a little figure I found at a street market in Seoul collects me. A reproduction of a thousand-year-old statue of the female bodhisattva of compassion, she sits in lotus posture upon a great fish. Mustaches and fins curling upward in rhythm with the waves, this Asian Leviathan grins with the honor of carrying such a passenger. Her subtle smile, strong and kind, her hands dancing a mudra of blessing, this Guan Yin sits facing me as I write. She floats there neither impressed nor offended by my foreignness. Her eyes remain closed, mercifully. She does not confront but grants me immense space.

I did not at first realize her connection to this very essay, provoked by the invitation to take part in an interreligious conversation in Kyoto on the *Lotus Sutra*. This two-thousand-year-old sutra, one of the major and most

---

Published in an earlier form as "The Place of Multiple Meanings: The Dragon Daughter Rides Today," *Journal of Chinese Philosophy* 32, no. 2 (June 2005).

beloved of Mahayana texts, was recognized by the Chinese Buddhist master Zhi Yi as the ultimate teaching of the Tiantai lineage, which through it spread to exercise great influence also in Korea and Japan. It announces the true dharma of compassion to all sentient beings, as distinguished from the inferior dharma of mere personal liberation. The compassion is boundless, infinite, encompassing all beings, all worlds, in their fathomless multiplicity. Not just men, not just the virtuous, not even just humans can become Buddhas, but even animals, in a munificence that circles through a fabulous manifold of bodies, of lives, of ages, of universes.

Let me confess up front that this essay, by an alien to the ancient sutra's profound traditions of practice and scholarship, remains an act of naïve dialogical spontaneity. I was surprised by the invitation, and grateful. Yet I admit that in this raw textual encounter I found myself at first getting impatient with the sutra's repetitious and multiplying invocations of multiplicities. But then this blossoming multiplicity turned out to be precisely what fascinated me. By way of extraordinary, indeed extreme, hyperboles the Sakyamuni Buddha teaches the new way of spiritual egalitarianism: the way of a radical compassion for the countless multitudes, in their incalculable and varied sufferings. This is not a condescending charity. It means your "capacity to be a buddha for someone else." It means, as Gene Reeves emphasizes, introducing his gripping translation—itself a work of compassion to nonspecialized readers—"that everyone without exception has the potential to be a buddha."[1]

Opening with "The Sutra of Innumerable Meanings," this ancient work minds its manifolds at every level, as content and as perspective. Multiplicity presents itself in the sutra as absolutely irreducible to any "One" (one Buddha, one world, one way) and so as unthinkable in traditional Western categories. Whether our One be God, the subject, the truth of speculation or of science, we habitually either divide multiplicities into "ones" or add them up to a totality of One. I do not mean to reduce "the West" from antiquity forward to one thing. Suffice it for now to note that whatever illumining and prophetic purposes the One has served, an aggressively bounded unit of unity services our ideologies of power: the unifying One over and against the multiplicity of the Other, bodies of the many, be they gods, barbarians, pagans, be they the masses of the poor, the dark, the female, the nonhuman. Or the Asian. From the vantage point of a Western autodeconstruction, the One subduing and subsuming the many permeates our fundamental spirituality, lending multiplicity the taint of fragmentation, chaos, and a readily feminized, naturalized dissipation.

Whitehead was one of the first to challenge the metaphysical priority of the one over the many. It can be no coincidence that Reeves was a noted early scholar of Whiteheadian process thought.[2] Influenced by British empiricism, with its early modern critique of the prevailing metaphysics of unitary substance, Whitehead began to theorize "multiplicities," as such, as "a category of existence." "On the one side, the one becomes many; and on the other side, the many become one."[3] If indeed "the many become one and are increased by one," the universe—or perhaps, as James had coined it, the pluriverse—neither begins nor ends as a simple unity. But Whitehead's fluent pluralism, so sympathetic to East Asian Buddhist and Daoist sensibilities, indeed so attractive among a widening circle of thinkers in Japan, in South Korea, and in China, is still beginning, after almost a century, to find resonance in the West beyond certain robust fringes of theological and interreligious thought.[4] In order to supplement the process sense of multiplicity in its multilayered and generational investments in religious pluralism, I lean in this essay on the philosopher of science Michel Serres. He works from a continental tradition that, with its insistent deconstruction of all bounded unities, can help, more than it yet has, experiments in interreligious as well as ontological multiplicity.

Such a reading offers a way, a shortcut, into the bottomless resource of liberation that is the *Lotus Sutra*. Its petals teach the practice of overcoming all patterns that obstruct or trivialize mindfulness of the ever-growing, aching, and conflicting multiplicities of our own planet. What we may call the "multiplicative matrix" of this sutra presses for transformation rather than transcendence—at least that familiar Western version, which may go vertical or horizontal in its transcending but remains dissociative in its dynamism. The multidimensionality of the *Lotus Sutra* diffracts rather than dissociates. Liberation happens not *from* but *within* an ongoing history. If in the end I ask certain questions of the sutra itself, pertaining to its views on gender, it is in solidarity with its own egalitarian intensity. Inasmuch as interreligious dialogue has come to mean more than conversation between the elites of the great patriarchal spiritual traditions, I trust that a certain resistance even to its gracious, ecumenically unifying masculinity may also be met with "compassion." If in such feminist interventions we practice "skillful means," an essay such as this then cannot claim to represent "woman." Woman is no more "one" than Man.[5] Our gender need neither unify nor divide us. It may, however, offer a fresh clue to enlightenment. One clue among many.

It is the many that offers the first clue.

Grace of the Multiple

> The multiple as such. Here's a set undefined by boundaries. Locally, it is not individuated; globally, it is not summed up. So it's neither a flock, nor a school, nor a heap, nor a swarm, nor a herd, nor a pack. It is not an aggregate; it is not discrete. It's a bit viscous perhaps. A lake under the mist, the sea, a white plain, background noise, the murmur of a crowd, time.
>
> <div align="right">MICHEL SERRES, <i>Genesis</i></div>

What rises off the pages of the *Lotus Sutra*, what billows and balloons and fills the reading gaze, is its crowd of multiplicities, its multiplicity of crowds. These multiples multiply mountainously, vertiginously. These lists start with the great audience of Buddha on Holy Eagle Peak, an audience of millions: of so many categories of worthies, starting, strategically with individual arhats representing the very ideal about to be superseded. Women are named from the start, two famous nuns and their thousands of followers. Then the eighty thousand bodhisattvas and the tens of thousands of various kings and deities—Indra alone is accompanied by "twenty thousand children of heaven"—and such marvelous collectives as the dragon kings and the centaur kings and the wheel-rolling kings and each of their tens of thousands of followers. "This is what I heard," opens the narrator.[6]

Why do these multiples matter? They materialize much of the bulk of the sutra. The *multiplicity as such* gets and holds the attention of the readers (the thousands, the hundreds of thousands, the millions of readers). But it also makes attention difficult. To the Western novice (such as this one), such lists sound like narrative hyperbole, reminiscent of more ancient, Hindu mythologies or like Mahayana missionary propaganda. At any rate, it does not offer that clean stroke of iconic minimalism Western intellectuals have coveted in Buddhism. The text is long-winded, ritually repeating every major passage: At each narrative turn we are told that we hear what a particular speaker, "wanting to restate what he had said, said in verse."[7] Yet these transpositions of prose into poetry do not read out as repetitions of the same, rather "repetition inhabits difference."[8] The iterative excess of the text, the multiplying of discourses, at once mesmerizes and enervates, it prolongs and repeats in order to move forward to each new chapter. In the process it creates a spiraling pluriverse of discourse.

Amid the oscillating styles, the multiplying audiences of the Buddha merge with the crowd of potential Buddhas: among them, the readers and hearers of the text. Thus Shariputra pleads with the Buddha to speak to the assembly: "Why? Because in this gathering there are countless hundreds of thousands of billions of living beings who have already seen buddhas. Their faculties are excellent and their wisdom is clear. If they hear the Buddha preach, they will be able to believe respectfully."[9] The crowds do not remain exterior to the multiple subjects of the text, of the Buddha-way. The multiple as such thus floods off the page, becomes viscous, invites us, takes us in: It demands attention. Can the multiple be said to constitute the doctrinal subject of the text? For its novel emphasis and good news is the dharma of Skillful Means—which is defined as precisely, yes, multiple, proliferating strategies with which to meet every sincere effort, however childish or distracted or culturally obstructed. (However Westernized, foreign, modern, postmodern . . .) As "every Buddha has been closely associated with hundreds of thousands of billions of buddhas in the past, fully practicing the way of the immeasurable *dharma*," so the Buddha has "*countless skillful means* to lead living beings."[10]

For the *Lotus Sutra*, the point of the multiple multiples would not seem to be what Serres calls the "multiple as such," the multiple for its own sake. The point is the advancement of the practice of the dharma. The sutra does seem to require a relentless and, for the West, far more recent attention to the multiple as such. As Serres makes clear, the multiple is not an aggregate of discrete entities, which do not exactly exist anyway: "We've never hit upon truly atomic, ultimate, indivisible terms that were not themselves, once again, composite."[11] Mere diversity—mere aggregates of discrete individuals, or indivisibles—would not conform to what Reeves calls the sutra's "strategy of integration." He characterizes the *Lotus* dharma as a middle way "between utter diversity and sheer unity. The infinite variety of ways of teaching have the one purpose of leading all living beings to pursue the goal of becoming a buddha, a goal that everyone without exception can reach, though the time may be very long and the way far from smooth or easy."[12]

Differently as to the formulation of one purpose, but not unrelated in sensibility, the emergent Western philosophy of the multiple as such resists not only mere unity but the mere many. Yet it does come close (very close, in Serres, as in all poststructuralists) to the latter. For diversity all too readily reduces to atomic units of difference. Indeed, Whitehead's definition of a multiplicity, as a "pure disjunction of diverse entities,"[13] might also tend toward the atomization of momentary actual entities. But this disjunction obtains in the mode of contemporaneousness before each causal connection, between moments of mutual immanence, philosophically protecting difference from any omnivorous unity.

Might such a meditation on the "multiple as such" at least belong among the "skillful means" of *Lotus Sutra* interpretation? Perhaps only then if we bear in mind that this sutra does not belong to the rich genre of the metaphysical or cosmological treatises of Buddhism. The international Tientai movement for which it is the primary text was not soliciting from it an abstract category of multiplicity but the particular and potential communities and practices of enlightening compassion.

The text can be read as one long argument against the competing Buddhist tradition of an atomizing, or "arrogant" arhatism, with its single-minded stress upon the path of the one individual to the one end of nirvana. In this it encodes an ancient argument against the elite, exclusionary claims of the Theravadan approach to the arhat (or *shravaka*) as the perfected or enlightened one. "Monks and nuns full of arrogance, proud laymen and laywomen of little faith . . . these people of little wisdom have already left."[14] (I resist the temptation to draw any comparisons to the Protestant Reformation.) But Reeves resists this reading of the sutra as a polemic written "to give its readers ammunition against other Buddhists."[15] The *Lotus Sutra*, consistently with its compassionate outreach, *includes* the arhats' accomplishment in a provisional nirvana. It does not ultimately exclude the arhats who are depicted as those traditionalists who march out of the assembly in pre-emptive refusal, not wishing to hear the new dharma of skillful means. The Tiantai vision of a future paradise always includes *shravakas* as well as bodhisattvas. The sutra is ecstatically compassionate in its pluralization. All the pomp and ceremony of the iterative enumerations of the hundreds of thousands of already realized and of becoming buddhas, bodhisattvas, the monks and nuns, etc., does not add up to any top-down hierarchy of being or religious privilege—even of an antihierarchical hierarchy.

The multiplicative matrix of the *Lotus* materializes the graciousness of the Buddha-way. It evinces the radical generosity of a "tender care that nothing be lost" (as Whitehead put it in theological form).[16] Indeed, as has long been noted, the Buddhist emphasis on skillful means bears a resemblance to the Christian language of grace (in the distinction, formative of Protestantism, from the arrogance of self-saving works). But in Christianity the background soteriology of a singular and omnipotent deity gives grace a heavy hand. We have tried to say, from Augustine on, that without this loving support, with its many "means of grace," we cannot even choose grace itself. The grace must first be *given* to me, as a gift that shapes me before "I" receive it, for "me" even to aspire to liberation from the incurred ego. But the unilateralism of the gift turned all too readily into "God does

"The Place of Multiple Meanings"

it *for* me." Grace then becomes indistinguishable from power, and the aggressive hierarchies of Christendom, modeled on that sovereign omnipotence, justify themselves as the means of "His" grace. This grace of a God who does it *to* or *for* me then bears little resemblance to the graciousness of the *Lotus* way, in which the agency of each becoming-subject is never in doubt. The skillful means[17] are skillful precisely in the endless patience and subtlety with which the bodhisattva coaxes a being into its agency of liberation.

Consider, for instance, the sutra's parable of a rich man who disguises himself as a worker for several years, just in order to re-establish connection with his destitute and alienated son. The parable does bear startling comparison to the gospel parable of the prodigal son. But the sutra's version is not just more elaborate but more subtle. For the father does not merely welcome but painstakingly, craftily, enters the son's own world just in order to lure him into relationship. (Whitehead systematizes the trope of the divine lure as the "initial aim," the relevant possibility for a moment of creaturely actualization.) In this the *Lotus Sutra* displays an extraordinarily high level of consciousness of the viscosity or interdependence (*chou* in Chinese) of our linked lives. Might this relationality be a key to the significance of the multiplying multiples?

The dissemination of the saving potentials or "Buddha-seeds" serve not merely as the blessing of innumerable increase but as the means of interrelation within the multiplicities, for the sake of a dharma of interdependence. And yet the *Lotus Sutra*, like most Mahayana teachings, does not relinquish all rhetoric of oneness:

> Though buddhas in ages to come,
> May teach millions and millions
> Of countless gateways to the dharma,
> This will actually be for the sake of the One-vehicle. (95)

Can we read the "oneness" sought in Tiantai as code precisely *not* for a simplifying, homogenizing unity, an annihilation of difference that assures the eventual collapse of the multiple, but instead for a dynamic relationality? Such a reading seems to be less a postmodern projection than a demand of the text itself, which continues:

> The buddhas the most honored ones,
> Know that nothing exists independently,
> And that Buddha-seeds grow interdependently.
> This is why they teach the One-vehicle. (95)

The Multiplicative Matrix

In the *Lotus Sutra* I count four main categories of multiplicity (aware that in fact one cannot successfully break the text into countable categories, as all the collectives overlap and expand constantly): buddhas, eons, skillful means, suffering multitudes. (1) There are the innumerable buddhas and becoming or future buddhas, the whole pantheon of realized personages. (2) There are the times, the "innumerable hundreds of millions of eons." These multiples holographically diffract the content of the new dharma, as (3) the multiplication of skillful means—whereby all these Buddha-natures or instances of the Buddha-nature are affected and themselves are affecting others. (4) The crowd of those others—the "countless multitudes for whom I teach"—constitutes the purpose and the recipients of the teaching: The Way is not a way of self-salvation but always (also) the salvation of the other, of any and all others.[18] So the insistence on the multiple media of these means is powerful and reflected, of course, in the multiple styles of the sutra itself. The stunningly conscious intentionality of this multistylistic strategy must be cited:

> With a variety of explanations,
> Parables and other kinds of expression,
> Through the power of skillful means
> He causes all to rejoice.
> He teaches sutras, poetry,
> Stories of disciples' previous lives,
> Stories of buddhas' previous lives
> And of unprecedented things,
> As well as causal explanations,
> Parables and similes,
> Verses which repeat them,
> And passages of dialogue. (86)

All of these genres are enacted in the sutra itself. So a multiplication of styles is necessary for the multiplication of buddhas and for the amplification of the joy of the process itself.

Climactically, the Buddha of the *Lotus* declares the Dharma of Innumerable Meanings. This suggestive phrase (which has another, kindred sutra dedicated to it) really does sound suspiciously postmodern! Without ever swaying toward meaninglessness, the sutra resists any homogenizing or exclusivist meaning. On such deconstruction the *Lotus* seems to insist. Others have explored the possible affinities of Buddhism with the continental philosophy of difference—as the disruption of any substantial or self-present subject by otherness.[19] This resemblance might focus especially in the discourse of absence, gap, fissure—in its resemblance to the emptiness of all selves or dharmas.

The *Lotus*, however, offers a practice—between awareness and activity—that both precedes and exceeds any Western models of which I am aware: "As soon as he had taught this Sutra, he sat cross-legged in the midst of the great assembly and entered the kind of concentration called *the place of innumerable meanings*, in which his body and mind were motionless."[20] This is an intriguing concept: that of a form of concentration or attention that is itself understood to be a *place*—something like the current English colloquial use of "place" to mean "state" (as in "she seems to be in a good place these days"). What would it mean for us pluralists of the postmodern to pause and contemplate the multiplicity—in its ever-shifting, turbulent, kaleidoscoping diversities—in utter stillness? Does this freeze its dynamism, as we must surely suspect? Or, to the contrary, does it embrace and permit it? Does its immobility host a simultaneity of speeds too fast and too slow to measure each other? In this perhaps it bears a resemblance to the space or *khora* of all contemplative practice.

The extraordinary disclosure of this place of innumerable meanings is marked as more than a psychic space by a cosmological event—again framed in a plurality of plurals: "At this moment mandarava, great mandarava, manjushaka and great manjushaka flowers rained down from the sky over the Buddha and the whole great assembly, while the whole Buddha-world trembled in six different ways."[21] In the stillness amid the immense flux, there is no stasis but rather a wondrously sensuous rain of flowers and a trembling, *tremens*, itself a rhythmic repetition. Might this tremble be related to the "repetition" that in Whitehead breaks up substantialist self-sameness while composing an alternative continuity? In this flower-drenched, fragrant sutra, the *tremendum* is felt not as a threat to foundations but as joyous peacefulness.

Perhaps we may sense that this place of innumerable meanings offers new meaning in the chronotope of trembling that is the present eon. If the postmodern place of multiple meanings has long since expanded to include the many religions, religious multiplicity itself points beyond religion, in a nexus crisscrossed by the secular pluralism without which any religious claim in the West drifts toward totality. The multiplicative matrix of the *Lotus* promotes the grace of a cohesiveness that happens only in and through the disjunctions of diversity.

Eco-Cosmic Multiplicity

Might we now open this "place" into an even wider, indeed the widest, sense of place? Throughout the sutra there are references to vast scales of space and time. These were characteristic of ancient Indian thought. Such scales were not at all indigenous to biblical or later Christian cosmologies, tiny by comparison (until the fifteenth century).[22] The place of the universe, and then perhaps the multiverse, has only gradually been pried open by astronomy. The *Lotus Sutra* develops neither cosmology nor cosmogony as such. Nonetheless, the oscillation between its multiple multiples often illumines gargantuan sweeps of time and space. The narrator takes such vision as a gift, the beam of awakened perception that allows the disciple to perceive through the Buddha-nature all of these "worlds beyond worlds." Both space and time expand in a virtual infinity closer to contemporary calculations of the age and size of the universe than to prior Western assumptions. Thus of the "hundreds of billions of myriads of buddhas, as numerous as the sands of the Ganges," it is said that

> The blessings of such people
> Are so beyond calculation
> That tens of millions of billions of eons
> Would not be enough to describe them. (211)

One may, of course, insist that this is not cosmology but hyperbole. Yet it is the awesome expansiveness of space-time relationality that seems to be internalized, "concentrated," precisely as the "place of innumerable meaning."

At the opening of this new millennium we are living in a golden age of astronomy, in which if we pay any attention we hear descriptions that sound just as hyperbolic in their extremities: We hear of fourteen billion years, of a hundred billion stars within each of a hundred billion galaxies. And that is just one universe. Speculation is scientifically now kosher that theorizes parallel or multiple or infinite universes.[23] All such calculations unfurl at the edge of the incalculable. The scientific postulations, however, often still manage to purge the sense of wonder, let alone of meaning. But is it not high time that we begin to outgrow *spiritually*—not just scientifically—our perilously parochial little world? Without resorting to a version of Monty Python's satiric prayer: "O lord you are so very very big," can the heirs of Abraham contemplating every now and then the unfathomable scales of space-time?

"The Place of Multiple Meanings" 157

The multiples of the *Lotus Sutra* never convey mere size or quantity but always also a complex variation, unfolding innumerable meanings in space-time. Reading the sutra through the diffracting lens of Serres's *Genesis*, with its attempt to think "the multiple as such," I begin to see it everywhere. In the urban crowds in the city, in the unique faces of the crowd, in the clouds overhead and the clouds in my head. Not a set of countable *ones*, or a single *One* divisible into *ones*, but the multiple of multiples.

> The cosmos is not a structure, it is a pure multiplicity of ordered multiplicities and pure multiplicities. It is the global basis of all structures, it is the background noise of all form and information, it is the milky noise of the whole of our messages gathered together. We must give it a new name, definitely: it is a mixture, tiger-striped, motley, mottled, zebra-streaked, variegated, and I don't know what all, it is a mix or a crasis, it is a mixed aggregate, it is an intermittence.[24]

Actually, Serres is thinking here with chaos theory. He continues: "The most global concept, by good fortune and freedom, is not a unitary one. Order is never more than an island or an archipelago. In the midst of the multiple, one finds universe-isles."[25]

I pause and feel: this city around me as an island, bursting in its ecological fragility with its innumerables of population, history, oozing and flying across the seas in global interdependence with other universe-isles. This interlinked chaosmos of interconnection, the pure multiple, is not inherently good or beautiful. Neither is it evil or ugly. But it *matters*. Renarration lines up the linkages into its hierarchy of dominance, from the One down through the motley manys. Yet in an originative alternative, the multiplicity of the creation emerges in a collaboration of "letting be," not ordered from above but emerging from the space—the deep—of multiplicity. There the spirit—*ruach*, breath—that "vibrates over the face of the waters" in Genesis 1:2 suggests the path that Western theology might have taken and might yet take. Intermittence of our reality has the character of trembling, of self-organizing in a rhythm of iteration and multiplication, self-birthing and dying to self, expanding beyond calculation. Of course, we within this process can, like modern Western Man, continue to shake a fist in defiance of our own smallness in the face of an impersonal, too-big Totality. Or we might practice emptying our selves, rhythmically and intermittently, breath by breath, into the immensity that is never an empty void but that dis/closes itself as "the place of innumerable meanings."

Such a practice does not confine itself to private meditation. It circulates in a vast ecology potentially more important now than ever. In the *Lotus Sutra* a wonderfully nonhuman parable captures this multiplicity that *matters*, that takes material form, that is to be respected, nurtured in its specificity. I quote it at length, in delight at the bodily aliveness and the mysterious cloud of this complex topography:

> Kashyapa, suppose that in the three-thousand-great-thousandfold world, growing on mountains, along rivers and streams, in valleys and in different soils, there are plants, trees, thickets, forests and medicinal herbs of various and numerous kinds, with different names and colors. A dense cloud spreads over all of them, covering the whole three-thousand-great-thousandfold world, and pours rain down on all equally and at the same time. The moisture reaches all the plants, trees, thickets, forests, and medicinal herbs, with their little roots, little stems, little branches, little leaves, their medium-sized roots, medium-sized stems, medium-sized branches, medium-sized leaves [etc.]. Every tree, large or small . . . receives its share. The rain from the same cloud goes to each according to its nature and kind, causing it to grow, bloom and bear fruit. Though all grow in the same soil and are moistened by the same rain, these plants and trees are all different.
>
> You should understand, Kashyapa, that the Tathagata is like this. He *appears in this world like the rising of a great cloud*, and extends his great voice universally over the world of human and heavenly beings and titans, just like the great cloud covers the three thousand-great-thousandfold world. (160–61)

This great moist cloud spreads over the world like the *ruach* over the primal waters of Genesis, misty, proliferative, breathy. The Buddha's attention to the particularity of every creature in its circumstance and capacity is at once intimate and impersonal. It waters them all, as perhaps in the gospels God shines like the sun and falls like the rain on good and evil alike. The parable (which continues this thick description of a forest environment at much greater length) manifests the multiplicative medium of the sutra in the form of highly specific biodiversity. The place of multiple meanings incarnates as the place of multiple species. The multiplicative matrix manifests in the terrestrial form of our actual living space. Might the cloud metaphor materialize now, ecologically, and so point to the needed global practices: indeed, the way of "Bodhisattva Earth Holder," hearing "Bodhisattva Regarder of the Cries of the Worlds."[26]

Nobody's Transformation

We can only read such a sutra from a great distance of historical time and, in my case, of geocultural space as well—even if such distance appears minuscule relative to the sutra's sense of scale. My difference does not collapse into, cannot become one with, and so appropriate, this text. Nor does this difference leave me merely outside of the text—for its margins are moist, fecund, cloudlike, shot through with transcontextual radiance. Despite or because of my Euro-American and Abrahamic roots I grow in the soil of the same earth, watered by that same cloud cover. The multiplicity of our cultural difference, like the ecological, can become a matter of mere otherness or can fold, intermittently, rhythmically, the multiplicities into mindful interdependence. But then this is a transformation—not a transcendence—of difference. As Serres says, "the work of transformation is that of the multiple."[27]

Of course, the unitary ego, particularly in its Western and masculine format, obstructs that transformation as surely as it thwarts its own prophetic patrilineage of eco-social justice. It neither perceives nor desires the place of innumerable meanings. Serres offers a radical answer to that Cartesianized substance, one that would make a *Lotus Sutra* Buddha smile: "I think, therefore I am Nobody. The I is nobody in particular, it is not a singularity, it has no contours, it is the blankness of all colors and all nuances, an open and translucent welcome of a multiplicity of thoughts, it is therefore the possible. I am, indeterminately, nobody."[28]

An old feminist voice in me, however, mutters back that the inflection of multiplicity as nobodiness works best for empowered egos West or East, needing emancipation from themselves, not for those who never got a confident sense of "I am." This question of no-self is also an issue that I raised long before in a context of Christian-Buddhist dialogue.[29] I had argued ('80s style) that the construction of the self *or* the no-self in terms of a rigid gender hierarchy and the maintenance of the symbols of "the tradition" that continually reinscribe the supremacy of the male—as God the Father or Son, as Buddha or arhat—and the subjection of the female to male egos serves as the lowest common denominator of the major world religions. Yet such a critique does not, must not, dispute the transformative value of self-emptying, of no-thingness, *sunyata* or kenosis—inasmuch as they are teachings inscribed upon the multiplicative matrix, the cloud, of interdependence. Then the nihilism of an abstract void does not threaten to swallow up the richness of the innumerable diversities. Then, as Serres imagines from the vantage point of science, multiplicity does the work of transformation. Then those groups and those persons who suffer from involuntary no-bodiness may benefit from the liberating wisdom of the many means and the innumerable meanings. Now, therefore, I would not dream of making any argument against the Buddhist doctrine of nothingness, no-thingness. It is another way of disassembling the ego-thingness of Cartesian substance and its making of others into mere things. The question is rather one precisely of finding "skillful means" for different people, different groups, in different contexts of suffering. Otherwise the multiple collapses, and with it the compassion that sustains social change.

As it turns out, however, the *Lotus Sutra* does not emphasize the teaching of *sunyata*, of *no-self*, anyway but rather "wisdom" and "enlightenment." The Buddha in "his great mercy and compassion" seeks always "the good and whatever will enrich all beings." Is it the teaching of compassion that softens or perhaps rather moistens and clouds the more stringent teaching of no-self—thus displaying at the deepest level the practice of skillful means? Indeed, this sutra does not directly articulate fresh insights into the four noble truths, the dialectics of *sunyata* or the elements of *pratitya samutpada*. It embraces a densely populated, mythological imaginary, reminiscent of ancient Indian and also Tibetan pantheons, philosophy, and aeonic immensities. Yet all these Buddhas and becoming-Buddhas (etc.) appear in the multiples only to repeat, repeat, to cosmically chorus: *All* can become Buddhas. And women, like the nuns Mahaprajapati and Yashodhara, are prominent among Buddha-candidates.

Is the sutra in this sense a metatext—not just a commentary rich in intertextuality with prior texts but an offering of a new way of practicing and thus of reading the Buddha-way itself? It seems indeed to offer a kind of premodern pluralism—not in relation to other ways than the Buddha way but more urgently in relation to multiple forms of Buddhism.

It is striking that early Christianity was forming at the same time, in its own rush of multiple forms. Its solutions would by the fourth century trend in the opposite direction from the *Lotus Sutra*, toward a singularizing, centering, and top-down orthodoxy. Here and there—in Augustine's earlier hermeneutics of "multiple true interpretations," in Trinitarian paradoxes of one and many, in the Pseudo-Dionysius's "multiplication of names"—would appear hints of a pluralizing first principle. But for the most part, the multiple, the innumerable, became identified with the fallen, dissipative multiplicity of the world over and against the one God, one Son, one true religion.

Sex, Power, and Dragons

If, however, I overdraw this contrast, I risk a misleading idealization of the Other, rendered a weapon in one's own oedipal struggles. So it is good to note that a unifying power-drive and its specifically patriarchal propulsion is evident in the *Lotus Sutra*'s teaching as well. Its pluralism is contained within the proclamation of one all-encompassing way. Indeed, not unlike the Book of Revelation, it occasionally stoops to curses against those who malign its teachers or teachings:

> If they become camels or are born as asses,
> They will always carry burdens on their backs,
> Be beaten with sticks, think only of water and grass,
> And know nothing else.
> For slandering this Sutra.
> They will have to suffer. (133)

And it offers rewarding enticements for those who teach its way:

> Wherever such a teacher lives or stays,
> Walks, sits, or lies down,
> Or teaches even a stanza,
> There a stupa should be erected.
> It should be wonderfully
> And beautifully adorned.
> And offerings of many kinds
> Should be made to it. (313)

I do not wish here to risk reincarnation as an abused ass. Nonetheless, in the mode of interreligious honesty let me also note that among the innumerables I did *not* hear any liberation for women as such but only *in spite of* our being women. Spite indeed: The misogynist view of women and their bodies at moments resembles that of Christianity, which, though it early on held many ascetic women at high levels of esteem, widely held all women qua women to be inferior and disturbing to the celibate male subject. The true subject of most Christian and Buddhist discourse.

This tension is evident, and not subliminal, in the final chapter of the sutra. Here it is intriguing that the possibility of an instantaneous leap to enlightenment is marked by the Dragon Princess, an eight-year-old girl. It is a leap depicted in almost unfathomable contrast to the eons of the Buddha's own contemplation. She seems to arise as the mythic image of the

Lotus Sutra way's radicality. But she must o'erleap a great abyss of masculine prejudice. By a familiar strategy, that prejudice is at once transcended and reinscribed within the same text:

> Then Shariputra said to the dragon girl: "You think that in no time at all you attained the supreme way. This is hard to believe. Why? Because the *body of a woman is filthy and impure, not a vessel for the dharma.* How could you attain unsurpassable awakening? The Buddha way is long and extensive. Only after innumerable eons of enduring hardship, accumulating good works, and thoroughly practicing all the practices can it be reached. Moreover, a woman's body has five hindrances: first, she cannot become a king of the Brahma heaven; second, she cannot become king Indra; third, she cannot become a Mara-king; fourth, she cannot become a holy wheel-rolling king; and fifth, she cannot have the body of a buddha. How then could a woman's body so quickly become a buddha? (252)

A discouragingly rhetorical question. And yet it is dramatically answered: "The dragon girl instantly transformed into a male, took up bodhisattva practice, and immediately went to a world called Spotless, in the southern region, where, sitting on a precious lotus blossom, she attained impartial, proper awakening." And she then, in her trans-carnation as he, proceeds to preach the *Lotus Sutra* to all beings in the ten directions.[30]

This is precisely the solution of the gnostic Gospel of Thomas (otherwise such a mystically attractive, perhaps Buddhist-influenced gospel) to the same problem: "if the female becomes as a male." These new movements attract some gifted, strong women, also some great female donors. In response, the leadership does not seek liberation from the shackles of their own delusional male supremacism—apparently such an insidious work of *maya* that these great texts remain trapped within its presuppositions. But it does graciously extend women the privilege of masculinization. Really, the gesture is meant generously, indeed compassionately; it is part of the expansive, universalizing spirit of the reform. And it runs parallel to Christianity's extending to all others, ethnic, cultural, religious, the opportunity to be saved by conversion; an inclusiveness that turns oppressive only when the movement becomes the religion. I do not mean to belabor the *Lotus Sutra*'s imperfect liberation at the threshold of gender. As Reeves comments, this story "is obviously intended to persuade monks, who would have been its only early auditors and readers, that women as well as men have the potential of being buddhas, common prejudice and informed opinion to the contrary." One might hear a response to an entrenched twentieth-century identity politics when he adds: "The story is not designed merely to criticize male assumptions, though it does do that; it also affirms the positive potential to be a buddha in the very men it also criticizes."[31] There are many Buddhist scholars working to make the feminist critique truly internal to Buddhism and thus far more skillful in its *upaya*.[32] And who—without committing an ahistorical delusion of our own—can dismiss the originative radicality of Paul's "in Christ there is neither male nor female," despite the frequent sexism of his epistles? Or by the same token: "The dharma is neither male nor female."[33]

My gaze returns to my Guan Yin sitting in fishy lotus-grace upon the waves. It is not, then, insignificant that Guan Yin is none other than the Chinese name for the Sanskrit Avalokitesvara, the bodhisattva of compassion. Only in China, under Daoist influence, did this "he" become a "she"—an intriguing inversion of the sex change of the Dragon Girl. In the *Lotus Sutra* Guan Yin/Avalokitesvara (Kannon in Japanese) appears in thirty-three manifestations, seven of which are female. And in Japan, this popular figure has increasingly taken female form in recent centuries. Of course, in this millennium the multiplicative matrix of our species' gender and sex opens all around us. The transgender mobilities of Guan Yin and the *Lotus* will open into a new multiplicity of meanings. They shift shape like the Dragon Daughter—an early queen of enlightened drag![34]

On our watery planet, new forms of dharmic fluidity are needed. "Because the Buddha and his Dharma are alive in such bodhisattvas," Gene Reeves writes, "the Buddha continues to live. The fantastically long life of the Buddha, in other words, is at least partly a function of and dependent on his being embodied in others."[35]

The intercarnation of the Buddha? The *Lotus Sutra* teaches an interdependence so intimate and immense—so implicitly and easily interreligious—that it can only blossom in and as each one of us. In its moist cloud of endless, endlessly valued, diversity, might we now at last and not too late learn how to make space for each other—for our impossibly many qualities and quantities of bodies? How shall we find the skillful means to do it but by way of the contemplation and the materialization of that place of multiple meanings?

CHAPTER 10

The Cosmopolitan Body of Christ. Postcoloniality and Process Cosmology: A View from Bogotá

> Like God's salvation plan with its math of punishment and expiation, globalization offers wealth to some but a calculus of destitution, starvation and exclusion to far too many.
>
> —EDUARDO MENDIETA, *Global Fragments*

> The Church gave unto God the attributes which belonged exclusively to Caesar.
>
> —ALFRED NORTH WHITEHEAD, *Process and Reality*

In gratitude for hospitality that welcomes multiple discourses and dimensions, that embraces a cosmos of vulnerabilities, nationalities, and even cosmologies, I wish to share thoughts today on the notion of the cosmopolitan. As we are gathered to consider the value of process theology for a Latin American context, I will propose a cosmopolitanism—a "world citizenship"—in process within this very conversation.

"Ethics is hospitality," as Derrida summarizes the long cosmopolitan countertradition.[1] The trope of the world citizen was launched by Diogenes the Cynic and carried by Stoicism. Then Paul enfolds the cosmopolitan ideal, thereby globalizing the biblical imperative of hospitality for the stranger: "You are no longer strangers and migrants but *sympolitai*," cocitizens (Eph. 2:19). Kant had revived this ancient tradition with his last dictum, "The law of cosmopolitanism must be restricted to the condi-

---

This lecture was delivered at a conference on Latin America and Process Theology hosted by the philosophy faculty of the Pontificia Universidad Javeriana de Bogotá and sponsored by the Center for Process Studies at the Claremont School of Theology in April 2008.

tions of universal hospitality."[2] As every new crisis of immigration in the North reveals, this imperative drifts far from the laws of nations and from the rules of the global economy. Still, in the wake of a tragically unheeded imperative and its history of Christian betrayals, the ethic of cosmopolis refuses to disappear. Instead it finds new voices.

Eduardo Mendieta sets forth in *Global Fragments* a proposal for a "dialogical cosmopolitanism." His diasporic discourse will help to develop this Bogotá conversation. "Dialogical cosmopolitanism situates us in our global fragments, but also turns our moral look to our global responsibilities and duties toward others."[3] Mendieta here engages "the critical and dialogical cosmopolitanism" of Walter Mignolo, which he pulls into a formal conversation with Judith Butler, Enrique Dussel, Jürgen Habermas, and Cornel West. These theorists represent, along with many others, the recently renewed interest in the ancient idea of the cosmopolitan.[4] The discourse arises in confrontation with the new face of what we can call imperial cosmopolitanism, in its dual forms of economic neoliberal globalization and the manifest militarism of the *pax Americana*. The cosmopolitan comes under consideration for its capacity to make ethical claims strong enough, global enough, indeed universal enough, to counter in the third millennium what Richard Falk has long called "globalization from above." And it had entered Whiteheadian thought through the process theologian David Ray Griffin's intensive engagement of Michael Walzer's "communitarian cosmopolitanism."[5]

All of these thinkers recognize that the globalization from above has wrapped itself in the mantle of the *mission civilatrice*. It offers hospitality but holds the world hostage to a homogenizing universal. The postmodern temptation to a reactive *anti*-universalism is therefore hard to resist. Yet these thinkers do resist it. They argue for a universality articulated through the challenges to universalism itself. For they recognize the universalizing logic also at work in the refusal of the universal. So Judith Butler takes up Karl-Otto Apel's "performative contradiction" between the prior claim to universality and those who have been excluded by such a claim: the subaltern, the marginalized, the stranger. The new cosmopolitanism would provide "a basis for *resisting* the homogenization now being ruthlessly carried out by the corporation-led 'globalization.'"[6]

It is important to notice how the imperial cosmopolitanism colludes with the profound *anti*-cosmopolitanism of fundamentalism. In the United States the absolute faith in unrestrained capitalism only finds electoral success in conjunction with Christian fundamentalism and a variety of boundary-fixated patriotisms that can be marketed as "grassroots." Thus

Kwame Anthony Appiah: "If cosmopolitanism is, in a slogan, universality plus difference, there is the possibility of another kind of enemy, one who rejects universality altogether. 'Not everybody matters' would be their slogan."[7] Both religious fundamentalism and economic globalization—while operating from the basis of their own sovereign and exclusionary universals—depend on this unstated anti-universalism. In the indifference that uses its universals to repress difference and its difference to monopolize the universal, only those of the right religion or of the right class can actually matter. So then in response the emergent cosmopolitanism materializes in the interstices of fractured worlds. It fosters the very diversity that the Eurocentric universal has metaphysically colonized. Mignolo nicknames this new universality "diversality."[8]

I want to lift up what should be more obvious than it is, even among the marvelous array of thinkers I have so far named: This inviting universality does not escape its actual material universe. Indeed, universality can mean nothing apart from a reflection on what the "universe" means. Here is where process thought might be helpful: It offers a cosmology capable of hosting in theory the hospitable cosmopolitanism that we need in practice. The relation of the *polis* to the rest of the cosmos may be obvious here, up in Bogotá, 2600 *metros más cerca de las estrella*.[9] Yet in most cities those stars are hardly visible. Stellar deprivation and light pollution are, of course, not high on anyone's list of global crises! But what Mendieta calls "megaurbaniztion" is. It dominates a planet that in the past century crossed the threshold after which more humans live in the city—the *polis*—than in the country. We suffer from a "detranscendentalized alterity," writes Mendieta (with echoes of Dussel's reading of Levinas).[10] We become mere strangers to each other. We matter ever less. But is that detranscendentalization reducible to other humans? When the nonhuman alterity is eclipsed—the nonhuman that surrounds us and that composes us in our complex animality and our stardust, our matter, our *mattering*—what sort of humanity remains? A posthumanity describable less by its animate embodiment than by its info-techno-global economics?

A rigorously dialogical cosmopolitanism must therefore become ever more attentive to the ecological depredations of economic globalization. Let me suggest that it requires, indeed already implies, a decolonization of cosmos. For without a cosmological supplement, our answers to the predatory globalization will tend to slide back into the Eurocentrism that presumes (with Kant and the modernity of Enlightenment) a foundationally anthropocentric ethic.

A decolonial cosmology will, in what follows, counter the dissociation of the human from its universe at seven points: (1) as globalizing modernity; (2) as ethical disembodiment; (3) as repulsion of indigenous "cosmovision"; (4) as androcentrism; (5) as ecological anthropocide; (6) as the theodicy of a Christian power drive; and (7) as anthropocentric displacement of responsibility, Christologically reinforced.

(1) *Modernization is radicalized anthropocentrism.* Mignolo distinguishes three global-imperial projects according to their cosmopolitan imaginaries. The global thrust of the Spanish and Portuguese empires from the sixteenth through the seventeenth centuries was infused with the indubitable cosmopolitanism of Christian mission, understood as evangelization and conversion of the heathens. In the eighteenth and nineteenth centuries the British and French imperial aggressions expressed their cosmopolitanism as the mission to civilize—to initiate into the global *polis*—the "barbarians." And in the twentieth century, the United States developed the global and neocolonial form of its imperial designs. Universalism then conveys the modernization of the premodern, the traditional, the backward. If a decolonized and decolonizing cosmopolitanism is possible, it is only possible to the extent it makes audible the voices of the local histories that have been silenced by the imperial globalization. That suppression continues all the more vociferously under the conditions of a twenty-first century that in its incipience "heeds the call of 'you're either with us or against us,' to use the language of George W. Bush's Manichean theodicy."[11]

All of these forms of cosmopolitan imperialism carry the traces of the ancient imperialization of the Christian universal. That is, they are all infused with the strangely successful conversion of the church to the globality of world empire. This entailed the inversion of the Pauline counter-imperial imaginary of global "co-citizens" into the cosmos of Rome. The metaphysics enabling the translation of the biblical metaphors into a cosmopolitan language could go and did go both ways—toward empire or the radically hospitable alternative. But either way it carried with it a classical cosmology. The universe did thus contextualize human social existence. But that cosmos and its Logos was increasingly ordered to "Man" as its measure; "his" matter was subordinated to a universal reason presumed separable from its own body.

Reason, identified as the *imago dei*—which thus forfeits the intensively cosmological constellation of Genesis 1—hosted a sharply anthropocentric turn in Christianity that would have been inconceivable within the Hebrew and early Christian sense of the creaturely. Early modernity and the lurch into a Cartesian and Newtonian science clinched the deal. If, then, Western anthropocentrism grows from a deep Christian root, it continues in the United States to call upon a politico-theological force for its supposed projects of modernization. Modernization thus requires a double alienation: the ongoing dissociation of the colonizer both from "nature" (while clinging oxymoronically to our own oddly reified "human nature") and from those judged "closer to nature," whether with romantic or degrading associations.

(2) *However "materialist," a liberative ethics that repeats the modern anthropocentrism cannot come to terms with the materiality it embraces.* I am suggesting not that we eschew the reasoning universalism of the West but that we build a cosmological consciousness into its self-correcting process.

The aim of all liberation thinking is the well-being of the persons, peoples, who have been cast to the margins of the human cosmos. And it insists, as did Marx universally, on the materiality of that well-being, as the condition of the dignity and diversification of life. "Man lives from nature, i.e. *nature is his body*, and he must remain in a continuous process with it if he is not to die."[12] The germ of a radical incarnationalism! How Marx, constrained by a Newtonian physics and an instrumentalized earth, could not adequately address the complexity of that life and the dynamism of its ecology I will not attempt to discuss. Socialism in its more "scientific" form may have come hobbled with a modern notion of matter as "simply located," a species, according to Whitehead, of "the fallacy of misplaced concreteness."

Nature is my body, my process. The heirs of the social-justice tradition will surely want to evolve rather than jettison this bodiliness so promisingly extended by an unbounded and inhuman "nature." What happens to liberation discourse as it begins to internalize a new reason, a new physics? Whitehead would explain "the steady endurance of matter" as an abstraction from the "startling discontinuity" of the quanta. We have still barely learned to think, to sense, the discontinuity, the difference, whereby "each primordial element will be an organized system of vibratory streaming of energy."[13] It is a difference not of independent atoms but of radical interdependence. If "every location involves an aspect of itself in every other location,"[14] might this cosmos not be worked for greater solidarity in the cosmopolitan struggle against a profit-driven individualism and its smoothly homogenized globe?

Certainly it has been only with great difficulty that emancipatory reasoning has begun to thematize our creaturely condition as such, as enmeshed in the life processes that compose the planet as a live system of systems. But it has done so, and in a primary way it has done so through the theological gifts of Latin American Catholicism. From Brazil, Leonardo Boff and Ivone Gebara mark breakthroughs of liberation theology into ecological thinking; in Nicaragua, Ernesto Cardenal relates science and ecology to social justice through the immense poetry of his *Cántico Cósmico*.[15] They practice a visionary eco-cosmology that does not attenuate or distract from but rather amplifies their passion for the poor.

The antifoundationalist critical theories, including postcolonial theory, in the United States, lag behind—and so, therefore, does our cosmopolitan discourse. For instance, Judith Butler's feminist/queer "denaturalization," indispensable and radical as it is, remains Kantian in its dissociation from the nonhuman.[16] We correctly deconstruct "nature" as constructed in and of culture; but we miss the corollary truth: "culture" is constructed in and of nature.[17]

(3) *An anthropocentric modernism represses indigenous material sensibilities.* Its colonialism transmits everywhere an allergy to the traces and traditions of what the Mexican thinker Sylvia Marcos calls "cosmovision." Of Mesoamerican civilization she narrates the "fragments that here and there escaped the inquisitional filter." She finds that "even vestiges of it can begin to reveal incarnate universes that escape the master narrative of the disdainful superiority of spirit over flesh."[18] Incarnate universes: impossible for the Christo-colonial paradigm, early or late. That disdain is emitted by a Christian and modern ideal of the human, an anthropocentrism that is always already Eurocentrism, cleansing the spirit of its fleshly, dusty local *kosmoi*.

Gayatri Chakravorty Spivak's *A Critique of Postcolonial Reason* approaches this insight, offering one of the rare moments in which Latin American liberation theology appears on the secular Asian American screen of postcolonial theory: "Having seen the powerful and risky role played by Christian liberation theology, some of us have dreamed of animist liberation theologies to girdle the perhaps impossible vision of an ecologically just world." She has in mind the tribal people with whom she works in India. Her realization of the importance of their cosmological sensibility marks a turning point within or beyond postcolonial theory. "For nature, the sacred other of the human community, is in this thinking also bound by the structure of ethical responsibility." However, her appeal to liberation theology carries this caveat: "No individual transcendence theology, of being just in this world in view of the next, however the next is underplayed, can bring us to this."[19] Thinking without theological interlocutors, she naïvely presumes that liberation theology has failed to critique such individualist otherworldliness.[20]

Yet as secular critics begin to recognize the more spirited, if endangered, cosmos inhabited by so many subalterns, a more truly dialogical cosmopolitanism becomes possible. Insights of postcolonial theory can then get woven together with the longstanding decolonial traditions of Latin America, with waves of liberation theology themselves evolving through the activism and the thought of ecological and feminist cosmovision articulating more incarnational universes. The animating nonseparability of the indigenous and the indigent becomes manifest.

(4) *As the universal has served overwhelmingly as a male construct, the dominant anthropocentrism is almost invariably androcentrism.* Is this already evident enough? What is not perhaps evident is the peculiar cosmopolitanism of a Latin American ethos inflected by a feminist cosmology. Marcos, for example, describes her work as that of "a cosmopolitan Mexican intellectual, a feminist long connected to the struggle of Mexican women, particularly in Chiapas."[21] In its recovery of an ancient and still partially surviving cosmovision, her project learns from its "native informants" of a body alien to the individualism, the anthropocentrism and the oppositionalism of the northern women's movement: "The body, abode and axis of delights and pleasures, the dual body of women and men, fluid and permeable corporeality, the body as the principle of being on earth, fusion with the immediate surroundings and also with the origin of the cosmos."[22] Immediately we may suspect such a cosmological duality of presuming a heterosexist romanticism, a binary essentialism. But does the very suspicion not symptomatize the presumption of Eurocentric privilege? It may be that all attention to indigenous narrations of embodiment must risk the charge of essentialism. Not to take this risk knowingly and self-critically may assure that we fail to hear the local voices and to amplify their translocal resonances.

Certainly this fluent relational body cannot be confined to the category of the indigenous religious alien. The planetary feminist contribution to the emergent cosmopolitanism may lie in a subversive relationalism grounded in a corporeality, an incarnationalism, that hosts social and ecological justice. In theology, therefore, feminism lays claim to the biblical prophetic traditions. For me and for others, the Christ of process theology—the logos as "creative transformation"[23]—has delivered an indispensable key to a radically interfluent universe. At the same time, Ivone Gebara, writing her liberative ecofeminist theology from the context of a Brazilian slum, prophetically announces that "our Sacred Body is ailing."[24] In this embodiment of the divine in the situation of the earth, she is developing the panentheistic metaphor of the "universe as God's Body," as she draws it from Sallie McFague, who took it from the process thinker Charles Hartshorne.[25]

(5) *Most important, it has become rather evident that anthropocentrism at the global scale now spells "anthropocide."* The feedback loops of climate change will devastate and produce ever-greater populations of the poor, first of all. But now—as though in a mockery of our universalisms—the human species as a whole is at risk. It is noteworthy that our interhuman solidarity can only come into its own now as an exemplification and embodiment of our interdependence with the whole spectrum of species that inhabit the earth. Theologically I have dubbed this complicated solidarity "the Genesis collective." The real test of a decolonial and cosmopolitan diversality will be its capacity to recognize, rue, and resist the unsustainable contradictions between human and nonhuman diversity. In this regard, Bogotá is not only a stellar city but the capital of a "megadiverse" nation, one of twelve signatories of the Cancun Declaration of Like-Minded Megadiversity Countries.[26]

The savage reduction of nonhuman diversity corresponds to the homogenizing impetus of the imperial cosmopolitanism. It is important, therefore, that a cosmopolitan thinker like Mendieta, while not focused on the nonhuman, does not ignore the ecological crisis. He points to "the growing scarcity of potable water, rising populations and decreasing arable lands" as the legacy of the so-called green revolution, that great globalizing mission of technoscientific modernity.[27] He does not, however, articulate a link between the cosmopolitan and its living ecological cosmos. The diversity of nature is treated as instrumental to human well-being. This is understandably characteristic, at least until recently, of most of the discursive genres of social justice.

From Whitehead and his ecological progeny, we learn to consider the intrinsic as well as the instrumental value of every becoming, human or nonhuman. Our boundlessly diverse entanglement may become unlivable apart from the spread of cosmovision. Among Christians it will take theological form. Conversely, our theologies will now be tested by ecological crisis. Some join the ranks, swelling now for decades (praise the Lord), of those environmentally minded evangelicals committed to "the stewardship of creation."[28] More of us may be learning to inhabit our hospitable planet as though it is itself a living body amid the immense mystery of the universe-body. We are "members of each other" (Rom. 12:5)—cocitizens—only as its members. The cosmopolitan body of Christ was never a mere global church but always a cosmos-body, enjoying and suffering the life of a vulnerable world. Yes, our sacred body, our host body, is ailing.

(6) *The theodicy of the Christian imperialism that legitimated the colonial missions underlies the secularized economy of globalization.* Mendieta opens his book with a remarkable political theologem that will help me conclude these remarks. If the current globalization is the latest point in a "world-historical narrative and time line," it "hearkens back to the idea of a divine history (Heilsgeschichte), which has as its underbelly a theodicy that exonerates humans of all culpability for their inequity and injustice."[29] The omnipotent God of classical theism, revved up in modernity through Calvinism, the Sovereign without whom nothing happens that happens, legitimates every Christian power drive. The deprivations of the poor and the economic rewards of the rich are all part of God's providential plan. Who are we to question the arrangement?

And so in the context of this gathering we must return to that crucial passage at the end of *Process and Reality*. Here the idea of the "transcendent creator, at whose fiat the world came into being, and whose imposed will it obeys," is exposed as "the fallacy which has infused tragedy into the histories of Christianity and of Mahometanism." These great world movements were themselves converted to empire even as they converted empires. "When the Western world accepted Christianity, Caesar conquered; and the received text of Western theology was edited by his lawyers."[30]

And so vast inequity became not only fate but gospel. "Today globalization is the name of this gospel," writes Mendieta. "It promises salvation, but also the convenient alibi that globalization's devastating effects and exacting costs are both inevitable, and, in the end, worth the sacrifice."[31] If the neoliberal orthodoxy of globalization operates an economy of sacrifice, it thereby deems the devastation of the diverse majorities of human and nonhuman lives expendable. The power of the market seems to parody the omnipotent providence of an earlier Western mission.

(7) *The theodicy of omnipotence funds anthropocentric irresponsibility.* Human responsibility seems not to be heightened by the *imago dei* but displaced by divine control. I may not in this context offer the needed reading of Job's whirlwind vision. With its refusal of the theological justification, the theodicies of power, offered by the well-meaning comforters and presumed by the older legend that frames the epic poetry, it ministers to the beginnings of our ethical dissociation from the wild universe. For it sweeps away the language of divine control with a vast cosmological vision of sheer divine delight in the complicated, even leviathanic, diversities of the creation. "I will not keep silence concerning its limbs, or its mighty strength, or its splendid frame," YHWH exults over the sea monster, culminating a long hymn of cosmological exuberance (Job 41:12).[32] But the unifying calculus

"of punishment and expiation" gradually overwhelmed the prophetic and sophic traditions.

Eventually the singular God-Man, enshrined as the exclusive revelation of the relation between God and world, would become the sole incarnation of an anthropomorphic (not to mention *andro*morphic) God, concerned only with human salvation, as a salvation *from* rather than *of* the cosmos. If, to the contrary, our bodies—like that of Jesus—are endlessly entangled in each other and in the creation, incarnation cannot be thus isolated in one body. The attempt only multiplies the sacrifice. Then theodicy justifies human injustice as omnipotent necessity. It can never find enough victims, enough sacrifices, enough resources, profits, and products, to satisfy.

Theologically, the incarnation itself gets sabotaged; it cannot quite deliver on its promise. Not at any rate on behalf of the God who "so loved the world," the God of the new creation, the new heaven (atmosphere, sky) and earth. Yet what can salvation possibly mean for Christian theology apart from its biblical matrix: that of a transformation that signifies nothing in abstraction from the Genesis collective, nothing separable from the salvaging—the radical renewal—of the earth?

The decolonial cosmology needs at once an intensified human responsibility and a deconstructed anthropocentrism—and not by displacing the God-relation. Divinity does not become distant or diminished. Thus, for instance, in the interest of a feminist postcolonialism in league with liberation theology, Mayra Rivera proposes a divine transcendence that cannot be opposed to the materiality of immanence: "God is 'over all,' we might say, following Irenaeus. Not above, but over all, everywhere—as one who envelops the immense organism of which we are all part, a divine envelope through which God and creation touch each other."[33]

Only in the interfluent pleasures and vulnerabilities of a shared flesh, a *diversal* planet, a collective life as "members one of another," does what Whitehead calls the Eros of the Universe find embodiment in our particular cosmos. Love, whether or not we worship it, remains, as Spivak writes with reference to liberation theology, the "strongest mobilizing discourse in the world in a certain way, for the globe, not merely for Fourth World uplift."[34] The church may yet hear its own gospel of planetary love. Christ is "in but not of this world"—inasmuch as the world is controlled by the worldly Procurators of the Caesar-system. If "a better world is possible," a decolonial cosmopolitanism, so turbulently in process, will accompany it.

CHAPTER 11

Toward a Political Theology of the Earth

> Whereas Gaia could be taken as having a somewhat leisurely pace, to the point of being considered as some sort of homeostatic system maintaining equilibrium over immensely long geological time spans, it has taken on—because of this sudden change in the human dimension—a feverish form of palsy, falling catastrophically from tipping point to tipping point, from one positive feedback to the next, in a rhythm that frightens climatologists even more with the publication of each new data set.
>
> —BRUNO LATOUR, "Facing Gaia," Gifford Lectures

This newly terrifying temporality of *terra*—is there a chance that it will tip politics toward planetary responsibility? Can such a conversion be conceived outside of something resembling a theological imagination? The adamantly secular Latour, here invoking the palsied rhythms of climate change, offered his Gifford Lectures of 2013 under the banner of "a political theology of nature." While he lifts up the notion of nature only to dismiss it as hopelessly confused with religion, he keeps political theology in play. Yet the discourse of political theology pulses across a heterogeneous conceptual history: from classical Christian theocracy to its reception in the conservative political theory of the twentieth century, crisscrossed by the social justice theologies and in this century again appropriated as a burgeoning site of progressive political philosophy, secular or postsecular but widely irreligious. But even recently it is rare that this interdisciplinary conversation lurches into the question of climate.

Delivered at "Political Theology: The Liberation of the Postsecular?," a conference of Liverpool Hope University, Liverpool, July 2015.

Political theology can rarely be mistaken for ecotheology. At least in its guise as political theory, it leaves concern for the matter of the earth to ecological science, activism, and religion. Indeed, politics and ecology seem to move in different spatiotemporalities, at different rates of speed. As do their theologically entangled theories. The current conversation in political theology has been unfolding with the rush of a theoretical currency fueled by old, indeed ancient, theopolitical language. Ecological theology seems to slow theory down, capturing it in a geological time far older than language, and at the same time to lurch into the terrifying speed of climate destabilization.

This essay, in other words, is undertaking a concomitance of incongruent temporalities in the form of a political theology not of nature but of the earth. But doesn't the very word *earth* seem to slow discourse down to its inhuman, indeed inorganic temporalities, inhospitable to the high speeds of politics or of theory? But at the same time doesn't *earth* now conjure up a scale of catastrophe that is happening too fast for politics and too late for theory? Too quickly, that is, for us to change paths planetarily, not just to wean ourselves off of fossil fuels but to undo the global economy that is committed to extracting them no matter what climate scientists say. It seems that ten-thousand-year epoch of climate stability is coming to a high-speed conclusion. Yet the collapse of the Holocene does not take place at the pulse-quickening speed of an emergency, like a massacre or a financial collapse—unless you happen to find yourself in the path of the hurricane. Most of us, without being climate deniers, can go about our business most of the time. And business as usual is now all it takes to usher in the apocalypse. "Bad timing" Naomi Klein calls it in her great climate opus, the title of which performs its own action: *This Changes Everything: Capitalism vs the Climate*. The emergency of the so-called Anthropocene remains, even in the time of its tipping point, eerily imperceptible.

Key to political theology has been its readings of the German legal theorist Carl Schmitt's definition of sovereignty in terms of emergency. "Sovereign is he who decides in the exception"—that is, in the face of emergency. "The exception, which is not codified in the existing legal order, can at best be characterized as a case of extreme peril."[1] If global warming and its likely ruination of civilization does not count as extreme peril, then my correlation of political and ecological theology will not be worth the effort. Schmitt's own political ideal of the sovereign remains indissociable from his support for the Führer. However, if climate catastrophe does constitute an uncodified "exception," then we had best not avoid reflection on what sort of power can address "extreme emergency." But it is the succinct theology of Schmitt's view that has cracked open certain vital transdisciplinary conversations from which secularism normally excludes theology itself. "All significant concepts of the modern state" now count as "secularized theological concepts." The territorial authority of the sovereign is recognized as a rendition of the "omnipotent lawgiver." Any political theology that seeks ecosocial justice through democratic means and sans omnipotence (including this present effort) may need to confront Schmitt—if we want our ecology *political* and our political ecology *theological*.

But a political theology *of the earth*? The phrase suffers from an irreducible bidirectionality. It is one thing to address the perils of what Pope Francis's climate encyclical calls "the common home."[2] It is quite another to imply that the theology is in some sense the *earth's*: that the earth might have some agency, some voice, some subjectivity. Some Gaia? Either a mythological subject, the earth goddess for aging new-age consumers? Or more likely a new front for the reduction of everything, of politics, of discourse, of theory, to sublinguistic matter, in a moralizing essentialism that would unify and green us all in the name of this emergency finally, an excuse for the imposition of some ontotheological Nature? But of course it is the very Latour who calls in the name of Gaia for "a political theology of nature," who had already splendidly exposed the semantic mash-up of "nature, this jumble of Greek philosophy, French Cartesianism and American parks."[3]

Latour will discard "nature" in the Gifford Lectures for the sake of "Gaia." But usually, and differently, the dismissal of the natural as a totalizing notion, the pursuit of "denaturalization," marks a range of theory that, while politically progressive, has still barely begun to outgrow its ecological indifference. In this the politics of the left has oddly colluded with the right-wing sense of climate change as a totalitarian plot. So an *eco*-political theology must surface not only subliminally operative theological patterns but also a certain ecophobic resistance endemic to progressive political theory. In other words, does the present avowal of a theology, a perspective, *of the earth* threaten theory with some environmentalist totalization of thinking, spurred on by emergency? In the guise of thinking for and as *terra*, would we territorialize politics itself?

What I do have in mind when it comes to the agency of terra as the terrain or territory of a political theology is something more like this: "The earth constantly carries out a movement of deterritorialization on the spot by which it goes beyond any territory: it is deterritorializing and deterritorialized. It merges with the movement of those who leave their territory en masse, with crayfish that set off walking in file at the bottom of the water...." Deleuze and Guattari ply here their "geophilosophy." "The earth is not one element among others but rather brings together all the elements within a single embrace while using one or another of them to deterritorialize territory."[4] With this trope of a migrant embrace in and by this deterritorializing terra, they dispel every notion of a passive, inert earth external to the intensities of language and history. In the force field of an endlessly branching multiplicity, the enfolding of all the elements in one deterritorializing togetherness, far from monopolizing or monocropping or monotheizing, does not ground any sovereign territorialism. But capitalism too deterritorializes, fails to respect territories, and so imposes a sovereign deterritorialization. This earth enfolds at once the territorialities and their mutual undoing. As this deterritorializing and deterritorialized matter, the earth is lively, vital, active, though certainly not as a single agent or a unified subjectivity. Its "embrace" echoes precisely the Deleuzian sense of "the fold," the *pli* of a complication derived from an ancient apophasis of enfolding and unfolding, in which God is translated as the infinite *complicatio*.[5] As God deterritorializes God within negative theology, here terra deterritorializes itself.

So yes, I do want to commit the complication encoded in that double genitive of the political theology *of the earth*. We have to do not only with the earth as the object, even the surrounding object, of the operative discourse but also as participant in it. This would mean minimally that the earth cannot be separated from the activities, including the geologies and theologies, of earthlings. This earth reads not as a conscious subject or single entity but as an embracing process, indeed, in the politically charged language of Deleuze and Guattari, as an assemblage. We might call the earth, then, our planetary assemblage of all assemblages. So then, if we are what the phenomenologist Glen Mazis calls "earthbodies," we are inhabited and surrounded by countless other earthbodies.[6] In our interactions with them as an assembled collective, a multitemporal assemblage, the earth itself may be said to be engaged in our political theology—however unconscious our politics or our theology remains of its earth. More, the double genitive means that as embodied in those humans performing an ecologically political theology, earth comes into a con/sciousness—a knowing-together—that can at no level be extracted from the nonhuman.

The question is whether we are oblivious to an embrace that by ignoring, we refuse. Note that the verb turns to the noun, refuse, as we trash our common home. Such dumping is a byproduct of precisely the sovereignty empowered by a theology of human dominion. Lynn White Jr., in his endlessly cited essay of 1976, "The Roots of our Environmental Crisis," made clear the danger for the earth posed by this biblically warranted anthropocentrism.[7] It is often forgotten that, far from merely debunking religion, he was (as though preparing the way for Pope Francis) lifting up Saint Francis as revolutionary Christian alternative to the sovereign hierarchy. It was an alternative that, as he notes ruefully, failed in its time. If an actually *theological* political theology has a current alternative to teach, it will depend upon the Christian deterritorialization of Christianity. The church is no more unitary than the earth. The Christian uniformity that triumphed is not identifiable as a denomination or an epoch but as the impulse to political theocracy. In the sovereignty derived from the image of the divine ruler, its political theology advanced the force of the Western exploitation of the *imago dei*. Eventually, in time for modernity, this theology—always contested, complicated—reinforced state power with a competitive territorialization of both the human and the nonhuman. White has shown the late Medieval origination of technologies crucial to modernity; Weber has tracked the capitalist economics of the Protestant ethic. We find ourselves now in another time, the time with too little time merely to demythologize the achievements, too little time merely to deterritorialize the lingering theology of a false triumph. The space of this time invites more complicating, more embracing, solidarities.

If the earth signifies no inert object that waited for billions of years for us to arise and take charge of it, then perhaps its unthinkably intricate creaturely assemblage does, after all, conjure the figure of Gaia. The tragic defeat of Gaia and her children staged mythologically as an Olympian triumph haunts the atmosphere of climate change.[8] If the mythic name can be used now, however, it would be the Gaia of something very like the sense that Latour's political theology would rescue. Whimsically noting that friends warned him away from the Gaia hypothesis of Lovelock and Margulis—not because it can any longer be dismissed scientifically but because the idea of the earth as a complex homeostatic system still conjures a disreputable animism—he takes the chance. In *Facing Gaia*, Latour speaks of a "multiplicity of engagements, of strategic assemblies of humans and nonhumans," as the only way "to cope with what the multiple loops traced by the instruments of science reveal of *the narrative complexity and entanglement of Gaia*."[9]

The Gaia hypothesis has long been named and developed in such diverse ecosocial justice theologies as those of Rosemary Radford Ruether, Anne Primavesi, and Jürgen Moltmann. In his ironic choice of the terms *nature* and *theology*, Latour is proposing precisely a *"political theology of nature."* Latour wants a political theology after religion. But it is "by facing

Gaia, that *wholly secularized and earthbound* set of processes, that there is a dim possibility that we could 'let the Spirit renew the Face of the Earth.'"[10] His secular pneumatology for the "earthbound" actually channels biblical energy to climate activism. In other words, this liturgical reference to Psalm 104, itself echoing the spirit that pulses over the face of the deep, reads as a highly *theological* secularization. By "political theology" he does not necessarily mean to subtract the *theos*—but certainly the supernatural transcendence, the providential sovereign, of believers who flee the earth, who indeed mistook it for a pagan mama deity. Latour performs a secularity that is not identical with a reductive secular*ism* and that therefore some of us might welcome as already postsecular.[11] So it offers an important analogue to a political theology of the earth.

Latour also captures—with apocalyptic flair, indeed with a nod to the Book of Revelation—the bad timing of our current moment. The contrast of the slow and stately pace of geological time spans with the "feverish form of palsy falling catastrophically from tipping point to tipping point" and only getting more terrifying "with the publication of each new data set" stimulates fearful metaphors. "So much so that, in Lovelock's own terms, Gaia reveals Itself as something that is 'at war' and that is even ready to take Its 'revenge.'"[12]

Obviously the risk of such rhetoric—as it tries to break through the armored surface of collective denial—is that it makes the earth the enemy. Terra becomes terror. But at this moment in history the bifurcation of culture from nature that founds the infotechnoeconomy is all set to unify a globe of consumers against an increasingly dangerous Gaia—the hostile, not the hospitable, earth mother. Of course the binary of friend/foe structures Schmitt's political theology around the unifying power that a worthy enemy lends the state. Riffing on Schmitt, Latour's political theology of nature recognizes that any possible political answer to catastrophe will require decisive action. That will inevitably involve the naming of enemies, whom he finds not only in reactionaries but in those modernists who construe the spokespeople of Gaia precisely as the enemy.

> Funnily enough, the more progress-oriented modernizers are, the more they are ready to deny that ecology could even be an issue; the more rabid is their contempt for those they call "prophets of doom," "apocalypse mongers." If you push them a bit more, they will even tell you that all the talk about the End of Time or the Irruption of Gaia is nothing but so many schemes to exploit the poor developing countries even more—if the modernizers are from the Left—or, if they are from

the Right, that it's nothing but a plot to impose communism on the rich developed nations. It's as if they were all saying: "Progress-minded of all nations and of all parties, let's unite in the denial of climatology as our new horizon. We need neither a territory nor a soil. There is no limit!"[13]

The caricature pokes at something uncomfortably real, does it not? This subliminal unity of the illimitable, right and left, against the common foe Gaia and her proponents has for three decades inhibited the development of a strong progressive alliance for ecosocial justice. Spookily, the premodern, the modern, and the postmodern can lock into unity in their resentment of the earth. The anthropocentrism of our civilizational sovereignty has shaped the whole political spectrum.

Surely not to equal effect, however. Latour remains cagey in naming the primary form of this denial of limits, of territory. I would more bluntly designate it as neoliberal capitalism, *not* symmetrically distributed between left and right. Though it is true that much of the left traditionally acquiesces to the god of growth, that the centrist Democratic party worships at its altar, and that many anticapitalist activists still avert their gaze from the nonhuman, these all variously seek forms of restraint and taxation of capital. Neoliberalism is the version of economics that Deleuze and Guattari tracked as a "new deterritorialization" of the earth. Their politics has been deftly characterized by Shakespeare and Moody: "The contemporary political machine of global capitalism manifests itself in specific strata—inorganic (or geological), organic (biological) and alloplastic (social), which stratify life and determine the forms of subjective possibility open to it." A mode of organization such as corporatization structures what we say and are "in order to configure and codify life into forms that are especially recognizable in the consumer market and expedient for its efficient operation." Drawing Foucault into the conversation, they juxtapose the corporate power, disciplining subjects by forming them immanently, to the transcendent sovereign power of a state. "Sovereign power had the right to life and death, manifest in the power to *make die and let live*." But the modernized technopower enabling transnational corporate control over all of life now can *"make live and let die."*[14]

To make live: Indeed, to produce life itself, to claim monopolies on life, to impose with economic sanctions technologically produced and patented life forms, as in Monsanto's increasing control of global agriculture by the elimination of plant fertility.[15] So surely one would not want to infer from transition from the earlier sovereign power that the institutions of global capitalism lack their own new kind of sovereignty. One may need to argue that transnational corporations exercise a neoliberal sovereignty precisely as legally enabled to transgress national laws.[16] But then the *de*territorialization of nations by corporate sovereignty drives its own *re*territorialization, precisely as globalization. In this triumphant global constellation of the omnipresent corporate power, we witness the deterritorialization that is first a dynamism of the earth now moving autoallergically against the earth. Its embracing ecosystems are being left to die. Corporate "persons" are being made to live.

So the register of doom will reverberate in the voices of those who see in this global imperium of capital the enemy of the earth, of its vulnerable populations—and so of us all. For finally the beast will turn on the voracious world empire, that Whore of Babylon, and devour her. Oh dear. That is bitter old misogynist John of Patmos. *Apocalypse Now and Then* is a whole feminist "counter-apocalypse" (not quite an anti-apocalypse) exorcising his ghost. Yet now I cannot fail to recognize the ever more *real* realization of that ancient prophecy of a sovereign global power sucking the life out of the human and nonhuman earth, bringing on the fires, storms, droughts, starvation, war, death of the life of the seas. However, none of his verses add up to the end of the earth or even of the species. It is a much later fundamentalism that writes "the end of the world." Apocalypse does, however, certainly predict catastrophe: the collapse, pretty much, of the hospitable Holocene world.

Catastrophe, etymologically "down-turning," is answered in the Apocalypse by the trope of the new heaven and earth, or the new Jerusalem, adapted from the prior prophetic responses to times of political catastrophe for the Jews. It is catastrophe that catalyzes new creation. In the Apocalypse the messianic event of the New Jerusalem is that of a down-turning, a coming down to earth. It has the hierarchical trappings of a hyper-triumph, a top-down reterritorialization. And by contrast to an earth of verdant wild spaces, this one is drily ordered. "No more sea." As the New Testament scholar Stephen Moore puts it (just as drily), "this continent-sized, lightly landscaped megamall contains but one named animal, sole companion to the single stream and the lone tree."[17] Indeed, a new global Christo-sovereignty quickly replaces the corrupt, collapsed empire. Its ecology is that of a planet-sized city. Theopolitical sovereignty is resurrected.

The New Jerusalem wants deterritorialization in advance. Nonetheless, counter-apocalypse is not anti-apocalypse. Perhaps, then, counter-sovereignty is not simple anti-sovereignty. In this time we may want to acknowledge a certain *apokalypto*, a spooky truth, in the old emergency revelation. The lascivious Rome-Babylon foreshadows all too accurately the voracious imperial enmity toward the populations and territories of the earth exhibited by the current neoliberalism. And in both this time of exploitative enmity renders the earth a scary place. To grant old John of Patmos some prophetic credibility is not to grant him wisdom. Nor is it to reduce the unpredictability, indeed the indeterminacy, of time. It is not to declare any final outcome but to recognize the pattern of power. It is to acknowledge the force of the friend/foe pattern, indeed, to recognize the devilish difficulty of gathering friends of the earth against (yes, against) those who would lay it waste.

Enemies exist. It may be well to remember not just how the apocalypse but how the gospel approaches them. And in that latter, more gracious, vein one may think here of Derrida, reflecting on Schmitt's political theology of antagonism—"not a woman in sight."[18] A pure phallogocentrism. To render the friend/foe distinction the very condition of politics is to commit "the political crime against the political itself."[19] It makes an enemy, therefore, of the future, of what is—in the messianic register of deconstruction—to come, perchance the "democracy to come." This messianic coming is not—unlike that of the Apocalypse and more like that of the classical Hebrew prophets—a guarantee but a promise. A promise comes covenantally conditioned in its very unconditional: Its fulfilment requires mutual fidelity. The difference between the possibility of the promise and the certainty of the guarantee lands in terms of temporalities as that between an open future and a determinist providence. Not surprisingly, the apocalyptic dramatization of the moral dualism of the elect friends of Christ and their absolute foe, the anti-Christ, has proven a dangerously unifying and self-fulfilling prophecy, favored by right-wing theopolitics but shadowing the left.

Eschatology deterritorializes as prophecy and gets reterritorialized as apocalypse. And we can no more do without it than we can without hope. Meditating on Paul's "time that remains," Giorgio Agamben notes that "the most insidious misunderstanding of the messianic announcement does not consist in mistaking it for prophecy, which is turned toward the future, but for apocalypse, which contemplates the end of time."[20] Yet one cannot quite so neatly oppose the two. All along apocalypse, precisely as prophecy, fuels the progressive potentialities of the West. As Ernst Bloch in his *Principle of Hope* demonstrates in the form of a Marxist philosophy of history, all Western revolutions originate in Hebrew eschatology and in what he calls the "Christian social utopias."[21] Bloch, contemporary with

Schmitt and inhabiting the opposite side of the European political spectrum, is less recognized for his analysis of the religious motifs that translated into modern politics. This may be because (in this close to Walter Benjamin) he focused on the forces of messianic revolution rather than of transcendent sovereignty. Jürgen Moltmann can be said to have returned Bloch's political philosophy to theology proper by redefining Christianity as eschatology: "forward looking and forward moving, and therefore also revolutionizing and transforming the present." The *Theology of Hope* can be read as one exuberant meditation on Kierkegaard's "passion for what is possible."[22] Moltmann, Metz, and Sölle were the German theologians who in the '70s rescued the phrase "political theology" from the fascist taint of the Schmitt brand.

But does hope *work* for a political theology now and of the earth? Latour recognizes that hope itself can pacify, can become the problem. So at the entranceway to climate hell, he paraphrases Dante: "Abandon hype, all ye who enter here."[23] We may infer that if hope is not hype it is not the same as optimism. Eco-Pollyanna can be dangerous. But surely no more so than the hopelessness that numbs our earthbodies, tightens our individualism, plugs us into comfort-consumptions. On the intellectual left it emits a toxic cloud of nihilism and politically hardens difference into the zero-sum game of treating as foe some neighboring claimant to radicalism—rather than creating a network of friends across the immense differences that will sustain a strong-enough assemblage. Strong enough, that is, to take on the real foe: the neoliberal economics for which "nature" appears only as resource or as enemy. Alliances across the boundaries of religions, across the fence between secular and religious, and indeed between academic disciplines do not arise out of hopelessness. Transdisciplinarity itself requires enlivening transgressions of those territorial criteria with which careers, and so business as usual, continue numbingly to advance. Yet as John Cobb with the economist Herman Daly argued already in 1989, no university discipline is *less* interdisciplinary than economics. Its deterritorializing globalism depends upon the strict territorialization of thought that permits the systemic substitution of abstractions for material realities, of, for instance, quantifiable profit for quality of lives.

By contrast, the more that divergent fields get into conversation, the more they form networks of imaginative resistance to disciplinary habits. Then they may, with an illumined pragmatism, stimulate and support planetary alliances for a just ecosociality—even with catastrophe "coming down." Is such creativity the hope of a messianic *coming*? If so, for a political theology of the earth that coming does not replay a singular incarnation. The coming amid the down-coming is also a *becoming*: a genesis unfolding in the entangled emergences of our earthbodied intercarnation.

In the multitemporality of its materializations, the hope of such earthbound emergence finds itself nonetheless caught in *planetary emergency*. And here converge three reasons that Schmitt's thinking will continue to haunt any political theology of the earth. First, the notion of decision in the exception might actually justify effectual—and right—action in the face of collective emergency (as in the case of climate change).[24] Second, he recognized with eerie prescience how the US dominance of the globe would, in the name of democracy, spell a neutralization of politics by *economics*. And third, he maps the chance of a peaceful future onto what he calls, and titles a later book, *The Nomos of the Earth in the International Law of the Jus Publicum Europaeum*.[25] It lays out a startling postwar geopolitics of land, ocean, and air. Yet his interest is not in the nonhuman earth in its interdependencies with the human but only as appropriated, "taken." The theologian Michael Northcott, author of *A Political Theology of Climate Change*, finds Schmitt "alone among twentieth century political theorists" in situating "the political in the interstices between air, earth, and sea, and in the agential role of earthly forces in the formation of the borders and laws of the nations, and hence of the political."[26] If Northcott infers more of an ecology than I can discern in Schmitt, this may be in part because Northcott's own theology sits better with the symbol of sovereignty, allowing him to voice strong arguments for ecosocial justice in terms of the Creator God's "ownership" of the world. Such ecological theology with a sovereign Lord—which would include *Laudato Si'*—can reach certain orthodox Christian publics that this political theology of the earth cannot. So even as the multiplicity of the intercarnation presses against the exceptionalist Christologies of orthodoxy, it considers their ecosocial avatars to be friends.

Yet as one less smitten by Schmitt, I find theological help sorting his influence in the "radical political theology" of Jeffrey Robbins, as it conjoins the conversations of radical theology and political theology. The project arises out of two mutually reinforcing insights key to thinking through the related possibility of a political theology of the earth. First, he judges the tradition of radical theology, with which he has long been allied, "insufficiently political." And then he claims that the predominant employment of political theology "has been antidemocratic in its thrust."[27]

Political theology in the shadow of Schmitt "is a response to the perceived crisis of political neutralization" represented by the liberalism of the

Weimar Republic. It thus finds modern democracy "naturally and inevitably giving way to the purely administrative economic state" represented above all by the growth of American influence. In this, Schmitt reverses the political theology of Spinoza. "Whereas Spinoza heralds the beginning of the modern, liberal democratic order, Schmitt chronicles, or exposes, or perhaps even hastens its end."[28] The secularized theology that for Schmitt defines the modern state is not that of a radical immanence but of a "transcendent and omnipotent God operating outside the bounds of natural law." Thus the sovereign may exercise a monopoly upon decision-making in times of national crisis. Schmitt characterizes the exception as "a case of extreme peril." The sovereign is he who "decides whether there is an extreme emergency as well as what must be done to eliminate it." Such "principally unlimited authority then suspends the entire existing order."[29] The juristic order of the state remains while "preformed law" recedes. Only so can an emergency be met effectually. Robbins shares certain elements of Schmitt's critique of liberalism in the guises of modern secular humanism and neoliberal economism. But Schmitt, he avers, throws out the baby of a politically robust democracy with the bathwater of modern liberalism.

An alternative might be to distinguish radical democracy from modern, ipso facto secular, liberalism. Then there appears a hospitable opening for feminist and other theological experiments, often drawn from a Christianity alien to Schmitt's nostalgia for theocracy. But more: This postsecular critique might also empower surprising alliances, for instance, with the Mosque movement in Cairo, the organization of women Saba Mahmood has intensively engaged in *Politics of Piety*. She exposes how the certainties presumed by liberal secularism made Western feminism useful to the imperial US Islamophobia that opened the millennium (and thereby, I would emphasize, to its continuing apocalyptic brew of sovereign militarism and *neo*liberal economics). So might a radical democracy allow for specific solidarities with communities working for women's flourishing through orthodox religious and, indeed, non-Western, nondemocratic polities? Her conclusion suggests how: "This attempt at comprehension offers the slim hope in this embattled and imperious climate, one in which feminist politics runs the danger of being reduced to a rhetorical display of the placard of Islam's abuses, that analysis as a mode of conversation, rather than mastery, can yield a vision of coexistence that does not require making other lifeworlds extinct or provisional."[30]

In this subsequent moment her metaphors of climate, of rendering other lifeworlds extinct or provisional, emit unintended but meaningful ecological resonances. For the liberal humanist project, feminist when convenient and for the most part phallogocentrically sovereign, remains aggressively anthropocentric. So then a political theology of the earth must embrace conversations that deterritorialize some of our own, my own, feminist egalitarianism. Ecofeminism has, therefore, long espoused radical democracy, engaged, as in the theology of Ivone Gebara or Rosemary Radford Ruether, in the lives of women in the Global South. And there is further climate resonance with the mounting crisis of the Muslim world. In the words of a report from 2014:

> As the Obama administration undertakes a . . . multilateral campaign to degrade and destroy the militant jihadists known as ISIS . . . many in the West remain unaware that climate played a significant role in the rise of Syria's extremists. A historic drought afflicted the country from 2006 through 2010, setting off a dire humanitarian crisis for millions of Syrians. Yet the four-year drought evoked little response from Bashar al-Assad's government. Rage at the regime's callousness boiled over in 2011, helping to fuel the popular uprising. In the ensuing chaos, ISIS stole onto the scene, proclaimed a caliphate in late June and accelerated its rampage of atrocities.[31]

Surely we can only meet such global emergencies, political and ecological, in their disturbing mutual entanglement. They are crises of an earth embracing and in this time, in new ways, shaking every territory, a terra including all manner of Abrahamic terrans, of earth, air, and sky terrans. And if our convulsive terrors are interlinked, so must be the alternatives. It is already hard enough to hold together transnational issues of sociopolitical and economic justice, let alone just, say, race, gender, class, religion—but then also ecology? Do we have time to break the habit of territorializing our differing and differently just causes? Here I take heart from Naomi Klein's activist wisdom: "The environmental crisis—if conceived sufficiently broadly—neither trumps nor distracts from our pressing political and economic causes: it supercharges each one of them with existential urgency."[32] For the breadth of the crisis—a multitemporally spatial breadth—also reveals the breadth, the embrace, of the common *oikos*, home, with its common wealth.

So then an earth politics must systematically interrupt the modern bifurcation of culture and nature that structures politics, liberal and illiberal, while it delivers most of us up to neoliberal economic dominance. As Schmitt expected, the liberalism of economics is neutralizing politics. Democracy is becoming corporatocracy. To fight this omniterritorial foe, we require, as Robbins urges, a radical democratization of our politics. This would make it radical enough to form versatile solidarities with variously nondemocratic—non-Western, nonmodern—communities (such as the mosque women) in the interest of the common home. And could it be so radical, I wonder, to locate us, in Whitehead's language, "amidst a democracy of fellow creatures"? Does the radix of such a radicality actually resemble a Deleuzian rhizome, a multiplicity of entanglements spreading quickly just below the surface? Rather than the heraldic image of the single tree rooted and growing on the axis of a vertical transcendence. A multiplicity, not a mere many—and so then politically appears the multitude in becoming, the biblical *ochlos*, the common crowd, the uncommonly diverse *demos*. What for this time, this time that comes, would the actual *theology* for such a rhizomatically radical political theology look like?

Robbins's second point was that radical theology is insufficiently political. He tracks the theology of crisis, then of the death of God, through that of the deconstructively insistent but inexistent God, marking the postmodern turn to the religious, perhaps the postsecular. These radicalisms remain philosophical and aesthetic in focus. He does not discount this root of radical theology but wants its heirs to claim an overtly political vision, one that would let us "counter the unrestrained and increasingly unregulated spread of global capital and to direct the energies of opposition toward a future beyond either dehumanization or terror."[33] And let us add: beyond collapse and extinction. But how can *God* help? Heidegger's "only a God can still save us" connotes for Robbins a "theopolitical fatalism." It seems to faint into the waiting arms of the old sovereign deity, who may—at last, after all—intervene. We are tempted to postulate a "God conceived to fill the void left vacant by the death of God"—which he rightly deems "at best a stopgap measure."[34] But the gap keeps yawning. So for Robbins the alternative is a political theology that can sustain "not only the political instantiation of the death of God but also a theological affirmation of the political power particular to humanity."[35]

A political theology of the earth—if it is meaningfully *political*—will not relax into some cosmic naturalism or ecotheology that fails to make precisely such an affirmation. But the power peculiar to humanity insistently redistributes itself across the other-than-human materializations of the earth. Only so does the tradition of the death of God escape its own orthodoxy, its unification of all God-talk under the sovereign omnipotence of old Nobodaddy. That particularly white male tradition of radicality may instead want to break into a more lively manifold. If that is to happen, however, an actually radical political theology will no longer disdain the chaotic multiplicity of Gods and spirits, of liberatory, animist or Abrahamic, orthodox or polydox practices that remain vibrant among the multitude. The test is no longer of "belief or unbelief" but "Can a particular theology energize that political power particular to humans as members of the democracy of fellow creatures?" Or put differently: Without a hospitality beyond condescension for active, lived theologies along with the varieties of nontheism, for some construction amid the deconstruction of God, Oedipal satisfaction may be reached. Nobodaddy may be killed again. But political theology then lacks any nonconservative future. At least as *theology*. And its radicality will be of no help in collecting the planetary alliance that gives us the hope of a common future.

How, then, does a theology forged in alliances of entangled difference help that alliance emerge—in the face of what may be mounting planetary emergency? I want to share an example of one theological move that answers rather precisely the would-be foundation of political theology in the sovereign power of the exception. "In the exception," writes Schmitt, "the power of real life breaks through the crust of a mechanism that has become torpid by repetition."[36] He is citing Kierkegaard on the vital intensity of the exception. This language, redolent of novelty, freshness, the opposite of the conservative (as Moltmann's Kierkegaard signifies), is hard to resist. Indeed, the various reactionary radicalisms appeal to collective affects impatient with the "bureaucracy" of liberalism, ready to trump democracy for the sake of "real life." Mainstream Christianity may have, by the twentieth century, absorbed that aura of torpid repetition. But is the only theological alternative the appeal to the sovereign exception—the power ready to be called on—despite repeated disappointment—in any emergency?

Intriguingly, Whitehead was writing in the same time as Schmitt, with no apparent link: "God is not to be treated as an exception to all metaphysical principles, invoked to save their collapse. He is their chief exemplification."[37] God, no longer the metaphysical exception, becomes the embodiment—of the principles, in this case, of a creative process in which anything that exists does so as an event of interdependent becoming. Each such becoming is an embodiment, a materialization of the creativity. And this obtains also of God, incessantly in time, in process, getting bodied in each entangled materialization of the universe. Each is a partial and partially self-determining incarnation; none is merely mechanical. There is no unilateral act of creation, no one-way Creator: "It is as true to say that God creates the world as that the world creates God."[38] The affirmation of this nonexceptional deity is of one who does not control creatures or step in to save them. It lures them all, even the quantum, toward a greater intensity of experience. And absorbs the outcomes.

So process theology always already undoes the sovereign omnipotence. Since the '60s it has conversed with the death of God thinkers. But it works from the precedent of a more overtly political theologoumenon. Like Schmitt, Whitehead's gaze sweeps back to the European theocratic lineage—with an incommensurate reading. It is one of the most quoted passages of *Process and Reality*:

> When the Western world accepted Christianity, Caesar conquered; and the received text of Western theology was edited by his lawyers. . . . The brief Galilean vision of humility flickered throughout the ages, uncertainly. In the official formulation of the religion it has assumed the trivial form of the mere attribution to the Jews that they cherished a misconception about their Messiah. But the deeper idolatry, of the fashioning of God in the image of the Egyptian, Persian and Roman rules, was retained. The Church gave unto God the attributes which belonged exclusively to Caesar.[39]

Rendering metaphysical tribute to its Lord Omni, imperial Christendom had beefed up His sovereignty and therefore its own. And did the West not abstract, nay extract, this infinite patriarch from the matter of the earth, releasing His energy to power an increasingly secular state and finally its economic neutralization?

I have found that for the contexts in which theology can make any difference, the process theological iconography of lure to possibility and of divine eros, of God "the poet of the world," as persuasive rather than coercive power, may feel at first iconoclastic. But then it proves far more fetching than the mere death of God. But is the language itself, well, persuasive? For me, now, it rings true only as rhythmically deterritorialized by a negative theology intensified through deconstruction. Then the nonexceptional divinity of the cosmic lure lets autodeconstructive theological metaphors circulate without sovereignty. But with unconditionality. Such an unconditional affirmation—promising, not guaranteeing, a greater aliveness—negates any unquestionable assertions. About God or world. Process thought, interested less in what is believed than in what is becoming, remains heir to the radical traditions of secularization and, therefore, of the postsecular.

In terms of the concrete effects of process theology on political theory in the postsecular specifically, none is more important than the work of William Connolly. As though tracking the political theology of capitalism, he exposes an entire economic theodicy, according to which true belief will be rewarded: The rising tide will float all boats. Increasingly alert to the political entanglement of climate change in "the human estate," he uses Whitehead to theorize the layered temporalities whose complex and climate-altering materializations are systematically obscured and manipulated by neoliberal capitalism. He tracks also the strange geological slowness with which global warming is—all too speedily—closing in on the human future.[40] In a related trajectory, political theorist Paulina Ochoa Espejo develops a notion of the people, the subject of sovereignty in a democracy, "as process."[41] From the perspective of the Global South, simply forfeiting a claim to sovereignty is to surrender to Northern hegemony. So she engages Schmitt's political theology with attention to the rich religiosity of Mexico. "The people" no longer conforms to the liberal model of a collection of individuals but collects itself as "an unfolding series of events" in an open-ended temporality that is on principle incompletable; "open-ended," experienced in its indeterminacy.[42] It is from the metaphysics of Whitehead that she derives her concept of process. The radically democratized and yet postsecular trope of the people as process must surely be taken into account by any radical political theology.

In terms of theology itself, process relational cosmology has instigated much of the emergence of ecotheology in the United States over the past half century. More broadly termed panentheism, it offers one model that is working to turn catastrophe into catalyst. The deity of process offers itself as one source for a radically rhizomatic political theology of the earth.[43] Of our common place, our commonwealth: our uncommonly lively site of mutual materialization. Panentheism, all in theos, makes divinity itself the most common place. Not, then, as a static container or the transcendent insulation of the creation but a deterritorializing embrace of the multiverse.

If the common deterritorializes, the commons is traditionally a territoriality that the propertied classes fight to reterritorialize (as in the enclosures of eighteenth-century England, then replicated in nineteenth-century colonial India). Vandana Shiva tracks this history in developing her argument that "commons are the highest expression of economic democracy."[44] Cobb had early on transmuted process theology into one of the first major critiques of globalized neoliberal capitalism in *For the Common Good*—which proposes a future in which all have at least a chance of flourishing, in which the planetary commons of earth, water, and air is protected from us and for us. Naomi Klein now writes—as an activist, not a theorist, and certainly no theologian—that "any attempt to rise to the climate challenge will be fruitless unless it is understood as part of a much broader battle of worldviews: a process of rebuilding and reinventing the very idea of the collective, the communal, the commons, the civil, and the civic after so many decades of attack and neglect."[45] Decades of time lost, enclosures gaining.

The socially democratic energetics of a planetary commons draws upon a popular power for its hope—not the theopolitical sovereignty of emergency powers. But in the face of emergency, can a political theology of the earth really afford to relinquish the model of exceptional power? This is a thorny question. I take seriously the argument of *Unprecedented*, the book on climate change where David Griffin calls on the president of the United States to declare a state of emergency. As the earth is an emergency, it does follow that the United States is in one too. So the president should use the kind of powers routinely used for military decisions to act to immediately transfer all subsidies to US-based fossil fuel companies to sustainable fuel industries, impose a carbon tax along with transitional provisions for lower-income households, etc. Klein recognizes the same emergency but places her hope in the new phenomenon irrupting from below, which she calls Blockadia—unprecedented new alliances of first nations, farmers, students, ecoactivists. (Especially active in the Pacific Northwest and Australia in blocking the shipment of coal.) It is this development—nothing coming from the sovereign above of nations or technologies—that makes her hopeful.

And then note a third strategy: The climate encyclical of Pope Francis comes from the traditionally most transcendent above in an appeal—to those within the range of magisterial authority but also simply to all humans—that identifies itself with those below. Indeed, if *Laudato Si'* targets with utter precision the economic foe of "the common home" it does so because the massively victimized poor of the world are in danger of ever-new levels of catastrophe, as droughts persist, the crops fail, oceans rise, migration multiplies . . . we hear "both the cry of the earth and the cry of the poor."[46] But what hope rises to meet such a double devastation?

With a prophetic credibility, Klein twists the inescapable emergency into an emergent possibility: "The double jeopardy of social injustice and global warming" should not discourage us. Climate change, with its rising flood waters, "could become a galvanizing force for humanity, leaving us all not just safer from extreme weather, but with societies that are safer and fairer in all kinds of other ways as well . . . ." She stirringly suggests that we collectively use "the crisis to leap somewhere that seems, frankly, better than where we are right now."[47] In other words, the double jeopardy of ecology and justice might actually be what tips emergency into emergence. Catastrophe into catalyst.

In the light of the slow-fast velocity of the crisis and the maddening multiplicity of our issues, we might insist that both political motions, the coming down of sovereignty to earthly responsibility and the becoming of new popular alliances, movements, strikes, cosmopolitics, must work in simultaneity. And in the earth, which—as its own cry is heard—becomes audible within all of our agencies. A political theology of the earth will attend with plasticity to the possibilities. If they may come increasingly beclouded by the impossible, what excuse is that for paralysis? Theologically we may translate the eschatological hope for the new heaven and earth, *hashamayim v haeretz*, quite literally, into the new atmosphere and earth. Or into what Deleuze prophecies—whether he is mindful of the messianism of his deterritorialization—as the movement from "the democratic State in the present" to "the new people and earth in the future."[48] In *"l'avenir," a venir*, "the people to come."[49] New—not as the exception but as the earthbound exemplar of what is already possible. It calls, it presses. For the becoming of the unlikely future is and was and can only be coming now.

CHAPTER 12

The Queer Multiplicity of Becoming

As this bit of cosmopolitan Berlin welcomes us to reflect upon the now-perennial question of genders vis-à-vis faiths, the actual moment intrusively imposes its own agendas. The images of Syrian immigrants, of the massacres, and of xenophobic reactions in Europe and the United States ricochet across the mind. The terror in Paris, and right now, there, the climate talks: Does the high velocity of human emergency threaten to keep the slower crisis of global warming in the background? Where the environment traditionally belongs? Global capitalism can continue to pump the human exceptionalism that defines our civilization's relation to the earth. And for the foreseeable future, emergencies of terror will permit the state power of the exception to tap the quite unexceptional, thousand-year

---

Delivered at an interdisciplinary conference on gender and faith at the Institute for Cultural Inquiry, Berlin, December 2015, organized by Zairong Xiang and Gero Bauer. The Paris climate talks were happening simultaneously, just two months after the Paris ISIL attacks. A monograph dealing with these and related themes, *The Political Theology of the Earth*, will soon follow.

history of Islamophobia in the West. So history returns us to this gathering's question of faith.

Of course faiths in God, in the state, and in the human future name very different projects, prone to distinctive exceptionalisms. Let us consider, however, that they unfold in a certain historical entanglement not just in each other but in an ancient exceptionalism—that by which Christ as God Incarnate supersedes all other faiths. Its secularization in modernity forms the subject matter of much current theory of secularization, or of the postsecular, or of political theology. The triumphalist version of the Christian faith can be read as enabling in its secularization the sovereign politics that results, in Europe and the United States, in forms of nationalized and racialized exceptionalism. And from the start this political theology of Christian dominion expresses the more fundamental dominion of Man [*sic*] over the earth.

This Mankind is refracted through a theology of the human as the exceptional, the Godlike, creature. Of course Man as Mankind, as *der Mensch*, in the image of the straight male God, *der Herr Gott*, somehow includes Woman—and simultaneously excludes her/me. Eve is Adam's state of emergency. Woman is both within and outside Mankind, included even as excluded, the mother of all Others. (Of course, there were always the exceptional women, granted sovereignty and following Athena; "I for one have always preferred the male.")[1] No, we have not quite gotten over it. But now it appears more insistently that this ambiguous gender exceptionalism could be maintained only by a permeable membrane of sexuality: a masculinity maintained against the pressure of both an external woman and an internal feminization. Sex/gender exceptions then end up proving the rule of heteronormative Man.

So you see that sniffing out this iterating, shifty, and multiplicitous logic of exceptionalism actually does keep us on the track of our topic. It will eventually lead to a theological moment of unexceptional but queer, indeed radical, entanglement. Even to a glimpse of divine queerness. Genders and faiths have, of course, been constructed in the West within the spatiotemporality and under the constraints of a long Christianized history of sovereign patriarchy. At this point in a history describable at once in terms of the secularization of faith itself and the postsecularity of multiple faiths, gender has undergone—is still undergoing—rapid cultural diversification. Ever since Judith Butler made *Gender Trouble* we have come to know that gender does not follow from sex as culture does from nature. Sex and gender can no more be identified than they can be decoupled. So then neither

The Queer Multiplicity of Becoming

can homophobia be neatly separated from gynophobia. And the dance of the drag queen performed the very permeability of the distinctions.

If when we now discuss "gender" it comes permeably linked with "sex," that link signifies the affirmative multiplication of genders beyond any fixed biological or cultural meaning of male and female. This discursive complexification gets enunciated at this moment in the alphabetic manifold of LGBTQI, roughly summed up in the Q of queer. But does that mean that queer theory has left behind, indeed *superseded*, feminist theory? What a self-defeating sort of queerness, casually kin to postfeminism, that would signify. Note that supersessionism itself characterizes precisely the temporality of the exception, normatively modeled on the sovereign Christian triumph. And unless queer theory argues that the power of the heteronormative male supremacism and the faith it inspires and requires—the patriarch that feminist movements have destabilized in religious and secular cultures—is now past history, the alliance of feminist and queer, first joined in the bodies of lesbian feminists, often theological ones, remains life-giving. In this moment, this time, amid its emergencies, its emergences.

Nonetheless, I do not in this millennium write feminist cues into my book titles. And the book forthcoming from a recent conference of Drew Theological School's Transdisciplinary Theological Colloquium is not on feminist faith or feminism vs. faith or vice versa but *Sexual Dis/orientations: Queer Temporalities, Affects, Theologies*. Temporality is precisely what is at stake in supersession, which dictates the straight-ahead time of teleological succession. So let me suggest that gender does not get superseded by sex, or feminist by queer, in practice, in theory or in theology. Instead of supersession there appears a multiplicity of becomings, multiplicities of multiples happening in a nonlinear movement whose events of becoming, massively iterative even in their novelties, do not cease to entangle each other. Sexually and otherwise—every other wise. Consider, for instance, Elizabeth Freeman's diagnosis of the *chrononormativity* of straight time—the time of civilization as we know it. As an alternative, J. Halberstam proposes the queer possibility of future times imagined "according to logics that lie outside of those paradigmatic [heteronormative] markers of life experience—namely, birth, marriage, reproduction and death."[2] Such a queer temporality is characterized in the Drew volume thus: "This timely body of work *on* time seeks to replace reliance on logics of repetition, linearity, periodicity, and teleology with counter-logics of hauntological historiography, erotohistoriography, and queer temporal drag."[3]

The subject of such a counter-logic does not, in other words, find itself ever complete, secure in some bounded—and exceptional—identity. It finds itself in a time in drag, a time that drags the future into encounters with its own spooky pasts, the present into relation to its hauntingly possible futures. It thus resists the triumphant supersessionism whereby the normative present marches toward its telos. The straight time of teleology may take the form of fundamentalist apocalypticism or of modern progress. The timely alternative, then, does not supersede the supersessionisms but recognizes their drag upon the present. And you do not need a theological education to hear the particularly theological echoes of supersession: The *novum* of the Christ-event—and surely Jeshua of Nazareth did materialize extraordinary novelty—got soon hyped as the supreme exception of human history.

Christian exceptionalism thus could sanctify a new model of imperial sovereignty, one that could be retroactively interpreted as the political theology at work, visibly or invisibly, in all modern Western powers: "Sovereign is he who decides in the exception."[4] And as Carl Schmitt (in)famously clarified this power of decision, it renders the friend-foe polarity the key to politics. The Christian supremacism of theocracy and of the divine right of kings may be thus read in the form of the explicit theological exceptionalism that entrenches us in a millennial arc of crusades, from Urban II in 1096 to Bush II invading Iraq nearly a millenium later. The temporality of the conquering cross thus extends through a manifold of political times and sovereignties. I have argued elsewhere that "the West" as such cannot be abstracted from the original crusader theology, which intentionally used enmity with Islam to forge a new amity between the mutually violent European principalities.[5] This form of Christian unity against the religious foe granted theological sanction to the sovereign exceptionalism of the secular state. If Jews historically served as its internal foe, Muslims provided the external menace. And as Agamben argues in *Homo Sacer*, the state of exception insidiously becomes the rule. He had in mind, particularly, the camps, the *lager*, of World War 2 but anticipated all too accurately other camps, massive refugee camps, becoming permanent. These are now mainly Muslim, inhabiting an inhospitable inside. One thinks of Palestinians within the borders of Israel, of the Africans and Syrians within the borders of Europe. At this moment Berlin's Tempelhof Airport is becoming the largest refugee camp in Germany, housing seven thousand. The Islamophobic arc of Western exceptionalism was not, after all, ending with its millennium.

So you may now admit there is a shared logic, indeed a theo-logic, to the homophobic and the Islamophobic exceptionalisms. But to climate change? The connection emerges as you reflect on the situation of mass climate migration that rising and acidified oceans, melting ice and water supplies, spreading fires and droughts has barely begun to unleash. The rise of ISIL amid the destabilization and desperation of five years of extreme drought conditions in Syria, compounded by the effects of long-term dictatorship and of our war with Iraq, must be read as a harbinger of a new eco-political climate of long-term Islamophobia. And what is driving climate catastrophe but the religio-secular spatiotemporality of *human* exceptionalism—and the relentless drag-time of a self-defeating dominion?

Is it all a still-falling Edenic drag? Our genders and our faiths circulate within an anthropocentrism that fitfully recharges its own androcentrism. In the time of the newly named Anthropocene, the lost epoch of the Holocene, the twelve thousand years of relative climate stability may indeed soon be looking like the lost garden. Should not a feminist theology provide the key to liberate us from all the sovereign exceptionalisms, to reconcile us with the trickily gendered Gaia?[6] Can faith in gender transformation solve the problems of gaiophobia, of Islamophobia, as well as of homophobia? Of course not—we can no longer turn to feminism, or to any single movement, however convincing its own identitarian exceptionalism, for salvation. But a certain rethinking of gender and faith may offer *a* key to our tangled current time of gnarly emergency.

We might put its counter-logic this way: It is our *entanglement* in each other and in the planet that *exceptionalism* represses. So if something planetarily better is to emerge from all this emergency, then might we mobilize, against the power of the exception, the performance of our entanglement? Entanglement is not a casual metaphor. It names the endlessly, ecosocially interlinked planetarity that materializes in mysteriously multiplying multiplicities. Indeed, it summons up an ancient margin of mysticism, as my recent exercise in apophatic entanglement tells it. Such a theology echoes an ontological entanglement materialized even at the level of quantum entanglement. Theology comes always entangled with God, but here contemplates—beyond and before the exclusive incarnation—a theos tangling with all the bodies of the universe.

If the classical Christian supersessionism has yielded in modernity a subjectivity cut free from the old collective forms of creaturely relationality, its individualism takes forms on both sides of the political spectrum. It allies itself readily with the ego of neoliberal capitalism but also perpetuates the sharp cuts of identity politics on the left. If a single social issue shapes the telos of a complete subject, essentially separable from its others, no wonder, for instance, a cisgender identity could form a simple unity with its "own" sexuality, abstractly separated from sex or gender alterity. But as Judith Butler demonstrates, the heteronormative identity is formed by a "constitutive exclusion": The relations being excluded actually form the boundary of such a subject. Butler illustrates her alternative with what Elizabeth Freeman calls "the classically queer practice of drag performance."[7] Butler's own now-classic analysis of the ironic mimicry of sex/gender roles exposes what the exclusion includes, upon what exterior other it depends. In its relationality it performs what Freeman means by "temporal drag" as an answer to chrononormativity. It drags us, tugs us, slows us, into contact with the troubling histories and identities that normative time works to supersede.[8] Temporal drag concerns less "the psychic time of the individual than...the movement time of collective political fantasy." It is "a way of forcing the present to touch its own disavowed past or seemingly outlandish possible futures."[9]

In the ambiguous permeability of the boundary appears an inescapable entanglement. To mind its dynamism is already to perform an alternative to the politics of friend vs. foe. For the constitutive exclusion only works because of an inescapable and repressed condition of *interdependence*—what Butler in this millennium acknowledges to be a relational ontology. Such an ontology had, in the previous millennium, fired up my own feminist theology as an account of the gendering of selves within a boundless spatiotemporal web of relations. I found gender to be an invaluable lens upon a relationality rendered abject, chaotic, monstrous by a warrior masculinity that predated and preformed the Abrahamic faiths. From within one branch of this heteropatriarchal faith I found resources for mobilizing a feminist faith against the straight male God and his hierarchies and secularizations; and for performing a feminist faith *in* a gender difference that, as time unfolded, revealed its creatively multiple sexualities.

This did not mean, for instance, that I needed then to shift my sexual identification so as to supersede a draggy old feminism. Lesbian feminists have experienced this tension as well. Freeman addresses the danger of this disconnection as one recent example of temporal drag; she cites "the gravitational pull that 'lesbian,' and even more so 'lesbian feminist,' sometimes seems to exert on 'queer.'"[10] In many queered classrooms and even in certain works of queer theory, "the lesbian feminist seems cast as the big drag," fated to conjure up "essentialized bodies, normative visions of women's sexuality, and single-issue identity politics that exclude people of color, the working class, and the transgendered [sic]."[11] Vital debates and developments, capable of strengthening complex alliances, on the left quickly crack into new supersessions. And so we are divided and conquered by an exceptionalism we never owned.

We might seek instead to perform the entanglement of our differences: to activate entanglement as solidarity. And in one fell swoop this makes possible more complicating engagements with other faiths, religious and irreligious, as we undo the impermeable boundary, the mighty fortress—not the difference—between faith traditions. This sense of entangled solidarity is anticipated by what the Black feminist Combahee River Collective forty years ago called "simultaneity," and then Kimberlé Crenshaw "intersectionality." It articulates the entanglement of gender in other registers of identity—in sex and race, in class and abledness, and, increasingly, as works of theological ecowomanism demonstrate, in ecology.[12] Yet it does not collapse these multiple registers or straighten them into mere parallels. The intersections crisscross multiple genres and divergent intensities, requiring in their perpetual simultaneity a constant work of decision, a suffering of priority, a drag dance of indeterminacy.

In the face of a climate catastrophe that will entangle all humans in all of the above registers in new ways, in ways we can only partly predict, must we not now also surface that simultaneity materializing beyond the human species? Not just in interhuman but also in interspecies entanglements? And these organic entanglements are apophatically entangled in the unknowable experiential registers of the inorganic, within the planetary intersectionality that is the earth. In the time of Christianized supersession, the theocratic and then the secularist subject perform a disentanglement from the nonhuman that means to render us sovereign in our Manhood, independent of the dark, dirty space-time drag of Gaia—of the multiplicitous manifestations of the earth-matter, *adamah*, of which we are constituted. Of the biogeology that slows us down to the speed of the elements. But, then, for all its advancing science, the human exceptionalism has only rendered our fleshly dependence upon the nonhuman dangerously invisible, denied even when known.

Not unlike the male abjection of the female and the straight abjection of the queer. But, again, our inevitable identitarian priorities can betray our own constitution. Thus queer theory may also collude in the human exceptionalism when it deploys a careless rhetoric of "denaturalization." Then it reinvests the culture/nature binary with the force of political fashion.

Perhaps, however, the exceptionalisms I have discussed are themselves too diverse to enfold in a single analysis. No doubt the multiple issues at stake require a multiplicity of strategic responses. But they do seem to come all embedded in the Russian doll of a political theology of sovereign power. And so to recapitulate: First comes God the omnipotent sovereign. He—totally He—rules through the Byzantine Pantocrator, the Son in his solo, his exceptional incarnation. Just beneath him and in His image is Man, the exceptional creature, with dominion over the other creatures; and somehow he is male and female, but he is a he with sovereign power over her until recently, a straight he from whom deviations make for emergencies of perversion, exceptions that prove his *rule*. His sovereignty over all the human others that have been marked as near to the female, the animal, the material that is his to form and to use.

This theology founds the sovereignty that makes laws and, in the exception, breaks them. In its distinctly postbiblical metanarrative, Christianity has superseded Judaism and invalidated other ways. In what we may call an eschatological chrononormativity, it lays out time, after Irenaeus, in a straight line from *creatio ex nihilo* to final victory. The eschaton thus denuded of the prophetic teaching of justice or the gospel kingdom of God forms the ultimate exception, *ex-cipere* (to take out): It becomes the time when time itself is taken out. Its political theology sanctifies the divine right and exceptional authority of the Christian sovereign in time. If in its medieval format it produced "Europe" in a unification against the Muslim foe, it morphed then into subsequent globalizations. It takes its white racist turn in a departure from the Latinate Catholic order, and what Kelly Brown Douglas calls "Anglo-Saxon exceptionalism" comes to the fore.[13] This notion is a key for reading British expansion and the subsequent specific postrevolutionary legitimations of slavery and racial hierarchy that define US history. It yields, then, after World War 2 the anglobalization of the planet (linguistically so convenient for this speaker). US exceptionalism carries on as not just one but *the* one nation under God, defining our new millennium through 9/11/01 with the racialized Muslim terrorist as the galvanizing enemy of the longest war in US history. It is not that all issues come down to this one and all times are framed by the thousand-year arc of Western Islamophobia. But it is rather that right through the nationalist colonial and economic neocolonial expansions of Western sovereignty, our history expresses the political theology of the ultimate exceptionalism.

This does not render any major historic form of sovereignty simply and singly responsible—the foe of ecosocial justice faith today. It is not that the chrononormativity of an ancient sovereignty has managed to unfold its quite linear determinism in a way that would have been predictable from the start, as its own triumphal theology suggests. These multiple tensions and dynamisms of sovereignty run across conflicting, incongruent dimensions. It is not as though we can align Islamophobia, gynophobia, homophobia on one side against some glowing assemblage of just pluralists, feminist Muslims, eco-queers, etc., on the other. The tangles of difference, enfolded in our constitutive exclusions, prevent merely replicating the friend/foe binary from the opposite—the correctly emancipatory—side. It would, after all, fail to keep faith with the differences that make us up and certainly with the complication that is gender. It would fail in the faith that our entangled difference might be making possible.

So we can only share Derrida's denunciation of Schmitt's *Freund/Feind* politics as pure phallogocentrism—"not a woman in sight."[14] Actually Schmitt did *see* us: "When anarchists today see in the patriarchal family and in monogamy the actual state of sin, and when they preach the return of matriarchy, the supposedly paradisiacal original state, they are paralyzing politics along with the authority of the father and the transcendence of God."[15] The mockery of early utopian experiments in gender equality reminds us that the Eve-emergency had not yet faded into the past. Sovereignty, and with it, for Schmitt, all social order, depends upon the paternal norm. And the norm depends upon God the Father—a transcendence not at all apophatically unknown but (exceptionally) male. Exceptional women, of course, are not the problem but the deterioration of the patriarchal potency of politics itself. In the fear for lost potency—now threatening in the United States to trump politics itself, by way of an economic defeat of democracy that would not have surprised Schmitt[16]—sex and gender normativities fuse in one great temper tantrum. And so the rage against the racial minoritization and religious alterity projected as the "immigrant" carries an eerie phallic charge.

We will respond, I suspect, more effectively, which is to say, more coalitionally, if we avoid our own counter-simplifications. Because Islamophobia is pressing right now, and will continue to do so, interrogations of the way the supersessionism of the exception influences also liberal and progressive self-narrations, specifically of gender and sex, remain illumining. For instance, Jasbir Puar, writes in *Terrorist Assemblages* of how "state of exception discourses rationalize egregious violence in the name of the preservation of a way of life and those privileged to live it."[17] In the light of Abu Ghraib and other perverse sexualizations of the Muslim other, she draws upon Schmitt's theory of the suspension of law to show how biopolitics continuously seeks to redefine the boundaries between life and death. She is thinking with Agamben, who writes, "The state of exception is neither internal nor external to the juridical order, and the problem of defining it concerns precisely a threshold or a zone of indifference, where inside and outside do not exclude each other but rather blur with each other."[18]

We may hear resonances with the internalized exterior of gender formation in Butler's constitutive exclusion. What we may read as the permeable membrane of heteronormativity resembles this political zone of indifference, if that means not an absence of differences so much as the apophatic indivisibility between them. Agamben likens the externally internal space of exception to a Möbius strip: At the moment it is cast outside it becomes inside. Puar picks up here: "In the state of exception the exception insidiously becomes the rule. . . . Sexual exceptionalism works by glossing over its policing of the boundaries of acceptable gender, racial and class formations." So the mobilizing of the exceptional status of the homosexual within the United States and some European nations generates what she calls homonationalism: the exceptional, acceptable, properly Islamophobic—usually white and affluent—homosexual, produced in opposition at once to the "the colloquial deployment of Islamic sexual repression that plagues human rights, liberal queer, and feminist discourses, and the Orientalist wet dreams of lascivious excesses of pedophilia, sodomy, and perverse sexuality."[19] The membrane of heteronormativity is so flexible as to include the new homonormativity. Her analysis, while closely linked to the moment of Abu Ghraib, exercises a drag upon the temptation to queer triumphalism in a way that can only intensify the queer time of political theology.

In a related vein, Joseph Marchal, who writes between queer theory and biblical studies, warns of "the exceptionalism that is potentially endemic to queer studies, perhaps especially to those narratives that promote only one way of relating to temporality as queer."[20] Queerness does not mean just everything strange; but neither does it make LGBTQI identities mere exceptions to the norm. Otherwise, as we witnessed in Puar's disturbing analysis, it proves the very norm it exists to *reprove*. Marchal's internal critique of queer exceptionalism attends to the different velocities, now and then, of an apocalyptically inscribed history. It traces temporalities that in their convulsive revelations—male, female, in a Pauline text or in queer studies—do not converge upon one final chrononormative end. Even as all queerness does not center upon sex/gender performance. The queer multiplicity of becoming inscribes no teleological hope of closure but perhaps an honest chance of dis/closure—apokalypsis. But as the issues, the betrayals, the entangling ecologies of our time disclose their multiplicity and multiply their disclosures—what hope remains?

As Marchal reads it, the famous debate between the antisocial hypothesis of Lee Edelman and the critical utopianism of José Esteban Muñoz brilliantly surfaces the tension within queer theory. On the one side, resistance to queer normativity amounts to a denunciation of relationality itself and so of any collective hope: "no future." The antisocial hypothesis performs the time of a queer exceptionalism, as a polemic against the normative, reproductively driven futurity. If sociality in our civilization comes structured around the reproductive continuities of chrononormativity, why not stage exceptions to the social and to its temporality? Muñoz voices the alternative response, that of a queer relationalism. He joins it with queer person of color and also feminist critiques. He finds that "the field of utopian possibility *is one in which multiple forms of belonging in difference adhere to a belonging in collectivity.*"[21]

These belongings inhabit the multiplicity of becoming, queer indeed, as the space-time of an alternative hope. For theology, it is worthy of note that *Cruising Utopia* makes intensive use of Ernst Bloch and his utopian political *"not yet"*: thus Muñoz's "we are not yet queer."[22] In claiming Bloch's collective *not yet*, he blasts open an alternative—crucial to the theologian of hope Jürgen Moltmann—to the Schmittian political theology of the exception. Muñoz himself does not address Bloch's own richly theological historiography of the Hebrew prophets and the Christian social utopias as the inspiration of all Western revolutions. The eschatologically hopeful historiography of *Das Prinzip Hoffnung* had been key to the end of millennium meditation I called *Apocalypse Now and Then*: countering the misogynist end-times of closure with the radically dis/closive potentiality in which apocalypse itself comes entangled. Now I would solicit an apocalyptic drag for any politically viable hope: that of a queerness that constitutes and exceeds sexual identity and performance.

The excess signifies not the exception but the entangled—and no less novel—becoming of an alternative. It emerges in abnormalcy, indeed in the emergencies which test or burst the norm. And it carries the possibility for the ethical transmutation of the norm itself. Becoming bursts in upon the enclosures of the normal with the hope of robustly multiple belongings. Multiple forms of belonging in difference: In this space gender would be performed as a radically pluralist faith, irreducible to a liberal pluralism, which in religions or without them keeps its differences tolerantly separate. Instead, intersectional assemblages entangle us in a collectivity that pulses toward "the then and there of queer futurity." It feels the drag of profound histories and haunting losses. But there is a festivity also in the uncertainty: Doom is not certain! The terrestrial spiral of terror and territorialism is undeniably and irrevocably heating up with the climate. But is something else, something better than survival, something planetarily better than the here and now, perhaps at the same time, if within an altered temporality, nonetheless possible?

The question is not rhetorical. But I pose it within the rhetoric of a history and a practice, that of theology, that itself verges on the impossible. Yet I keep finding that the drag of a feminist relationalism initiated in the last millennium still makes theology, at least, possible. And with it a certain eschatologically entangled hope. In its own cloud of impossibility, theology exposes itself to the vast and mostly unknown spatiotemporality of our relations. Call it the drag of the universe. Its theos names neither a transcendent outside nor a bounded inside of its world, in which in our fragile socialities we participate in each other—inside out, outside in. Its participatory politics would challenge every sovereign game of omnipotence. These entanglements constitute a world, with the outside of the past becoming internal and the inside surging out into its future. Like Agamben's Möbius strip, read by Puar as an alternative to the political theology of sexual exceptionalism, it moves in its own infinity, *infini*, unfinished. The eschaton is its edge, not its end. Here, theologically speaking, infinity becomes always again creation. As it materializes, it undoes our human exceptionalism; it tangles us in the precarious possibilities of planetary belonging.

In this formulation of our interdependent and indeterminate becoming I also am feeling the drag of process theology on my thought. I have discussed earlier the affinity of Alfred North Whitehead's cosmology of process and relation from the '20s with Karen Barad's "new materialist" notion of quantum entanglement with its (and our) "agential intra-actions."[23] These cosmologies describe a responsiveness, a living, deciding, but not necessarily consciously thinking, connectivity that, far from the exclusive trait of exceptional human moments, characterizes the most elemental beings constituting matter. This relational ontology, in dialogue with Donna Haraway and Judith Butler, leads Barad more recently to articulate "the queer performativity of nature" through and beyond any known sexes and genders.[24] Such an enlivened mattering of matter undoes the nature/culture binaries on which the theological, Western, and, indeed, sexual exceptionalisms are historically based.

The cosmic drag of our becoming tugs not just the microcosmic but the macrocosmic responsiveness into play. If it sways with the queer multiplicity of the world, it keeps in play a theology of entangled difference. But theology does, after all, require some active, even intra-active, sense of theos—unless we stay within the patrilineage of the theology of the death of God.[25] A living theology may imply a more lively theo, thea, diffractively She/he/it, a queer God, there where a too-familiar transcendence, not nearly *trans* enough, had congealed. A divine multiplicity? Love materializing out of bounds? An erotic ultimate?

If a single logos of theos lured me as a fresh feminist into a theological life, it was Whitehead's figure of the "Eros of the universe." It unfolded in his thought as the divine lure—to life and more life, to greater complexity of interrelation and greater intensity of experience. It is God as sheer possibility, not yet actual; it seeks materialization in the multiplicity of becomings. In and through them the divine itself becomes. It is a becoming by affect—suffering with and enjoying the experiences of all material becoming. Really all. And so a receptive responsiveness replaces the icon of the paternal *actus purus*. And it is this receptivity—verboten by the orthodoxy of pure act—that undoes any model of sovereign omnipotence. And in so doing it also unhinges the hierarchy of exceptionalisms that issue from the paternal creator ex nihilo: For this "God is not to be treated as an exception" to the categories of interdependent becoming but rather as their "chief exemplification."[26] And so it deflates the doctrine of His exclusive Son Incarnate. Jesus appears in process theology instead as one fully attuned to the lure—the logos as "creative transformation."[27] He does not pose as the ontological exception, God temporarily disguised in Man's flesh. Instead, congruent with any responsible reading of the second Testament, Jesus teaches by example, expecting his friends to "also do the works that I do and, in fact, will do greater works than these" (John 14:12). But he is exemplifying the Eros of the universe not in order to harden a norm but rather to embody novel possibilities. For it is a desire that does not take us out, in *excipere* of the matter of world, but that calls us out and takes us in deep. It calls for becomings that matter, for the inception—*incipere*—of new modes of being together, of belonging here and now.

Let me relate the alternative power, the entangling force, of erotic affect to another bit of queer theory. Asking "where eros becomes important," Lynne Huffer writes that "in its etymology eros refers not only to a notion of passionate love but also to a life force, what Audre Lorde calls, like Nietzsche, 'the *yes* within ourselves.' Might an ethics of eros be articulated as a possibility of life to transform the violence of biopower?"[28] If that life possibility translates theologically into the eros of the universe, we get a clue for theology as such and so for any "new" political theology. That immanent affirmation, however stifled and denied, nonetheless lives in the nonexceptional space of life itself. And it is nowhere in this time more vibrantly exemplified—indeed, spelled out—than in the yes of LGBTQI experience. If we treat it not like the exception but let its difference—whatever our sexual or celibate practice—utter that yes, the embodied multiplicity of all our becomings is refreshed. Within ourselves, in a within that is also a without, the permeable membranes that entangle us in our differences find intercarnation.

But then the alternative of a God that does not model the archaic omnipotence or the modern biopower, indeed that does not descend from straight theological debate but comes out of the closets and the commons, the edges and the interstices, becomes along with us. Here Marcella Althaus-Reid, the late, great "indecent theologian," finds God coming "from the margins of sexual deviance and economic exclusion." Inspired by the transgressive spaces of Latin American spirituality, where the experiences of slum children merge with queer interpretations of grace and holiness, her *Queer God* challenges the oppressive powers of heterosexual orthodoxy, whiteness, and global capitalism: "Queering theology is the path of God's own liberation, apart from ours, and as such it constitutes a critique to what Heterosexual Theology has done with God by closeting the divine."[29]

The multiplicity of issues—economic, sexual, racial, theological—do not inhibit such theology, they inhabit it. In an interview—not naming the proximity to process theology and its becoming multiplicity—she announced an "unfinished God. One that is in process, ambiguous, one of multiple identities that we never quite get to know, because when we try they escape, there is more. I do not want a God of the hegemonic center, a king that comes to visit the slums, who extends his hand and says: 'I am God, I have a kingdom and I am so good that I come to visit. But now, I must return to the kingdom of heaven.' I speak of a God that opens his/her closet and entertains his/her friends saying: 'Now I'm Marlene Dietrich.'"[30] Quite a trans/lation of the incarnation.

Yet there is also queer theology that entertains the terms of classical trinitarianism. It admits of no feminist or queer exceptionalism vis-à-vis Christian doctrine. Linn Marie Tonstad's *God and Difference* concludes with an appeal to the hope of the resurrection as an apocalyptic end to the "continuation of ordinary time" and its reproductive projections. Again the eschaton is not a matter of the end of time but of heteronormative temporality. She rethinks the trinity through the spectral time—haunting indeed—of Spirit: "The Holy Ghost's sensuality is perhaps best represented by the wind, since its light caress reaches the surface that the divine phallus can only shatter, yet this light touch drives people wild."[31]

The light touch suspends the sovereign penetration. The lure does not sound like the Lord. Pneumatology thus tugs theology back through and before doctrine, to a space where we feel the drag of the prehuman time, where the wind/ruach/spirit pulses wildly over the face of the deep. And yet time does not stop, becomings build up possible futures, in the nonviolent apocalypse that is a counter-apocalypse, the queer time of a revivifying dis/closure.

Its breathy spirit, when its touch has been felt, has always opened ways beyond any one-way supersessionism. The great ninth-century Muslim theologian Ibn Arabi captured this precisely, in a reflection on the "path of Allah." He writes that "this path is that concerning which the Folk of Allah have said, 'The paths to God are as numerous as the breaths of the creatures.'" Thus "all religion comes from God, even if some of the rulings are diverse."[32] The point is not here to commit some impossible anachronism but to note that—with this lightness of touch, this inspiring breath—religious diversity is not just the subject of peacemaking ecumenism in times of religious violence. It materializes the multiplicity of the creation itself. In the Abrahamic imaginary the spirit/breath/wind haunts the cosmic multiplicity of becoming—*genesis*. A wild place, calling forth at all times the most diverse self-organizing processes possible.

A political theology of entangled difference hosts the widest and wildest sort of love. It resonates with what, in an important contribution to a queer ecotheology, Whitney Bauman calls "the polyamory of place." Allied with Althaus-Reid's polyamorous God, his *Religion and Ecology* lures us to a love not of world in the abstract but in the particular embodiments of spatiotemporality that we materially inhabit, that make us up as a world together. His polyamorous divinity is desiring "the emergence of planetary identities . . . for the becoming planetary community."[33] In the interest of such a cosmopolitics of becoming, the political theology of the earth creates the widest possible alliances—reaching endlessly beyond the human. Otherwise such emergence will be hidden or crushed by the exceptionalist powers of emergency. The eros of planetary identities, each of which is a multiplicitous collective within and without, calls every state of emergency toward the emergence, the yes, that is possible. Perhaps, indeed, toward what Lynn White Jr. called "the democracy of all God's creatures."[34] And for us that means the creatures of the earth, subjects of us, to us, in us, around us, sharing the emergency of our self-contradiction and, yes, the possible emergence from it.

If it is the eros of the world that instigates the hope of a democratic multiplicity of becoming, the polyamory of place locates the queer time of its becoming. And here the performance of our entanglement resists—in the Möbius strip of within and without—the phobic powers of the serial exceptionalisms. But what can power the performance, what gives it the energy—again—to resist, to persist, to create the planetary collective? Is it the power of the yes, for which faith is another word? The yes within all our entangled selves, so human and so nonhuman, so material and so ghostly, even holy? As theology it has no more settled for the exceptional incarnation than would Jesus or, indeed, that cosmic yes that he embodied. In its unpredictable comings and incessant becomings, the divine multiplicity (one, two, three for starts) neither exercises nor surrenders to the rule of the exception. Its eros is not dissipated by fear or hardened by foe. Among those who befriend this love, under whatever nickname, there blows and breathes an integral energy—an intercarnation—of wildly entangled difference. If its polytemporality drags and lures, it lets us end for now, like Muñoz's "flight plan for a collective political becoming," with "an insistence on something else, something better, something dawning."[35] The flight is not from but of the earth, in and through our queerly multiple bodies of earth. In and through an outside within us all that becomes the inside of what can have no outside.

After / Word Intercarnate

After the incarnate Word, what can come? As Word it precedes world. But what about the intercarnation, which has a tenuous grip even on the status of "word"? It certainly as a word comes long after the incarnation. But it works no supersession.

Gesturing ontologically, it may come just as much "before" as any mystery of inception, as any conception of the cosmic Logos, from which—after all—it remains indiscernible. Nothing begins without it. But it is unlikely to perform as solo origin. It voices something else now about the world, something intermittent, pulsating between beginnings: less the eternal principle that starts it all than the simultaneous entanglement of it all in all of the differences that compose it. The flesh of the intercarnation exceeds any particular body. It comes after by virtue of coming before; it precedes even as it follows.

Time will not stay straight, amid the pulsing bodies. Nor will time wash out; it vibrates at multiple frequencies. The diverse scales, intervals between comings, densities of becoming, may remain imperceptible to each other, too vague or too viscous, fast or slow, to be appreciated. Yet sometimes even wildly different bodies notice and complicate each other. They flesh out each others' worlds. What poetry. What ferocity.

What vulnerability.

As differences congeal, as they conceal their own interlacement, as productive rivalries lock into systemic contradictions, an epoch might end prematurely.

Thus saith the word intercarnate: we do not have much time, if we ever did. But we have the time we need.

We the people, we the earthlings.

ACKNOWLEDGMENTS

In a collection of essays written over a stretch of time, there is no way to surface and to thank all who form the buzzing clusters of conversation surrounding each piece, no way to name all who lend needed support, provocation, and inspiration. The indebtedness of *Intercarnations* is integral to its self-understanding, which only makes the problem worse: The crowd of witnesses clouds over quickly, precisely in the too-manyness of its offerings.

I can, however, thank first of all Helen Tartar of Fordham University Press for her original collusion with me on this project. To thank her is to mourn her untimely death. It is also to celebrate her spirit at work in the ongoing liveliness of the Press, as in this case manifest in the creative persistence of her successor, Richard Morrison. I also thank Bud Bynack for generous editorial advice at the needed moment. Over a discontinuous period of time, I have been dependent upon several Drew graduate students, current and former, for help with the work of selecting and editing these essays. Thank you for your gifts and for your time, Dhawn Martin, Elijah Prewitt Davis, Kyle Warren, Luke Grote, and—getting me to this moment—Winfield Goodwin.

It is Halloween as I write these acknowledgments, and so I give thanks for all of the spirited bodies, past and future, graciously haunting this text.

NOTES

INTRODUCTION

1. Lisa Isherwood and Elizabeth Stuart, *Introducing Body Theology*, Introductions in Feminist Theology (Sheffield, England: Sheffield Academic Press, 1998), 16.

2. While I do not deploy the method of phenomenology, I am much helped by the influence of Merleau-Ponty and his "flesh of the world" upon the works of Glen Mazis, Richard Kearney, and Mayra Rivera. See, as a recent example, Richard Kearney and Brian Treanor, eds., *Carnal Hermeneutics* (New York: Fordham University Press, 2015).

3. Mayra Rivera, *Poetics of the Flesh* (Durham, NC: Duke University Press, 2015), 26.

4. "For he [the Logos] became human that we might be made god." Athanasius, *De Incarnatione*, ed. and trans. Robert W. Thomson (Oxford: Clarendon Press, 1971), 54.3. On the relation of ancient theosis to Psalm 82, see Carl Mosser, "The Earliest Patristic Interpretations of Psalm 82, Jewish Antecedents, and the Origin of Christian Deification," *Journal of Theological Studies* 56, no. 1 (April 2005).

5. Daniel Boyarin, *Borderlines: The Partition of Judeo-Christianity* (Philadelphia: University of Pennsylvania Press, 2004).

6. J. Kameron Carter, *Race: A Theological Account* (Oxford: Oxford University Press, 2008).

7. Adrienne Rich, "Integrity," in *A Wild Patience Has Taken Me This Far: Poems 1978–1981* (New York: W. W. Norton, 1993), 8. Key to my first book, *From a Broken Web: Separation, Sexism and Self* (Boston: Beacon Press, 1986).

8. Nicholas of Cusa, "On the Summit of Contemplation," in *Nicholas of Cusa: Selected Spiritual Writings*, trans. H. Lawrence Boyd (Mahwah, NJ: Paulist Press, 2005).

9. See "After: Theopoetics of the Cloud," in Catherine Keller, *Cloud of the Impossible: Negative Theology and Planetary Entanglement* (New York: Columbia University Press, 2015).

10. Richard Kearney, *Anatheism: Returning to God after God* (New York: Columbia University Press, 2011).

11. John D. Caputo, *The Insistence of God: A Theology of Perhaps* (Bloomington: Indiana University Press, 2013), 22.

12. Laurel Schneider, "Promiscuous Incarnation," in *The Embrace of Eros: Bodies, Desires, and Sexuality in Christianity*, ed. Margaret Kamitsuka (Minneapolis: Fortress Press, 2010).

13. Karmen MacKendrick, *Word Made Skin: Figuring Language at the Surface of Flesh* (New York: Fordham University Press, 2004), 172.

14. Emily Dickinson, "We Learned the Whole of Love," in *Final Harvest: Emily Dickinson's Poems*, ed. Thomas H. Johnson (New York: Little, Brown, and Co., 1962), 144.

15. Saint John Damascene, *On Holy Images*, trans. Mary H. Allies (London: Thomas Baker, 1898), 15–16.

16. Catherine Keller, *Face of the Deep: A Theology of Becoming* (New York: Routledge, 2003).

17. "Skillful Means," in *The Lotus Sutra: A Contemporary Translation of a Buddhist Classic*, trans. Gene Reeves (Boston: Wisdom Publications, 2008), 95.

18. Gilles Deleuze and Felix Guattari, *What Is Philosophy?*, trans. Hugh Tomlinson and Graham Burchill (New York: Verso Books, 1994), 86.

1. RETURNING GOD: GIFT OF FEMINIST THEOLOGY

1. Biblical citations are taken from the New Revised Standard Version.

2. Ernst Bloch, *The Principle of Hope* (Cambridge, MA: MIT Press, 1986; German edition 1959). I explore Bloch and other apocalyptic posthistories in *Apocalypse Now and Then: A Feminist Guide to the End of the World* (Boston: Beacon Press, 1996).

3. Claire Démar, "Ma Loi d'avenir," cited in Leslie Wahl Rabine, "Essentialism and Its Contexts: Saint Simonian and Poststructuralist Feminists," in *The Essential Difference*, ed. Naomi Schor and Elizabeth Weed (Bloomington: Indiana University Press, 1994), 133.

4. Jacques Derrida, *The Gift of Death*, trans. David Willis (Chicago: University of Chicago Press, 1995), 80.

5. Alice Walker, *The Color Purple* (San Diego: Harcourt Brace Jovanovich, 1982), 168.

6. Nelle Morton, *The Journey Is Home* (Boston: Beacon Press, 1985), 50.

7. For example, classic texts of feminist theology: Mary Daly, *Beyond God the Father* (Boston: Beacon Press, 1973); Elizabeth Johnson, *She Who Is: The Mystery of God in Feminist Theological Discourse* (New York: Crossroad, 1992).

8. The theme of "the gift" has played a key role in the margins between poststructuralism and theology, for example, *God, the Gift and Postmodernism*,

ed. John D. Caputo and Michael J. Scanlon (Bloomington: Indiana University Press, 1999).

9. Jacques Derrida, *The Gift of Death*, 76.

10. Sarah Coakley's "In Defense of Sacrifice: Gender, Selfhood, and the Binding of Isaac," in which Isaac appears as a feminist hero, counterbalances any facile feminist dismissal of the Abrahamic sacrificial symbolism. In *Feminism, Sexuality, and the Return of the Religion*, ed. Linda Martin Alcoff and John D. Caputo (Bloomington: Indiana University Press, 2011).

11. Naomi R. Goldenberg, *Changing of the Gods: Feminism and the End of Traditional Religions* (Boston: Beacon Press, 1980), 3. It was to Syracuse, the site of the conference, that she returned.

12. See Cornel West, *Democracy Matters: Winning the Fight against Imperialism* (New York: Penguin Press, 2004).

13. George Lakoff, *Don't Think of an Elephant: Know Your Values and Frame the Debate* (White River Junction, VT: Chelsea Green Publishing, 2004).

14. Negative theology refers to the mystical tradition of the unknowability or unspeakability of the divine. For its theological genealogy, as well as an account of its reappearance in philosophical deconstruction, see Catherine Keller, *Cloud of the Impossible: Negative Theology and Planetary Entanglement* (New York: Columbia University Press, 2015). Key here is Jacques Derrida, *On the Name*, ed. Thomas Dutoit, trans. David Wood, John P. Leavey Jr., and Ian McLeod (Palo Alto, CA: Stanford University Press, 1995). For a rich introductory map of the relation of Derrida to the apophatic, see John D. Caputo, *The Prayers and Tears of Jacques Derrida: Religion without Religion* (Bloomington: Indiana University Press, 1997).

15. Building in feminist directions on the subtle tensions between the Christian apophatic discourse and poststructuralism, see the excellent essay by Sigridur Gudmarsdottir, "Feminist Apophasis: Beverly J. Lanzetta and Trinh T. Minh-ha in Dialog," *Feminist Theology: The Journal of the Britain & Ireland School of Feminist Theology* (January 2008); and Mary-Jane Rubenstein, "Unknow Thyself: Apophaticism, Deconstruction and Theology after Ontotheology," *Modern Theology* 19, no. 3 (July 2003).

16. See Kevin Hart's reflection on this bit of Derrida in *Trespass of the Sign: Deconstruction, Theology and Philosophy* (New York: Fordham University Press, 2000), 47. "My position," writes Hart indispensably, "is not that deconstruction is a form of negative theology but that negative theology is a form of deconstruction" (186).

17. See Catherine Keller, *Face of the Deep: A Theology of Becoming* (New York: Routledge, 2003).

18. Lydia York, "Chora: Feminist Theological Cosmology and Psychoanalysis in an Age of Teletechnology" (PhD diss., Drew University, 2016). ProQuest (AAT 10108939).

19. Ellen T. Armour, *Deconstruction, Feminist Theology, and the Problem of Difference: Subverting the Race/Gender Divide* (Chicago: University of Chicago Press, 1999), 183.

20. Judith Butler, *Undoing Gender* (New York: Routledge, 2004), 16.

21. Zadie Smith, *White Teeth* (New York: Vintage, 2000), 65.

22. Ibid., 438–39.

23. Marcella Althaus-Reid, *The Queer God* (New York: Routledge, 2003), 53. See especially chap. 3, "Queering God in Relationships: Trinitarians and God the Orgy."

24. As to the specifically same-sex effects, especially between women, see Bernadette Brooten, *Love between Women: Early Christian Responses to Female Homoeroticism* (Chicago: University of Chicago Press, 1996), and Antoinette Clark Wire, *The Corinthian Women Prophets: A Reconstruction through Paul's Rhetoric* (Minneapolis: Fortress, 1990).

25. For a discussion of the emergence of the Christian idea of infinity in the negative theology of Gregory of Nyssa and subsequent apophatic thinkers, see "Cloud-Writing: A Genealogy of the Luminous Dark," in my recent *Cloud of the Impossible: Negative Theology and Planetary Entanglement* (New York: Columbia University Press, 2015).

26. John Wesley, "Upon Our Lord's Sermon on the Mount, III," discussed in John B. Cobb Jr., *Grace and Responsibility: A Wesleyan Theology for Today* (Nashville, TN: Abingdon Press, 1995), 50.

27. For a discussion of Cusa, see "Enfolding and Unfolding God: Cusanic Complicatio," in my *Cloud of the Impossible*. Alfred North Whitehead's concept of "the primordial nature of God," which occurs in chiasmic relation to "the consequent nature," signifies the attractive force of pure possibility; see Whitehead's *Process and Reality*, ed. David Ray Griffin and Donald W. Sherburne, corr. ed. (New York: Free Press, 1978). Richard Kearney, *The God Who May Be: A Hermeneutics of Religion* (Bloomington: Indiana University Press, 2001).

28. Meister Eckhart, "Sermon 52: Beati paupers spiritu, quoniam ipsorum est regnum caelorum," in Meister Eckhart, *The Essential Sermons, Commentaries, Treatises, and Defense*, ed. Edmund Colledge and Bernard McGinn (New York: Paulist Press, 1981), 200, 202; John D. Caputo, *The Weakness of God: A Theology of the Event* (Bloomington: Indiana University Press, 2006), 33, 271–73, 277.

29. Gianni Vattimo, "Toward a Nonreligious Christianity," in John D. Caputo and Gianni Vatimo, *After the Death of God*, ed. Jeffrey W. Robbins (New York: Columbia University Press, 2007), 45.

30. Caputo, *The Weakness of God*, 269.

31. John B. Cobb Jr., "Commonwealth and Empire," in *The American Empire and the Commonwealth of God: A Political, Economic, Religious Statement*, ed. David Ray Griffin, John B. Cobb Jr., Richard A. Falk, and Catherine Keller (Louisville, KY: Westminster John Knox Press, 2006).

32. Caputo, *The Weakness of God*, 269.

33. John Milbank, *Being Reconciled: Ontology and Pardon* (London: Routledge, 2003), 160; see also my "Is That All? Gift and Reciprocity in Milbank's *Being Reconciled*," in *Interpreting the Postmodern: Responses to "Radical Orthodoxy*,*"* ed. Rosemary Radford Ruether and Marion Grau (New York: T & T Clark, 2006).

34. Rita Nakashima Brock, *Journeys by Heart: A Christology of Erotic Power* (New York: Crossroad, 1988); Rita Nakashima Brock and Rebecca Parker, *Proverbs of Ashes: Violence, Redemptive Suffering, and the Search for What Saves Us* (Boston: Beacon Press, 2001).

35. Vis-á-vis Mauss, the "primitive" gift, deconstruction, and radical orthodoxy, see Marion Grau's illumining "'We Must Give Ourselves to Voyaging': Regifting the Theological Present," in *Interpreting the Postmodern: Responses to "Radical Orthodoxy*,*"* ed. Rosemary Radford Ruether and Marion Grau (New York: T & T Clark, 2006).

36. For a multilayered analysis of the relations between deconstruction and ecology within theology and philosophy, see Laurel Kearns and Catherine Keller, eds., *Ecospirit: Religions and Philosophies for the Earth* (New York: Fordham University Press, 2007).

37. Catherine Keller, "The Flesh of God: A Metaphor in the Wild," in *Theology That Matters: Ecology, Economy, and God*, ed. Darby Kathleen Ray (Minneapolis: Fortress Press, 2006).

38. Laurel Schneider, *Beyond Monotheism: A Theology of Multiplicity* (New York: Routledge, 2007). See also her "Promiscuous Incarnation," in *The Embrace of Eros: Bodies, Desires, and Sexuality in Christianity*, ed. Margaret Kamitsuka (Minneapolis, MN: Fortress Press, 2010).

39. Sylvia Marcos, *Take from the Lips: Gender and Eros in Mesoamerican Religions* (Boston: Brill, 2006), 64.

40. Hadewijch, "Defense of Love," in *Hadewijch: The Complete Works*, trans. Columba Hart (New York: Paulist Press, 1980), 176.

41. Jean-Luc Marion, *God without Being*, trans. Thomas A. Carlson (Chicago: University of Chicago Press, 1991), 138.

42. Hadewijch, "The Noble Valiant Heart," in *Hadewijch*, 184.

43. Hadewijch, "Subjugation to Love," in *Hadewijch*, 194.

44. In *Face of the Deep*, I translate the *Elohim* of Genesis, which is grammatically plural yet takes the singular verb, as "Manyone" and as a cocreative plurisingularity.

45. Hélène Cixous, *"Coming to Writing" and Other Essays*, ed. Deborah Jenson, trans. Sarah Cornell, Ann Liddle, and Susan Sellers (Cambridge, MA: Harvard University Press, 1991), 41.

2. "AND TRUTH—SO MANIFOLD!": TRANSFEMINIST ENTANGLEMENTS

1. Emily Dickinson, *Final Harvest: Emily Dickinson's Poems*, ed. Thomas H. Johnson (New York: Little, Brown, and Co., 1962), 144.
2. I would like to claim to have had transgender developments more than faintly in mind when I wrote, but now gladly affirm the resonance. Others were already there. See, for instance, Emi Koyama, "Transfeminist Manifesto," in *Catching a Wave: Reclaiming Feminism for the Twenty-First Century*, ed. Rory Dicker and Alison Piepmeier (Boston: Northeastern University Press, 2003).
3. Robert Weisbuch, *Emily Dickinson's Poetry* (Chicago: University of Chicago Press, 1975), 74. I thank Robert, erstwhile president of Drew University, for rich conversation on Dickinson and Whitman.
4. Nicholas of Cusa, *De docta ignorantia*, in *Nicholas of Cusa: Selected Spiritual Writings*, trans. H. Lawrence Bond (New York: Paulist, 1997).
5. Augustine, *Confessions* XII.26. See also Catherine Keller, "'Mother Most Dear': Augustine's Dark Secrets," in *The Face of the Deep: A Theology of Becoming* (New York: Routledge, 2003).
6. Laurel Schneider, *Beyond Monotheism: A Theology of Multiplicity* (New York: Routledge, 2008).
7. Catherine Keller and Laurel Schneider, eds., *Polydoxy: Theology of Multiplicity and Relation* (New York: Routledge, 2011).
8. Catherine Keller, "The Entangled Cosmos: An Experiment in Physical Theopoetics," *Journal of Cosmology* 20 (2012); Catherine Keller, "Undoing and Unknowing: Judith Butler in Process," in *Butler on Whitehead: On the Occasion*, ed. Roland Faber, Michael Halewood, and Deena M. Lin (Lanham, MD: Lexington Books, 2012); Catherine Keller, *Cloud of the Impossible: Negative Theology and Planetary Entanglement* (New York: Columbia University Press, 2015).
9. Nelle Morton, *The Journey Is Home* (Boston: Beacon Press, 1985).
10. Catherine Keller, "The Apophasis of Gender: A Fourfold Unsaying of Feminist Theology," *Journal of the American Academy of Religion* 76, no. 4 (2008).
11. Ibid.
12. Kimberlé Crenshaw, "Mapping the Margins: Intersectionality, Identity Politics, and Violence against Women of Color," *Stanford Law Review* 42, no. 6 (1991).
13. Catherine Keller, "Be a Multiplicity: Ancestral Anticipations," in Keller and Schneider, *Polydoxy*.

14. Antoinette Brown Blackwell, *The Making of the Universe: Evolution, the Continuous Process Which Derives the Finite from the Infinite* (Boston: Gorham Press, 1914), 18.

15. Ibid., 20.

16. Ibid., 22.

17. Catherine Keller, *From a Broken Web: Separation, Sexism, and Self* (Boston: Beacon Press, 1986).

18. Karen Barad, "Posthumanist Performativity: Toward an Understanding of How Matter Comes to Matter," *Signs* 28, no. 3 (2008).

19. Sallie McFague, *The Body of God: An Ecological Theology* (Minneapolis, MN: Augsburg Press, 1993).

20. The phrase "body without organs"—first used by Deleuze to designate a body as resistant to any organization into parts in *The Logic of Sense*, ed. Constantin V. Boundas, trans. Mark Lester with Charles Stivale (New York: Columbia University Press, 1990)—is elaborated in Gilles Deleuze and Felix Guattari, *A Thousand Plateaus*, trans. Brian Massumi (Minneapolis: University of Minnesota Press, 1987). For example, see 160–61, as the site of nonhierarchical intensities produced by deterritorialization.

21. Gilles Deleuze, *Difference and Repetition*, trans. Paul Patton (New York: Columbia University Press, 1994); Michael Hardt and Antonio Negri, *Multitude: War and Democracy in the Age of Empire* (New York: Penguin Books, 2004). James Joyce's "chaosmos" recurs in Deleuze's works and also in my *Face of the Deep*.

22. Blackwell, *The Making of the Universe*, 32.

23. Alice Walker, preface to *The Color Purple* (New York: Harcourt Brace Jovanovich, 1992), xi.

24. Judith Butler, *Giving an Account of Oneself* (New York: Fordham University Press, 2005), 40.

25. Ivone Gebara, *Longing for Running Water: Ecofeminism and Liberation*, trans. David Molineaux (Minneapolis, MN: Augsburg Fortress Press, 1999), 132.

26. Ibid., 51.

27. Elliot Wolfson, *Language, Eros, Being: Kabbalistic Hermeneutics and Poetic Imagination* (New York: Fordham University Press, 2005), 289.

28. Alice Walker, *Overcoming Speechlessness: A Poet Encounters the Horror in Rwanda, Eastern Congo, and Palestine/Israel* (New York: Seven Stories Press, 2010).

29. John Thatamanil, "God as Ground, Contingency, and Relation," in Keller and Schneider, *Polydoxy*, 251.

30. For a discussion of the concept of the *complicatio*, "folding together" of all in the Infinite, see my discussion of Nicholas of Cusa, "Enfolding and Unfolding God: Cusanic *Complicatio*," in my *Cloud of the Impossible*.

31. This phrase from Tertullian is quoted in my *Face of the Deep*, 231.

32. Blackwell, *The Making of the Universe*, 28.

3. NUDA VERITAS: ICONOCLASH AND INCARNATION

1. Max Hollein, foreword to Tobias G. Natter and Max Hollein, eds., *The Naked Truth: Klimt, Schiele, Kokoschka and Other Scandals* (Berlin: Prestel, 2005), 10.

2. Ibid., 9.

3. Ibid., 9.

4. Frank Wedekind, quoted in Christina von Braun, "Shame and Shamelessness," in Natter and Hollein, *The Naked Truth*, 44.

5. Ibid., 54.

6. Marcella Althaus-Reid, *Indecent Theology* (London: Routledge, 2000).

7. Marie-José Mondzain, *Image, Icon, Economy* (Stanford, CA: Stanford University Press, 2004), 91.

8. At the turn of the century, this flattening of the visual plain, as an exploration of the aesthetic surface and its two dimensions, was revolutionary. If it reacts against the establishment, the academic style, with its two-dimensional effect of the third dimension, it is not a mere return to the flatness and irrealism of medieval images, themselves largely following the tradition of Byzantine iconography. But then modern art also in its abstraction will get inspiration from certain returns to icon, starting early with Picasso's inspiration by El Greco (whose father was an orthodox icon painter on Crete) and also of the decorative arts of Africa and other so-called primitive styles.

9. Klimt's startling use of oil and gold was popularized in the 2015 British movie, *Woman in Gold*. It tells the gripping narrative of a different painting, *Portrait of Adele Bloch-Bauer I*, seized by the Nazis and now on display in the Neue Galerie New York.

10. Mondzain, *Image, Icon, Economy*, 88, 90.

11. The First Iconoclasm, as it is sometimes called, lasted between about 726 and 787 CE. The Second Iconoclasm was between 814 and 842 CE.

12. Mondzain, *Image, Icon, Economy*, 88.

13. Saint John Damascene, *On Holy Images*, trans. Mary H. Allies (London: Thomas Baker, 1898), 15–16.

14. Pseudo-Dionysius, *The Mystical Theology*, in *Pseudo-Dionysius: The Complete Works*, trans. Colm Lubheid (Mahwah, NJ: Paulist, 1997), chaps. 1 and 3.

15. Dionysius the Areopagite, *On the Divine Names and the Mystical Theology*, trans. Clarence E. Rolt (New York: Cosimo Classics, 2007), 193.

16. For a succinct summation of the relation of icons to a subsequent tradition, largely apophatic, see Emil Ivanov, "Iconographic Interpretations of

Theological Themes in Pseudo-Dionysius the Areopagite and in St. Gregory Palamas and the Reception of these Themes by Meister Eckhart," *Studii Teologice* 7, no. 4 (October 2011).

17. Mondzain, *Image, Icon, Economy*, 90.

18. Michael Hardt and Antonio Negri, *Multitude: War and Democracy in the Age of Empire* (New York: Penguin Books, 2004), 325.

19. For a discussion of the politically charged effects of the Christian reception of prophetic hope, outlined in Norman Cohn's *Pursuit of the Millennium* and Ernst Bloch's "Christian Social Utopias" in *The Principle of Hope*, see Catherine Keller, *Apocalypse Now and Then* (Minneapolis, MN: Fortress Press, 1996), chaps. 3 and 5.

20. Damascene, *On Holy Images*, 15–16.

21. Berndt Apke, "A Farewell to Allegory," in Natter and Hollein, *The Naked Truth*, 104.

22. Ibid., 11.

23. Ibid., 108.

24. Ludwig Hevesi, quoted in Apke, "A Farewell to Allegory," in Natter and Hollein, *The Naked Truth*, 104.

25. Hollein, foreword to Natter and Hollein, *The Naked Truth*, 11.

26. Jean-Luc Marion, *In Excess: Studies of Saturated Phenomena* (New York: Fordham University Press, 2002), 75.

27. Ibid., 196.

28. Mondzain, *Image, Icon, Economy*, 90.

29. Jean-Luc Nancy, *The Ground of the Image* (New York: Fordham University Press, 2010), 10, 12, 9.

30. Ibid., 10.

31. Bruno Latour, "Clothing the Naked Truth," in *Dismantling Truth: Reality in the Post-Modern World*, ed. Hilary Lawson and Lisa Appignanesi (London: Weidenfeld & Nicholson, 1989), 115.

32. Bruno Latour and Peter Weibel, eds., *Iconoclash: Beyond the Image Wars in Science, Religion and Art* (Cambridge, MA: MIT Press, 2002), 37.

4. TINGLES OF MATTER, TANGLES OF THEOLOGY: BODIES OF THE NEW(ISH) MATERIALISM

1. Evgueny Pazukhin, "The Christian Materialism of Blessed Josemariá Escrivá," Opus Dei: Tutta la Verita, March 1997, http://www.escriva.it/Ing/19970301.htm. Also, José María Escrivá de Balaguer, *Conversations with Monsignor Escrivá de Balaguer* (Dublin: Scepter Books, 1968), 115.

2. Karen Barad, *Meeting the Universe Halfway: Quantum Physics and the Entanglement of Matter and Meaning* (Durham, NC: Duke University Press, 2007), 396.

3. Biblical materiality thus springs into play in the opening of Genesis, quickly yielding the bodily Edenic expulsion, the necessity of the law in all the Torah codes of the Pentateuch, then the prophets with a new vocalization of material threat (the collective injustice) and promise (the new heaven and earth). In the later texts (especially Ezekiel) the resurrection motif appears as the renewal of the people, gradually compressible into individual bodies.

4. Colleen McDannell, *Material Christianity: Religion and Popular Culture in America* (New Haven, CT: Yale University Press, 1995). See also Robert A. Orsi, *The Madonna of 115th Street: Faith and Community in Italian Harlem, 1880–1950* (New Haven, CT: Yale University Press, 1985).

5. Marie-José Mondzain, *Image, Icon, Economy: The Byzantine Origins of the Contemporary Imaginary* (Stanford, CA: Stanford University Press, 2005), 90.

6. Caroline Walker Bynum, *The Resurrection of the Body in Western Christianity, 200–1336* (New York: Columbia University Press, 1995), 186–87.

7. Dick Houtman and Birgit Meyer, *Things: Religion and the Question of Materiality* (New York: Fordham University Press, 2012).

8. For further discussions of the complex materialities of Christian practices, see Caroline Walker Bynum, *Christian Materiality: An Essay on Religion in Late Medieval Europe* (New York: Zone Books, 2011).

9. Jane Bennett, *Vibrant Matter: A Political Ecology of Things* (Durham, NC: Duke University Press, 2010), 121.

10. Ibid., ch. 6, "Stem Cells and the Culture of Life."

11. Slavoj Žižek, John Milbank, and Creston Davis, *The Monstrosity of Christ: Paradox or Dialectic?* (Cambridge, MA: MIT Press, 2009), 206.

12. Ibid., 111.

13. Ibid., 125.

14. Ibid., 131.

15. Slavoj Žižek, "Dialectical Clarity versus the Misty Conceit of Paradox," in Žižek, Milbank, and Davis, *The Monstrosity of Christ*, 240.

16. Quantum entanglement is the subject of the chapter "Spooky Entanglements: The Physics of Nonseparability," in Catherine Keller, *Cloud of the Impossible: Negative Theology and Planetary Entanglement* (New York: Columbia University Press, 2015). A shorter version has been published online: "The Entangled Cosmos: An Experiment in Physical Theopoetics," *Journal of Cosmology* (September 2012), http://journalofcosmology.com/JOC20/Keller_rev1.pdf.

17. Alfred North Whitehead, *Science and the Modern World*: Lowell Lectures, *1925* (New York: Free Press, 1925/1967), 35.

18. Alfred North Whitehead, *Process and Reality: An Essay in Cosmology*, ed. David Ray Griffin and Donald W. Sherburne (New York: Free Press, 1978), 94.

19. Whitehead, *Science and Modern World*, 49.
20. Ibid., 51.
21. Barad, *Meeting the Universe Halfway*, 184.
22. Whitehead, *Process and Reality*, 78, 79.
23. Whitehead, *Science and the Modern World*, 175–76.
24. Barad, *Meeting the Universe Halfway*, 139.
25. Whitehead, *Process and Reality*, 91.
26. Ibid., 40.
27. Bernard d'Espagnat, *On Physics and Philosophy* (Princeton, NJ: Princeton University Press, 2006), 19.
28. William E. Connolly, *The Fragility of Things: Self-Organizing Processes, Neoliberal Fantasies, and Democratic Activism* (Durham, NC: Duke University Press, 2013), 154.
29. Keller, *Cloud of the Impossible*, 263.
30. Connolly, *The Fragility of Things*, 154.
31. William Connolly, *Capitalism and Christianity, American Style* (Durham, NC: Duke University Press, 2009), 39–40.
32. Barad, *Meeting the Universe Halfway*, 122.
33. Ibid., 372.
34. Ibid., 375.
35. Ibid., 380.
36. Ibid., 381.
37. Isabelle Stengers, Michael Chase, and Bruno Latour, *Thinking with Whitehead: A Free and Wild Creation of Concepts* (Cambridge, MA: Harvard University Press, 2011).
38. John B. Cobb, *Christ in a Pluralistic Age* (Philadelphia, PA: Westminster Press, 1975).
39. "We find ourselves in a buzzing world, amid a democracy of fellow creatures, whereas, under some disguise or other, orthodox philosophy can only introduce us to solitary substances, each enjoying an illusory experience: 'O Botton, thou art changed! What do I see on thee?'" Whitehead, *Process and Reality*, 59.
40. Roland Faber and Catherine Keller, "A Taste for Multiplicity: The Skillful Means of Religious Pluralism," in *Religions in the Making: Whitehead and the Wisdom Traditions of the World*, ed. John Cobb (Eugene, OR: Cascade Books, 2012).
41. See Catherine Keller and Laurel C. Schneider, introduction to *Polydoxy: Theology of Multiplicity and Relation* (New York: Routledge, 2011). See also Mary-Jane Rubenstein and Kathryn Tanner, eds., *Polydox Reflections*, Directions in Modern Theology, vol. 30, no. 3 (Malden, MA: Wiley Blackwell, 2014).

42. A stream of thought unfolds the dialogue of science and religion in neighborly proximity to, but without direct dependence upon, Whiteheadian thought. Philip Clayton is the leading voice of this interdisciplinarity. See, for example, Clayton's recent works: *Signs of Solidarity: Mind and Emergence: From Quantum to Consciousness* (Oxford: Oxford University Press, 2006); *The Re-emergence of Emergence: The Emergentist Hypothesis from Science to Religion* (Oxford: Oxford University Press, 2008); *The Predicament of Belief: Science, Philosophy, and Christian Minimalism* (Oxford: Oxford University Press, 2011).

43. Whitehead, *Science and the Modern World*, 15–16.

44. See my recent *Cloud of the Impossible: Negative Theology and Plantery Entanglement* (New York: Columbia University Press, 2015). In particular, consider chap. 3, "Enfolding and Unfolding God: Cusanic Complicatio."

45. See Karsen Harries, *Infinity and Perspective* (Cambridge, MA: MIT Press, 2001). See also my chapter, "Enfolding and Unfolding God: Cusanic Complicatio," in *Cloud of the Impossible*; and Mary-Jane Rubenstein's *Worlds without End: The Many Lives of the Multiverse* (New York: Columbia University Press, 2014), esp. "End without End: Nicholas of Cusa."

46. Nicholas of Cusa, *De docta ignorantia*, in *Nicholas of Cusa: Selected Spiritual Writings*, trans. H. Lawrence Bond (New York: Paulist, 1997), 140.

47. Speaking of precarious opacities, fortunately even Judith Butler now also uses a language of ontological relationalism and has taken steps to correct her own anthropocentrism, in the context of a reading of Whitehead. See Roland Faber, Michael Halewood, and Deena Lin, *Butler on Whitehead: On the Occasion* (Lanham, MD: Lexington Books, 2012). See also my chapter on Butler, "Unsaying and Undoing: Judith Butler and the Ethics of Relational Ontology," in *Cloud of the Impossible*.

48. Sir Isaac Newton, *Opticks: Or, A Treatise of the Reflections, Refractions, Inflections and Colours of Light* (London: William Innys, 1730), 376.

49. Paul C. Davies and John Gribbin, *The Matter Myth: Dramatic Discoveries That Challenge Our Understanding of Physical Reality* (New York: Simon & Schuster, 1992), 17.

50. Louisa Gilder, *The Age of Entanglement: When Quantum Physics Was Reborn* (New York: Knopf, 2008), xv.

51. Richard Feynman, quoted in Michel Weber, *After Whitehead: Rescher on Process Metaphysics* (Frankfurt: Ontos, 2004), 100.

52. Meister Eckhart, *Meister Eckhart: The Essential Sermons, Commentaries, Treatises, and Defense*, trans. Edmund College and Bernard McGinn (Mahwah, NJ: Paulist, 1981), 53:208.

53. Chris Boesel and Catherine Keller, eds., *Apophatic Bodies: Negative Theology, Incarnation, and Relationality* (New York: Fordham University Press,

2010), esp. introduction and my essay, "The Cloud of the Impossible: Embodiment and Apophasis."

54. T. S. Eliot, "Burnt Norton," in *Four Quartets* (New York: Harcourt, Brace & World, 1936), 19.

55. Nicholas of Cusa, *De docta ignorantia*, 126. "Therefore the theology of negation is so necessary to the theology of affirmation that without it God would not be worshiped as the infinite God but as creature, and such worship is idolatry, for it gives to an image that which belongs only to truth itself."

56. Ibid., 140.

57. Mary-Jane Rubenstein asks, in her brilliant scan of multiverse theories past and present, if they "might mark the end of the fantasy that 'science' has wrested itself free from 'religion,' 'objectivity' free from subjectivity, and matter free from meaning?" Rubenstein, *Worlds without End*, 234.

58. Charles Hartshorne, *Omnipotence and Other Theological Mistakes* (Albany: SUNY Press, 1984). His briefly proposed metaphor of the "universe as the body of God" is then expanded by Sallie McFague as part of the ecofeminist archive. Sallie McFague, *The Body of God: An Ecological Theology* (Minneapolis, MN: Fortress Press, 1993).

59. "The Most Moved Mover" is Hartshorne's answer to the classical Unmoved Mover of orthodoxy; a development of Whitehead's "consequent nature of God," the aspect of the divine that becomes, and so has actuality, through the materializations of actual occasions. See Hartshorne's *Omnipotence and Other Theological Mistakes*.

60. Henry P. Stapp, *Mindful Universe: Quantum Mechanics and the Participating Observer* (Berlin: Springer, 2007), 332. Emphasis added.

61. N. David Mermin, "Is the Moon There When Nobody Looks? Reality and the Quantum Theory," *Physics Today* (April 1985).

62. See Jane Bennett, "A Vitalist Stopover on the Way to a New Materialism," in *New Materialisms: Ontology, Agency, and Politics*, ed. Diana H. Cool and Samantha Frost (Durham, NC: Duke University Press, 2010); see also Bennett, *Vibrant Matter*, ch. 5, "Neither Vitalism nor Mechanism."

63. David Ray Griffin, *Unsnarling the World-Knot: Consciousness, Freedom, and the Mind-Body Problem* (Berkeley: University of California Press, 1998), esp. chs. 6–10.

64. I have written about two thinkers considered vitalists or panpsychists: Anne Conway, whom I discovered in Carol Wayne White's *The Legacy of Anne Conway* (Albany: SUNY Press, 2008) and discuss at length in my piece "Be a Multiplicity: Ancestral Anticipations," in *Polydoxy: Theology of Multiplicity and Relation*, ed. Laurel C. Schneider and Catherine Keller (New York: Routledge, 2010); and Gustav Fechner, in my "The Luxuriating Lily: Fechner's Cosmos in Mahler's World," in *Mahler im Kontext/Contextualizing*

Mahler, ed. Erich Wolfgang Partsch and Morten Solvik (Vienna: Boehlau Verlag, 2011).

65. Whitney A. Bauman, *Religion and Ecology: Developing a Planetary Ethic* (New York: Columbia University Press, 2014), 172.

66. Ibid., esp. ch 6, "Developing Planetary Environmental Ethics: A Nomadic Polyamory of Place."

67. Thomas Berry's "Great Work" is being carried on especially in the activist ecotheological work of Mary Evelyn Tucker and John Grim. See their edited volume, *Living Cosmology: Christian Responses to "Journey of the Universe"* (Maryknoll, NY: Orbis Books, 2016). See also Heather Eato, ed., *The Intellectual Journey of Thomas Berry: Imagining the Earth Community* (Lanham, MD: Lexington Books, 2014).

68. Literally "vibrating" in Genesis 1:2, *meherephet*. See my *The Face of the Deep: A Theology of Becoming* (New York: Routledge, 2003).

69. See Mayra Rivera Rivera on Merleau-Ponty in *Poetics of the Flesh* (Durham, NC: Duke University Press, 2015).

70. Marcella Althaus-Reid, *Indecent Theology: Theological Perversions in Sex, Gender and Politics* (London: Routledge, 2000), 53–54.

71. Bauman, *Religion and Ecology*, 128.

72. Alfred North Whitehead, *Adventures of Ideas* (New York: Macmillan, 1933).

73. Vicki Kirby, *Quantum Anthropologies: Life at Large* (Durham, NC: Duke University Press, 2011).

74. Mary-Jane Rubenstein, *Strange Wonder: The Closure of Metaphyics and the Opening of Awe* (New York: Columbia University Press, 2009).

75. Barad, *Meeting the Universe Halfway*, 396.

76. Ibid.

5. CONFESSING MONICA: READING AUGUSTINE READING HIS MOTHER

1. Translations of *Confessions* generally follow either R. S. Pine-Coffin (London: Penguin Books, 1961) or John K. Ryan (Garden City, NY: Image Books/Doubleday, 1960). The Latin critical edition is *Corpus Christianorum, Series Latina*, vol. 27 (Turnhout, Belgium: Brepolis, 1981), 33.

2. Danuta Shanzer, "Latent Narrative Patterns, Allegorical Choices, and Literary Unity in Augustine's *Confessions*," *Vigilae Christianae* 46, no. 1 (1992): 45.

3. Shanzer, "Latent Narrative Patterns," 53.

4. John J. Winkler, *Auctor and Actor: A Narratological Reading of Apuleius's "The Golden Ass"* (Berkeley: University of California Press, 1985), 273.

5. Winkler, *Auctor and Actor*, 179, 124.

6. Winkler, *Auctor and Actor*, 141.

Notes to pages 91–108

7. Peter Brown, *Augustine of Hippo: A Biography* (Berkeley: University of California Press, 1967), 164.

8. Luce Irigaray, *Speculum of the Other Woman*, trans. Gillian C. Gill (Ithaca, NY: Cornell University Press, 1985), 318.

9. Nelle Morton, *The Journey Is Home* (Boston: Beacon Press, 1985), 127–28.

10. Irigaray, *Speculum of the Other Woman*, 318.

11. *Creatio ex profundis* is the alternative to *creatio ex nihilo* offered in my *Face of the Deep: A Theology of Becoming* (New York: Routledge, 2003).

12. Hannah Arendt, *Love and St. Augustine*, ed. and with an interpretive essay by Joanna Vecchiarelli Scott and Judith Chelius Stark (Chicago: University of Chicago Press, 1996), 147. For a discussion on natality in Arendt as she reads Augustine, see Grace Jantzen, *Becoming Divine* (Bloomington: Indiana University Press, 1999), 145–55.

13. Arendt, *Love and St. Augustine*, 147.

6. THE BECOMING OF THEOPOETICS: A BRIEF, INCONGRUENT HISTORY

1. Richard Kearney, *Anatheism: Returning to God after God* (New York: Columbia University Press, 2010).

2. Clement of Alexandria, *The Miscellanies*, IV.23.

3. Saint Basil the Great of Caesarea (330–379 CE), cited in Michael Christensen, "The Problem, Promise, and Process of Theosis," in *Partakers of the Divine Nature: The History and Development of Deification in the Christian Traditions*, ed. Michael J. Christensen and Jeffrey Wittung (Madison, NJ: Fairleigh Dickinson University Press, 2007), 23.

4. Thomas Buchan, "Paradise as the Landscape of Salvation in Ephrem the Syrian," in Christensen and Wittung, *Partakers of the Divine Nature*, 147.

5. Athanasius, *De Incarnationes* 54.3, in *Contra Gentes and De Incarnatione*, ed. and trans. Robert W. Thompson, Oxford Early Christian Texts (Oxford: Clarendon Press, 1971), 268. See also the discussion of Irenaeus and Athanasius in Catherine Keller, *Face of the Deep: A Theology of Becoming* (New York: Routledge, 2003).

6. See especially my colleague Michael J. Christensen's "The Problem, Promise, and Process of Theosis," in Christensen and Wittung, *Partakers of the Divine Nature*, 25.

7. Yet there were traces of a more cosmic or mystical sense of participation in God all along, and before the Wesley brothers. For instance, the Finnish school of interpretation, including such theologians as Veli-Matti Kärkkäinen, has recently argued for an alternative interpretation of Luther, for instance, as offering a far more participatory sacramentalism than the later Luther and subsequent orthodoxy retained. For a superb disclosure and

development of this cosmologically participatory Protestantism see Terra Rowe, *Toward a Better Worldliness: Ecology, Economy, and the Protestant Tradition* (Minneapolis, MN: Fortress Press, 2017).

8. "And we the life of God shall know, For God is manifest below." John Wesley, quoted in Michael J. Christensen, "John Wesley: Christian Perfection as Faith Filled with the Energy of Love," in Christensen and Wittung, *Partakers of the Divine Nature*, 224.

9. Vladimir Kharlamov, *The Beauty of the Unity and the Harmony of the Whole: The Concept of* Theosis *in the Theology of Pseudo-Dionysius the Areopagite* (Eugene, OR: Wipf and Stock, 2009).

10. Luce Irigaray is here quoted in Morny Joy, Kathleen O'Grady, Judith L. Poxon, eds., *Religion in French Feminist Thought: Critical Perspectives* (London: Routledge, 2003), 8. Emphasis added.

11. Grace Jantzen, *Becoming Divine: Towards a Feminist Philosophy of Religion* (Bloomington: Indiana University Press, 1999).

12. Quoted in the text Roland Faber chooses as an epigraph to *God as Poet of the World: Exploring Process Theologies* (Louisville, KY: Westminster John Knox, 2008).

13. Alfred North Whitehead, *Adventures of Ideas* (New York: Free Press, 1933/1961), 253; Alfred North Whitehead, *Process and Reality*, ed. David Ray Griffin and Donald W. Sherburne (New York: Free Press, 1978), 346.

14. Faber, *God as Poet of the World*, 151.

15. Whitehead, *Process and Reality*, 346.

16. Amos Niven Wilder, *Theopoetic: Theology and the Religious Imagination* (Lima, OH: Academic Renewal Press, 2001), iv.

17. David Leroy Miller, "Theopoetry or Theopoetics?" *Cross Currents* 60, no. 1 (2010): 9.

18. Stanley Hopper, *Interpretation: The Poetry of Meaning*, ed. David L. Miller (New York: Harcourt Brace, 1967), xix–xxi. If the "nexus of events" seems to refer to Whitehead, it would today tend to signify a quite different conceptual web of, for instance, the philosophies of Deleuze, Badiou, and Derrida, hardly innocent of Heidegger. But then these are being brought to bear upon Whitehead's own event-nexus.

19. See discussion of Hopper's use of Wallace Stevens in David L. Miller, "Theopoiesis: A Perspective on the Work of Stanley Romaine Hopper," in *Why Persimmons and Other Poems: Transformation of Theology in Poetry*, by Stanley Romaine Hopper (Atlanta, GA: Scholars Press, 1987), 7.

20. Roland Faber, Henry Krips, and Daniel Pettus, *Event and Decision: Ontology and Politics Badiou, Deleuze and Whitehead* (Newcastle, UK: Cambridge Scholars Publishing, 2010).

21. Miller, "Theopoetry or Theopoetics?," 8.

22. Ibid., 10.
23. Ibid., 8.
24. John D. Caputo, *The Insistence of God: A Theology of Perhaps* (Bloomington: Indiana University Press, 2013), 67.
25. Ibid., 49.
26. Ibid.
27. Ibid.
28. Ibid., 27.
29. Faber, *God as Poet of the World*, 259–61. For a recapitulation of Faber's earlier thinking on God's insistence, see "'Insistenz'—Zum 'Nicht-Sein' Gottes bei Levinas, Deleuze und Whitehead," in *Das integrale und das gebrochene Gesetz. Zum 100. Geburtstag von Leo Gabriel*, ed. Y. B. Raynova and S. Moser (Frankfurt: Peter Lang, 2005).
30. "Out of the depths not out of nothing." This disputes Augustine's *non de deo sed ex nihilo*. See Keller, *Face of the Deep*.
31. Karen Barad, "Niels Bohr's Philosophy-Physics: Quantum Physics and the Nature of Knowledge and Reality," in *Meeting the Universe Halfway: Quantum Physics and the Entanglement of Matter and Meaning* (Durham, NC: Duke University Press, 2007).
32. Pope Francis, *Laudato Si': On Care for Our Common Home*, Encyclical letter (Huntington, IN: Our Sunday Visitor, 2015), 7. For an impressive and timely response to the encyclical, see John Cobb and Ignacio Castuera, eds., *For Our Common Home: Process-Relational Responses to Laudato Si'* (Anoka, MN: Process Century Press, 2015).
33. Nicholas of Cusa, *De docta ignorantia*, in *Nicholas of Cusa: Selected Spiritual Writings*, trans. H. Lawrence Bond (New York: Paulist, 1997), 140.
34. Quoted in Karsten Harries, *Infinity and Perspective* (Cambridge, MA: MIT Press, 2001), 59.
35. Nancy J. Hudson, *Becoming God: The Doctrine of Theosis in Nicholas of Cusa* (Lanham, MD: University of America Press).
36. Gilles Deleuze, *The Fold: Leibniz and the Baroque*, trans. Tom Conley (Minneapolis: University of Minnesota Press, 1993), 92.
37. Stephen Shaviro, *The Universe of Things: On Speculative Realism* (Minneapolis: University of Minnesota Press, 2014), 23.
38. Roland Faber, *The Divine Manifold* (Lanham, MD: Lexington Books, 2014), 125.
39. Chris Cillizza, "Pope Francis's Speech to Congress, Annotated," *Washington Post*, September 24, 2015, https://www.washingtonpost.com/news/the-fix/wp/2015/09/24/pope-franciss-speech-to-congress-annotated/.
40. Ernesto Cardenal, "Cantiga 2," in *Cosmic Canticle*, trans. John Lyons (Willimantic, CT: Curbstone Press, 2002), 17.

41. Ernesto Cardenal, "The Word," in *Pluriverse: New and Selected Poems*, ed. and trans. Jonathan Cohen et al. (New Directions: New York, 2009), 197.

7. DERRIDAPOCALYPSE

1. Jacques Derrida, "The Villanova Roundtable," in *Deconstruction in a Nutshell: A Conversation with Jacques Derrida*, ed. with a commentary by John D. Caputo (New York: Fordham University Press, 1997), 18.

2. Or was, at any rate, an auspicious day on which to tackle the Apocalypse of John: "I was in the spirit on the Lord's day" (Rev. 1:10).

3. Jacques Derrida, "Circumfession: Fifty-Nine Periods and Periphrases," in *Jacques Derrida*, by Geoffrey Bennington and Jacques Derrida (Chicago: University of Chicago Press, 1993), 155.

4. Derrida, "The Villanova Roundtable."

5. Derrida arrives at this conclusion through reflection on the inaugural moments of the Apocalypse in particular, in which the revelation passes from God to the seven churches by way of a circuitous series of relays: Jesus, an angel, John, John's written testimony . . . (Rev. 1:1–2). To this convoluted structure of relays—perpetually in danger of derailing or arriving at an unintended destination—Derrida perversely (re)attaches the term "apocalypse": "As soon as one no longer knows who speaks or who writes, the text becomes apocalyptic" (Jacques Derrida, "Of an Apocalyptic Tone Newly Adopted in Philosophy," trans. John P. Leavey Jr., in *Derrida and Negative Theology*, ed. Harold Coward and Toby Foshay [Albany: SUNY Press, 1992], 57). What apocalypse, thus reconceived, reveals is not, however, no one saying nothing to nobody but rather "a transcendental condition of all discourse, of all experience even, of every mark or every trace." As such, apocalypse is "an *exemplary* revelation of this transcendental structure" (ibid.). The essay was originally published as *D'un ton apocalyptique adopté naguère en philosophie* (Paris: Galilée, 1983)—unless we count the English translation of it that somehow managed to precede the French original by a year: see Jacques Derrida, "On a Newly Arisen Apocalyptic Tone in Philosophy," trans. John P. Leavey Jr., *Semeia* 23 (1982).

6. Jacques Derrida, "Faith and Knowledge: The Two Sources of 'Religion' at the Limits of Reason Alone," in *Acts of Religion*, ed. Gil Anidjar, trans. Mark Dooley and Michael Hughes (New York: Routledge, 2002), 98.

7. Jacques Derrida, *Memoirs of the Blind: The Self-Portrait and Other Ruins*, trans. Pascale Anne-Brault and Michael Naas (Chicago: University of Chicago Press, 1993), 12.

8. Ibid., 30; emphasis added.

9. "You do not realize that you are wretched, pitiable, poor, blind [tuphlos], and naked," the Son of Man harangues the Laodicean church.

"Therefore I counsel you to buy from me . . . salve to anoint your eyes so that you may see [hina blepe̅s]" (Rev. 3:17–18).

10. He continues: "Even the slightest testimony concerning the most plausible, ordinary or everyday thing cannot do otherwise: it must still appeal to faith as would a miracle" (Derrida, "Faith and Knowledge," 98).

11. Ibid., 99.

12. Ibid., 98.

13. Jacques Derrida, *On the Name*, ed. Thomas Dutoit, trans. David Wood, John P. Leavey Jr., and Ian McLeod (Stanford, CA: Stanford University Press, 1995), 59.

14. Jacques Lacan, *Feminine Sexuality: Jacques Lacan and the école freudienne*, ed. Juliet Mitchell and Jacqueline Rose, trans. Jacqueline Rose (New York: Norton, 1982), 152.

15. Jacques Lacan, *Écrits: The First Complete Edition in English*, trans. Bruce Fink (New York: Norton, 2006), 581.

16. Castration, in Lacanian terms, being the recognition that "the phallus, even the real phallus, is a *ghost*." Jacques Lacan, "Desire and the Interpretation of Desire in *Hamlet*," ed. Jacques-Alain Miller, trans. James Hulbert, in *Literature and Psychoanalysis: The Question of Reading, Otherwise*, ed. Shoshana Felman (Baltimore, MD: Johns Hopkins University Press, 1982), 50.

17. Especially as further pursuit of it would necessitate difficult passage through Derrida's own reading of Lacan (Jacques Derrida, "Le Facteur de la vérité," in *The Post Card: From Socrates to Freud and Beyond*, trans. Alan Bass [Chicago: University of Chicago Press, 1987]).

18. See David Aune, *Revelation 6–16*, Word Biblical Commentary 52B (Nashville, TN: Thomas Nelson, 1998), 393; Gregory Beale, *The Book of Revelation: A Commentary on the Greek Text*, The New International Greek New Testament Commentary (Grand Rapids, MI: Eerdmans, 1999), 375; William C. Weinrich, ed., *Revelation*, Ancient Christian Commentary on Scripture: New Testament 12 (Downers Grove, IL: InterVarsity Press, 2005), 82–83.

19. Revelations 5 describes the opening of a top-secret file and the breaking of its code. Chapters 6–9 and 14–16 display a series of spectacular, shock-and-awe–inducing air strikes. Chapter 19 reports on the last-resort, boots-on-the-ground operation, as the armies of heaven invade the kingdom of the beast.

20. Derrida, "Of an Apocalyptic Tone Newly Adopted in Philosophy," 64.

21. On justice, see: Jacques Derrida, *Acts of Religion*, ed. Gil Anidjar, trans. Mark Dooley and Michael Hughes (New York: Routledge, 2002). On hospitality: Jacques Derrida and Anne Dufourmantelle, *Of Hospitality: Anne Dufourmantelle Invites Jacques Derrida to Respond*, trans. Rachel Bowlby, Cultural

Memory in the Present (Stanford, CA: Stanford University Press, 2000); and Derrida, *Acts of Religion*. On the gift: Jacques Derrida, *Given Time I: Counterfeit Money*, trans. Peggy Kamuf (Chicago: University of Chicago Press, 1992), and Jacques Derrida, *The Gift of Death*, trans. David Wills (Chicago: University of Chicago Press, 1995). On democracy: Jacques Derrida, *Specters of Marx: The State of the Debt, the Work of Mourning, and the New International*, trans. Peggy Kamuf (New York: Routledge, 1994); Jacques Derrida, *Politics of Friendship*, trans. George Collins (London: Verso, 1997); and Jacques Derrida, *Rogues: Two Essays on Reason*, trans. Pascale-Anne Brault and Michael Naas, Meridian: Crossing Aesthetics (Stanford, CA: Stanford University Press, 2005). On the messianic: Jacques Derrida, *Specters of Marx*, 166–69; and Jacques Derrida, "Marx and Sons," in *Ghostly Demarcations: A Symposium on Jacques Derrida's* Specters of Marx, ed. Michael Sprinker, Radical Thinkers 33, (London: Verso, 1999), 250–56.

22. Maurice Blanchot, *The Writing of the Disaster*, trans. Ann Smock (Lincoln: University of Nebraska Press, 1986), 141–42; see also Derrida, *Politics of Friendship*, 46n14, 173–74; and Derrida, "The Villanova Roundtable," 24–25.

23. Derrida, "Marx and Sons," 250–51.

24. Derrida, *Politics of Friendship*, 174.

25. The *locus classicus* of this theme is Rev. 6:9–11, wherein "the souls of those who had been slaughtered for the word of God and for the testimony they had given [cry] out with a loud voice, 'Sovereign Lord, holy and true, how long will it be before you judge and avenge/exact justice for our blood [Heōs pote . . . ou krineis kai ekdikeis to haima hēmōn] on the inhabitants of the earth?'" They don't have long to wait, as it turns out (see Rev. 16:5–7; 19:1–2).

26. Although as *deute* rather than *erchou*.

27. His 1966 manifesto, "Structure, Sign, and Play in the Discourse of the Human Sciences," ended with "a glance toward those who . . . turn their eyes away when faced by the as yet unnamable which is proclaiming itself and which can do so . . . only under the species of the nonspecies, in the formless, mute, infant, and terrifying form of monstrosity" (Jacques Derrida, "Structure, Sign, and Play in the Discourse of the Human Sciences," in *Writing and Difference*, trans. Alan Bass [Chicago: University of Chicago Press, 1978], 293). And again a year later in *Of Grammatology*: "The future can only be anticipated in the form of an absolute danger. It is that which breaks absolutely with constituted normality and can only be proclaimed, *presented*, as a sort of monstrosity" (Jacques Derrida, *Of Grammatology*, trans. Gayatri Chakravorty Spivak [Baltimore, MD: Johns Hopkins University Press, 1976]).

28. Jacques Derrida, "Passages—from Traumatism to Promises," in *Points . . . Interviews, 1974–1994*, ed. Elisabeth Weber, trans. Peggy Kamuf

Notes to pages 127–30

et al., Meridian: Crossing Aesthetics (Stanford, CA: Stanford University Press, 1995), 387.

29. "It is happening everywhere, it is the world, it is today the singular figure of its being 'out of joint.'" If Derrida's presciently expansive "today" seems all too empirically correct, let us remember he is rereading its disjointedness by way of *Hamlet*. Derrida, *Specters of Marx*, 58.

30. Gayatri Chakravorty Spivak, *A Critique of Postcolonial Reason: Toward a History of the Vanishing Present* (Cambridge, MA: Harvard University Press, 1999), 431. In a posture not unfamiliar among certain theologians, she is straining toward an activist appropriation of Derrida and yet distancing herself from the taint of a merely academic deconstruction. Hence the last sentence of this hefty book: "The scholarship on Derrida's ethical turn and his relationship to Heidegger as well as on postcolonialism and deconstruction, when in the rare case it risks setting itself to work by breaking its frame, is still not identical with the setting to work of deconstruction outside the formalizing calculus specific to the academic institution."

31. See "Seeing Voices" in Catherine Keller, *Apocalypse Now and Then: A Feminist Guide to the End of the World* (Boston: Beacon, 1996). I did imagine a certain begrudging pneumatological kinship with John's anti-imperial vision/audition. For a Derridean afterthought to this counter-apocalypse, see Catherine Keller, "Eyeing the Apocalypse," in *Postmodern Interpretations of the Bible: A Reader*, ed. A. K. M. Adam (St. Louis, MO: Chalice, 2001).

32. Derrida, *Specters of Marx*, 89.

33. I will not rehearse here the case, which is not hard to make, for the anti-imperial intentions of the book, for the millennium-long history of politically revolutionary deployments of John's Apocalypse, and the twentieth-century liberation apocalypse among Christians of the so-called developing world. These are recapitulated in my *Apocalypse Now and Then*. Let me point only to Ernst Bloch's *Principle of Hope* (trans. Neville Plaice, Stephen Plaice, and Paul Knight [Cambridge, MA: MIT Press, 1995]) and, less enthusiastically, Norman Cohn's *Pursuit of the Millennium* (Oxford: Oxford University Press, 1970), as pivotal accounts of the political *Wirkungsgeschichte* of the text.

34. Derrida's "topology of mourning" as the "spectral spiritualization that is at work in any *techne*" may be as interminable as mourning itself and so extends, of course, indefinitely beyond, if one can, the contours of the specifically political: "A mourning in fact and by right interminable, without possible normality, without reliable limit, in its reality or in its concept, between introjection and incorporation. But the same logic . . . responds to the injunction of a justice which, beyond right or law, rises up in the very respect owed to whoever is not, no longer or not yet, living, presently living" (Derrida, *Specters of Marx*, 97).

35. See Derrida's Kierkegaardian meditation on responsibility, suggesting, of course, no ethical fix to a paradox that perhaps the invocation of "Bush" flattens but also tests (for at what point does the inevitability of "sacrifice" enable the most vulgar collusion with brutality?): "As soon as I enter into a relation with the other, with the gaze, look, request, love, command, or call of the other, I know that I can respond only by sacrificing ethics, that is, by sacrificing whatever obliges me to also respond, in the same way, in the same instant, to all the others. I offer a gift of death, I betray, I don't need to raise my knife over my son on Mount Moriah for that . . . . I am sacrificing and betraying at every moment all my other obligations: my obligations to the others whom I know or don't know, the billions of my fellows (without mentioning the animals that are even more other others than my fellows), my fellows who are dying of starvation or sickness." Derrida, *The Gift of Death*, 68–69.

36. I discuss the breathless compression of Hebrew poetry, especially Ezekiel, in this flashing proto-MTV vision in "Eyeing the Apocalypse" and *Apocalypse Now and Then*.

37. Derrida, *Specters of Marx*, 51.

38. For this invaluable formulation, I thank Nester Miguez for his unpublished keynote address for the Oxford Institute, "The Old Creation in the New, the New Creation in the Old" (August 2002).

39. Derrida, "Faith and Knowledge," 82.

40. Jacques Derrida and Maurizio Ferraris, *A Taste for the Secret*, trans. Giacomo Donis (Cambridge: Polity Press, 2001), 59.

41. "But the woman was given the two wings of the great eagle, so that she could fly from the serpent into the wilderness, to her place where she is nourished for a time, and times, and half a time. [Time out of joint indeed!] Then from his mouth the serpent poured water like a river after the woman, to sweep her away with the flood. But the earth came to the help of the woman: it opened its mouth and swallowed the river that the dragon had poured from his mouth" (Rev. 12:14–16). Amid the many graphic oralities of the Apocalypse, the nurturing desert and the vomiting yet voracious beast invoke the scene of a burning and many-orificed desire. See Keller, *Apocalypse Now and Then*, 70–73.

42. Derrida, *Specters of Marx*, 33.

43. Ibid., 65.

44. Derrida, *The Gift of Death*, 57.

45. Derrida and Ferraris, *A Taste for the Secret*, 21.

46. Ibid.

47. Jürgen Moltmann's *Theology of Hope* (New York: Harper & Row, 1965–67), a twentieth-century theological classic, made the key transitions:

"The more Christianity became an organization for discipleship under the auspices of the Roman state religion and persistently upheld the claims of that religion, the more eschatology and its mobilizing, revolutionizing and critical effects upon history as it has now to be lived were left to fanatical sects and revolutionary groups." But once we read the biblical testimonies as "full to the brim with future hope of a messianic kind for the world," we realize that "the eschatological is not one element of Christianity, but it is the medium of Christian faith as such" (15–16). His specific enunciation of the "coming" as *adventus/Zukunft* will be discussed below.

48. "God's Being is in his coming, not in his becoming. If it were in his becoming, then it would also be in his passing away. But as the Coming One (*ho erchomenos*), through his promises and his Spirit (which precede his coming and announce it) God now already sets present and past in the light of his eschatological arrival . . . . The coming of God means the coming of a being that no longer dies and a time that no longer passes away." Jürgen Moltmann, *The Coming of God*, trans. Margaret Koh (Minneapolis, MN: Fortress Press, 1996), 23, 24.

49. Jürgen Moltmann, *The Spirit of Life* (Minneapolis, MN: Fortress Press, 1992).

50. Derrida and Ferraris, *A Taste for the Secret*, 84.

8. MESSIANIC INDETERMINACY: A COMPARATIVE STUDY

1. I am thinking here especially of John J. Thatamanil's phrase "multiple religious participation." He writes, "The term *multiple religious participation* is the best generic term for modes of religious life in which persons take up ideas and practices drawn from the repertoires of discrete traditions. In some cases, such participation may so deeply shape personhood that one might wish to speak of multireligious identity or double belonging." See Thatamanil's "Eucharist Upstairs, Yoga Downstairs: On Multiple Religious Participation," in *Many Yet One? Multiple Religious Belonging*, ed. Peniel Jesudason Rufus Rajkumar and Joseph Prabhakar Dayam (Geneva: WCC Publications, 2016), 10.

2. "Contrast," as creative momentary synthesis of actual past with possibilities for actualization, comprises each actual entity as inherently composite.

3. Personal communication with author.

4. Jacques Derrida, *Acts of Religion*, trans. Gil Anidjar (New York: Routledge, 2002), 100.

5. I had not, in preparing this essay, yet encountered the magisterial exception to my claim that political and comparative theology have had little to do with each other: Hugh Nicholson, *Comparative Theology and the Problem of*

Religious Rivalry (Oxford: Oxford University Press, 2011). Nicholson pursues a critique of liberal universalism in religion in dialogue with Carl Schmitt's critique of the depoliticizing effects of liberalism.

6. Stated thus succinctly on the dust jacket of Giorgio Agamben's *Homo Sacer: Sovereign Power and Bare Life* (Stanford, CA: Stanford University Press, 1998).

7. Taubes wrote *The Political Theology of Paul*, trans. Dana Hollander (Stanford, CA: Stanford University Press, 2004). Also noteworthy is Daniel Boyarin's *A Radical Jew: Paul and the Politics of Identity* (Berkeley: University of California Press, 1994).

8. Eric Santner, "Miracles Happen: Benjamin, Rosenzweig, Freud and the Matter of the Neighbor," in *The Neighbor: Three Inquiries in Political Theology*, by Slavoj Žižek, Eric Santner, and Kenneth Reinhard (Chicago: University of Chicago Press, 2005), 132.

9. Žižek celebrates Che Guevara's insistence "that it is 'relentless hatred of the enemy that impels us over and beyond the natural limitations of man and transforms us into effective, violent, selective, and cold killing machines. Our soldiers must be thus; a people without hatred cannot vanquish a brutal enemy.'" This is part of "revolutionary love." I do not dispute the messianism of this option, only Žižek's identification of it with the Jesus of Luke 14:26. Slavoj Žižek, "Neighbors and Other Monsters," in Žižek, Santner, and Reinhard, *The Neighbor*, 186.

10. Ibid.

11. Ibid., 190.

12. John J. Thatamanil, "The Hospitality of Receiving: Mahatma Gandhi, Martin Luther King, Jr., and Interreligious Learning," in *"In an Inescapable Network of Mutuality": Martin Luther King, Jr. and the Globalization of an Ethical Ideal* (Eugene, OR: Cascade Books, 2013), 132.

13. Catherine Keller, *Apocalypse Now and Then* (Minneapolis, MN: Augsburg Fortress Press, 2004).

14. Pantelis Kalaitzidis, *Orthodoxy and Political Theology*, trans. Gregory Edwards (Geneva: WCC Publications, 2012), 18.

15. See John Cobb's *Process Theology as Political Theology* (Philadelphia, PA: Westminster Press, 1982) for the history of this theological conversation.

16. Jürgen Moltmann, *The Living God and the Fullness of Life*, trans. Margaret Kohl (Louisville, KY: Westminster John Knox, 2015), 170.

17. Giorgio Agamben, *The Time That Remains: A Commentary on the Letter to the Romans*, trans. Patricia Dailey (Stanford, CA: Stanford University Press, 2005), 104.

18. Marcella Maria Althaus-Reid, "Graffiti on the Walls of the Cathedral of Buenos Aires: Doing Theology, Love and Politics at the Margins," in

Religion and Political Thought, ed. Michael Hoelzl and Graham Ward (London: Bloomsbury, 2006), 244.

19. "Mysticism and messianism are twins!" exclaimed Jürgen Moltmann to me, in response to my question about the bifurcation of the mystical and the political, when I was a young seminarian and he a visiting lecturer.

20. Judith Butler, *Parting Ways: Jewishness and the Critique of Zionism* (New York: Columbia University Press, 2012), 46.

21. Of the disturbing tension in the application of Levinas's messianic ethics, Butler writes: "So what has happened to the face in this essay by Levinas? Where is its humanizing directive, its commandment to stay attuned to the precarious life of the other, its demand that I become dispossessed in a relationality that always puts the other first? Suddenly, there is a figure not of a face but of a faceless horde, and the horde threatens not only to engulf this me, but a collective 'we' who has, contrary to the understanding messianism, found itself in the historical position of carrying alone, or with it Christian kin, the spirit of universality itself. There is no nameable Islam here, there is no nameable Arab here, only something vaguely *Asiatic*, without a face, threatening engulfment." Butler, *Parting Ways*, 48.

22. See Emmanuel Levinas, *Difficult Freedom: Essays on Judaism*, trans. Sean Hand (Baltimore, MD: Johns Hopkins University Press, 1990), 89, quoted in Butler, *Parting Ways*, 41.

23. The irreversibility of "emanation" or dispersal now implies a revalorization of exile. Butler beautifully surfaces Arendt's mystical sources (Butler, *Parting Ways*, 122).

24. Judith Butler, "Is Judaism Zionism?" in *The Power of Religion in the Public Sphere*, by Judith Butler, Jürgen Habermas, Charles Taylor, and Cornel West (New York: Columbia University Press, 2011), 81.

25. William E. Connolly, *A World of Becoming* (Durham, NC: Duke University Press, 2011), 9.

26. Elliot Wolfson, *Open Secret: Postmessianic Messianism and the Mystical Revision of Menahem Mendel Schneerson* (New York: Columbia University Press, 2009), 122.

27. Ibn al-'Arabi, in the translation and study of William C. Chittick, *The Sufi Path of Knowledge: Ibn al-'Arabi's Metaphysics of Imagination* (Binghamton: SUNY Press, 1989), 303.

28. Ibid.

29. Walter Benjamin, *The Arcades Project*, ed. Hannah Arendt, trans. Howard Eiland and Kevin McLaughlin (Cambridge, MA: Harvard University Press, 2002), 463.

30. See Christian Parenti, *Tropic of Chaos: Climate Change and the New Geography of Violence* (New York: Nation Books, 2011).

31. Jeffrey W. Robbins, *Radical Democracy and Political Theology* (New York: Columbia University Press, 2011), 176–79.

9. "THE PLACE OF MULTIPLE MEANINGS": THE DRAGON DAUGHTER REREADS THE *LOTUS SUTRA*

1. Gene Reeves, trans. and intro., *The Lotus Sutra: A Contemporary Translation of a Buddhist Classic* (Boston: Wisdom Publications, 2008), 5.

2. Gene Reeves, review of *Whitehead's Philosophy: Selected Essays, 1935–1970*, by Charles Hartshorne, and *Two Process Philosophers: Hartshorne's Encounter with Whitehead*, by Lewis Ford, *Journal of Religion* 55, no. 1 (January 1975).

3. Alfred North Whitehead, *Process and Reality* (New York: Free Press, 1929/1978), 22, 167.

4. In "A Postmodern China in the Making," Weifu Wu and Gene Wallace describe the flowering of process thought in China (*Process Studies* 43, no. 1 [Spring/Summer 2014]). There are currently about two dozen centers for process thought, in a Whiteheadian but not theistic vein, in China.

5. For a discussion of the inherent multiplicity of selfhood, as well as its specifically female manifestations, see my *From a Broken Web: Separation, Sexism and Self* (Boston: Beacon, 1986). Feminist theory, often in this century operating under more recent banners as indicated in the first three essays of this volume, can in theology and religion be systematically identified with a "polydoxy" or entire teaching of multiplicity. See Catherine Keller and Laurel Schneider, *Polydoxy: Theology of Multiplicity and Relation* (London: Routledge, 2011).

6. Reeves, *The Lotus Sutra*, 54, 53.

7. Ibid., 56.

8. Gilles Deleuze, *Difference and Repetition*, trans. Paul Patton (New York: Columbia University Press, 1994), 76.

9. Reeves, *The Lotus Sutra*, 81.

10. Ibid., 21.

11. Michel Serres, *Genesis*, trans. Genevieve James and James Nelson (Ann Arbor: University of Michigan Press, 1995), 3.

12. Reeves, *The Lotus Sutra*, 13.

13. Whitehead, *Process and Reality*, 22.

14. Reeves, *The Lotus Sutra*, 85.

15. Reeves notes that while the *Lotus Sutra* can be read as the assertion of "the superiority of the Great Vehicle, the Mahayana over more conservative traditions while disparaging the smaller vehicle. . . . It is certainly not as a record of Indian Buddhist history that this sutra has been read over many

centuries by the peoples of East Asia, where it has almost universally been regarded as a religious text, recited as a devotional practice . . . [as] one of the world's great religious scriptures and most influential books. It did not acquire that renown as a polemic against people or schools largely unknown to East Asian readers" (ibid., 5).

16. Whitehead, *Process and Reality*, 346.

17. Roland Faber and I have since written on *upaya*, or "skillful means," as a strategy for comparative religious thought. See Catherine Keller with Roland Faber, "A Taste for Multiplicity: The Skillful Means of Religious Pluralism," in *Religions in the Making: Whitehead and the Wisdom Traditions of the World*, ed. John Cobb (Eugene, OR: Wipf and Stock Publishers, 2012).

18. Reeves, introduction to *The Lotus Sutra*, 5.

19. Leo D. Lefebure, "Derrida and Buddha: A Review of *Buddhisms and Deconstructions*," *Concentric: Literary and Cultural Studies* 33, no. 2 (September 2007), http://www.concentric-literature.url.tw/issues/Ethics%20and%20Ethnicity/10.pdf.

20. Reeves, *The Lotus Sutra*, 55.

21. Ibid., 66.

22. The Stoics and Epicureans envisioned a space-time infinity, but Aristotle's finite universe prevailed in the West until Nicholas of Cusa. (See my discussion in "Messianic Indeterminacy" in this volume.)

23. Mary-Jane Rubenstein, *Worlds without End: The Many Lives of the Multiverse* (New York: Columbia University Press, 2014).

24. Serres, *Genesis*, 111.

25. Ibid.

26. Reeves, *The Lotus Sutra*, 379.

27. Serres, *Genesis*, 101.

28. Ibid., 31.

29. Catherine Keller, "Scoop up the Water and the Moon Is in Your Hands: On Feminist Theology and Dynamic Self-Emptying," in *The Emptying God: A Buddhist-Jewish-Christian Conversation*, ed. John Cobb Jr. and Christopher Ives (Maryknoll, NY: Orbis Books, 1991). See also the sensitive challenge to such critique by Linyu Gu, "Process and Shin No Jiko ('True Self'): A Critique of a Feminist Interpretation of 'Self-Emptying,'" *Journal of Chinese Philosophy* 27, no. 2 (June 2000).

30. Reeves, *The Lotus Sutra*, 253.

31. Ibid., 6.

32. See Diana Paul, *Women in Buddhism: Images of the Feminine in Mahayana Tradition* (Berkeley, CA: Asian Humanities Press), 1979, and Rita M. Gross, *Buddhism after Patriarchy: A Feminist History, Analysis and Reconstruction* (Albany: SUNY Press), 1992.

33. Rita M. Gross analyzes this axiom from a Buddhist feminist perspective in "Strategies for a Feminist Revalorization of Buddhism," in *Feminism and World Religions*, ed. Arvind Sharma and Katherine K. Young (Albany: SUNY Press, 1999).

34. See this volume's Chapter 12, "The Queer Multiplicity of Becoming," for further allusions to Judith Butler's trope of the drag queen, so key to queer theory, and to Elizabeth Freeman's concept of "queer temporal drag."

35. Reeves, *The Lotus Sutra*, 1.

10. THE COSMOPOLITAN BODY OF CHRIST. POSTCOLONIALITY AND PROCESS COSMOLOGY: A VIEW FROM BOGOTÁ

1. Jacques Derrida, *On Cosmopolitanism and Forgiveness* (New York: Routledge, 2001), 17.

2. Immanuel Kant, *Perpetual Peace: A Philosophical Essay*, trans. M. Campbell Smith (New York: Garland, 1972), 137.

3. Judith Butler, Jürgen Habermas, Charles Taylor, and Cornel West, *The Power of Religion in the Public Sphere*, ed. Eduardo Mendieta and Jonathan VanAntwerpen (New York: Columbia University Press, 2011), 13.

4. Other thinkers recently engaged in the trope of the cosmopolitan include Karl-Otto Apel, Martha Nussbaum, and Richard Falk. See also Pheng Chean and Bruce Robbins, eds., *Cosmopolitics: Thinking and Feeling beyond the Nation* (Minneapolis: University of Minnesota Press, 1998). Also Daniele Archibugi, ed., *Debating Cosmopolitics* (London: Verso, 2003). And for powerful theological reflections see Namsoon Kang, *Cosmopolitan Theology: Reconstituting Planetary Hospitality, Neighbor-Love, and Solidarity in an Uneven World* (Duluth, GA: Chalice, 2011).

5. David Ray Griffin discusses cosmopolitanism in terms of "global democracy." See Griffin's "Is a Global Ethic Possible?," in *Global Governance, Global Government: Institutional Visions for an Evolving World System*, ed. Luis Cabrera (Albany: SUNY Press, 2011). Also see David Ray Griffin, John B. Cobb, Richard A. Falk, and Catherine Keller, eds., *The American Empire and the Commonwealth of God: A Political, Economic, Religious Statement* (Louisville, KY: Westminster John Knox Press, 2006).

6. Judith Butler, "Is Judaism Zionism," in *The Power of Religion in the Public Sphere*, ed. Eduardo Mendieta and Jonathan Vanantwerpen (New York: Columbia University Press, 2011).

7. Kwame Anthony Appiah, *Cosmopolitanism: Ethics in a World of Strangers* (New York: Norton, 2006), 151.

8. Walter Mignolo, "The Many Faces of Cosmo-polis: Border Thinking and Critical Cosmopolitanism," *Public Culture* 12, no. 3 (Fall 2000).

9. "2,600 meters closer to the stars": a common Colombian self-description.

10. Eduardo Mendieta, *Global Fragments: Latinamericanisms, Globalizations, and Critical Theory* (Albany: SUNY Press, 2011), 21.

11. Ibid., 11.

12. Marx continues, "To say that man's physical and mental life is linked to nature simply means that nature is linked to itself, for man is a part of nature." Karl Marx, "Estranged Labor," in *Marx on Religion*, ed. John Raines (Philadelphia, PA: Temple University Press, 2002), 122.

13. Alfred North Whitehead, *Science and the Modern World* (New York: Free Press, 1925), 34.

14. Ibid., 91.

15. See my discussion of Cardenal toward the end of "The Becoming of Theopoetics" in this volume.

16. As I show in "Unsaying and Undoing: Judith Butler and the Ethics of Relational Ontology," chap. 7 of *Cloud of the Impossible: Negative Theology and Planetary Entanglement* (New York: Columbia University Press, 2015). However, I note there that the more recent work of Butler indeed "begins to enfold the earth" (233).

17. See Catherine Keller, "Talking Dirty: Ground Is Not Foundation," in *Ecospirit: Religions and Philosophies for the Earth*, ed. Laurel Kearns and Catherine Keller (New York: Fordham University Press, 2007).

18. Sylvia Marcos, *Taken from the Lips: Gender and Eros in Mesoamerican Religions* (Boston: Brill, 2006), 76.

19. Gayatri Chakravorty Spivak, *A Critique of Postcolonial Reason: Toward a History of the Vanishing Present* (Cambridge, MA: Harvard University Press, 1999), 382.

20. Catherine Keller, *God and Power: Counter-Apocalyptic Journeys* (Minneapolis, MN: Fortress Press, 2006).

21. From my preface to Marcos, *Taken from the Lips*, xiii.

22. Marcos, *Taken from the Lips*, 112.

23. John Cobb, *Christ in a Pluralistic Age* (Louisville, KY: Westminster John Knox, 1998).

24. Ivone Gebara, *Longing for Running Water: Ecofeminism and Liberation* (Minneapolis, MN: Fortress Press, 1999), 214.

25. Charles Hartshorne, *Omnipotence and Other Theological Mistakes* (Albany: SUNY Press, 1984); Sallie McFague, *The Body of God: An Ecological Theology* (Minneapolis, MN: Fortress Press, 1993); Gebara, *Longing for Running Water*.

26. Cancun Declaration of Like-Minded Megadiversity Countries. The ministers in charge of the environment and the delegates of Brazil, China,

Colombia, Costa Rica, Ecuador, India, Indonesia, Kenya, Mexico, Peru, South Africa and Venezuela, assembled in Cancun, Mexico, on February 18, 2002:

> Reaffirming the sovereign rights of the States over their own natural resources and according to the provisions of the Convention on Biological Diversity and our commitment to meet its objectives, in particular Articles 8(j), 15, 16 and 19; Underlining the need to guide our actions based on a new ethic, where equity prevails in relations among nations and between men and women, and where responsible attitudes must ensure the conservation and sustainable use of biological diversity, taking into consideration the precautionary principle; Acknowledging our important natural heritage, which represents nearly 70% of the planet's biological diversity, associated with our cultural wealth and diversity, and which must be preserved and utilized in a sustainable manner.

27. Mendieta tracks the "ecological footprints" of the wealthy nations by contrast to the poor ones. "This is not to suggest that human poverty is not as catastrophic as the destruction of habitats," he writes carefully. "Rather, the point is to put in perspective the fact that this poverty is not only growing but can only continue to grow precisely because environments are being exploited beyond their ability to regenerate" (Mendieta, *Global Fragments*, 32).

28. Laurel Kearns, "Noah's Ark Goes to Washington: A Profile of Evangelical Environmentalism," *Social Compass* 44 (1997).

29. Mendieta, *Global Fragments*, 32.

30. Whitehead, *Process and Reality*, 342.

31. Mendieta, *Global Fragments*, 2.

32. See Catherine Keller, "'Recesses of the Deep': Job's Comi-Cosmic Epiphany," in *Face of the Deep: A Theology of Becoming* (New York: Routledge, 2003). Its ecological hermeneutics is in league with Bill McKibben's *The Comforting Whirlwind: God, Job, and the Scale of Creation* (Lanham, MD: Cowley, 2005).

33. Mayra Rivera, *The Touch of Transcendence: A Postcolonial Theology of God* (Louisville, KY: Westminster John Knox, 2007), 136.

34. "We are talking about using the strongest mobilizing discourse in the world in a certain way, for the globe, not merely for Fourth World uplift . . . . This learning can only be attempted through the supplementation of collective effort by love" (Spivak, *A Critique of Postcolonial Reason*, 383).

11. TOWARD A POLITICAL THEOLOGY OF THE EARTH

1. Carl Schmitt, *Political Theology* (Chicago: University of Chicago Press, 2006), 5–6.

2. The encyclical had just been issued when I wrote this and was so very much in mind here. For an important, process theological response to the Pope's encyclical, see John Cobb and Ignatio Castuera, eds., *Our Common Home: Process-Relational Responses to Laudato Si'* (Anoka, MN: Process Century Press, 2015).

3. Bruno Latour, *Politics of Nature: How to Bring the Sciences into Democracy* (Cambridge, MA: Harvard University Press, 2004), 4, 5.

4. Gilles Deleuze and Felix Guattari, *What Is Philosophy?*, trans. Hugh Tomlinson and Graham Burchill (New York: Verso Books, 1994), 86.

5. *Complicatio* is a Cusanic term for the enfolding of all things in God. This is described in detail in "Enfolding and Unfolding God," chap. 3 of my *Cloud of the Impossible: Negative Theology and Planetary Entanglement* (New York: Columbia University Press, 2015). In chap. 5, "The Fold in Process," I show how Deleuze makes use of Cusa.

6. Glen Mazis, *Earthbodies: Rediscovering Our Planetary Senses* (Albany: SUNY Press, 2002).

7. Matthew T. Riley's dissertation exposes the widely misunderstood clarity, historically and prophetically, of White's work. Matthew T. Riley, "The Weberian Roots of the Lynn White Thesis: Religion, Ecology, and Max Weber's Social Theory" (PhD diss., Drew University, 2016).

8. See "Broken Touch: Ecology of the Im/possible," chap. 9 in Keller, *Cloud of the Impossible*.

9. Bruno Latour, "Facing Gaia: A New Enquiry into Natural Religion," Gifford Lecture Series at the University of Edinburgh, February 2013. For lecture videos and abstracts, see http://www.ed.ac.uk/arts-humanities-soc-sci/news-events/lectures/gifford-lectures/archive/series-2012–2013/bruno-latour.

10. Ibid.

11. John B. Cobb Jr. has long worked with a strong distinction between secularity, as the appropriate work of prophetic and wisdom traditions, and secularism, which is its own modern religion. See most recently *Spiritual Bankruptcy: A Prophetic Call to Action* (Nashville, TN: Abingdon, 2010). This distinction can be read as a development of a comment of Alfred North Whitehead: "The secularization of the concept of God's functions in the world is at least as urgent a requisite of thought as is the secularization of other elements in experience." From Whitehead's *Process and Reality: An Essay in Cosmology*, ed. D. R. Griffin and S. Sherburne (New York: Free Press 1929/78), 207.

12. Latour, "Facing Gaia."

13. Ibid.

14. Stephen Shakespeare and Katharine Sarah Moody, eds., *Intensities: Philosophy, Religion and the Affirmation of Life* (Farnham, UK: Ashgate, 2012), 8.

15. See especially the work of Vandana Shiva, *Stolen Harvest: The Hijacking of the Global Food Supply* (Cambridge, MA: South End Press, 2000), and *Earth Democracy: Justice, Sustainability, and Peace* (Berkeley, CA: North Atlantic Books, 2015).

16. Joshua Barker, *Corporate Sovereignty: Law and Government under Capitalism* (Minneapolis: University of Minnesota Press, 2013).

17. Stephen D. Moore, *Untold Tales from the Book of Revelation: Sex and Gender, Empire and Ecology* (Atlanta, GA: SBL Press, 2011), 240.

18. Jacques Derrida, *The Politics of Friendship*, trans. George Collins (New York: Verso, 1997), 155.

19. Ibid., 83.

20. Giorgio Agamben, *The Time That Remains: A Commentary on the Letter to the Romans*, trans. Patricia Daley (Stanford, CA: Stanford University Press, 2005), 62.

21. See Ernst Bloch's *The Principle of Hope*, trans. Neville Plaice, Stephen Plaice, and Paul Knight (Cambridge, MA: MIT Press, 1995). For a critical commentary on Bloch's study of the secular/revolutionary effects of the eschatology of the prophets and the "Christian social utopias," see my *Apocalypse Now and Then: A Feminist Guide to the End of the World* (Boston: Beacon Press, 1996), esp. chaps. 3 and 5.

22. Jürgen Moltmann, *Theology of Hope: On the Ground and the Implications of a Christian Eschatology*, trans. James Leitch (New York: Harper & Row, 1965), 16, 20.

23. Latour, "Facing Gaia."

24. David Ray Griffin, *Unprecedented: Can Civilization Survive the CO_2 Crisis?* (Atlanta, GA: Clarity Press, 2015). Griffin here proposes that the US president use emergency powers to declare the climate emergency a national emergency. He cites a letter written in 2011 by Bill McKibben and other environmental leaders to the presidents of the United States and China, saying, "It is time to publicly acknowledge that the continual burning of fossil fuels threatens the survival of civilization . . . It is with a deepening sense of dread over the fate of future generations that we call on you to acknowledge the severity of the global climate emergency" (393).

25. Carl Schmitt, *The Nomos of the Earth in the International Law of the Jus Publicum Europaeum*, trans. G. L. Ulmen (Candor, NY: Telos Press, 2003).

26. Michael S. Northcott, *A Political Theology of Climate Change* (Grand Rapids, MI: Eerdmans, 2013), 219.

27. Jeffrey W. Robbins, *Radical Democracy and Political Theology* (New York: Columbia University Press, 2011).

28. Robbins, *Radical Democracy and Political Theology*, 13.

29. Schmitt, *Political Theology*, 14, 7.

30. Saba Mahmood, *Politics of Piety: The Islamic Revival and the Feminist Subject* (Princeton, NJ: Princeton University Press, 2005), 199.

31. Charles Strozier and Kelly A. Berkell, "How Climate Change Helped ISIS," *Huffington Post*, September 29, 2014, http://www.huffingtonpost.com/charles-b-strozier/how-climate-change-helped_b_5903170.html. Ironically, I read this piece the day after the great New York climate march, so exhilarating in its multiclass, multiracial, multireligious, and multiatheist solidarity. And yet the ISIS crisis let Obama and company at the UN event ignore us. The exceptional power of the state is readily mobilized for emergencies of war, now routinized in this new endless war on the deterritorialized states of terror.

32. Naomi Klein, *This Changes Everything: Capitalism vs. the Climate* (New York: Simon and Schuster, 2014), 153.

33. Robbins, *Radical Democracy and Political Theology*, 9–10.

34. Ibid., 18.

35. Ibid., 182, 190.

36. Schmitt, *Political Theology*, 15.

37. Whitehead, *Process and Reality*, 343.

38. Ibid., 348.

39. Ibid.

40. William E. Connolly, *The Fragility of Things* (Durham, NC: Duke University Press, 2013); and Paulina Ochoa Espejo, *The Time of Popular Sovereignty* (University Park: Penn State University Press, 2011).

41. Espejo, *The Time of Popular Sovereignty*, 196. She writes, "A people is a process, an unfolding series of events coordinated by the practices of constituting, governing, or changing a set of institutions."

42. Ibid., 81.

43. As I write, this model has given birth at a stunning speed, timed to precede Pope Francis's visit to the United States (I am meditating on speeds), to a capacious set of essays, *For Our Common Home: Process Relational Responses to Laudato Si'*, with an introduction by Bill McKibben, ed. John B. Cobb Jr. and Ignacio Castuera (Anoka, MN: Process Century Press, 2015). I mention this as an example of how this theology of the nonexceptional exemplification is materializing right now. See also David Griffin, John B. Cobb Jr., Richard A. Falk, and Catherine Keller, *American Empire and the Commonwealth of God: A Political, Economic, Religious Statement* (Louisville, KY: Westminster, John Knox), 2006.

44. Shiva, *Earth Democracy*, 3.

45. Klein, *This Changes Everything*, 460.

46. Pope Francis, *Laudato Si'*, Encyclical letter on care for our common home, Vatican Web site, May 24, 2015, http://w2.vatican.va/content/francesco/en/encyclicals/documents/papa-francesco_20150524_enciclica-laudato-si.html, sec. 49.

47. Klein, *This Changes Everything*, 7.

48. Deleuze and Guattari, *What Is Philosophy?*, 110.

49. Ibid., 218.

12. THE QUEER MULTIPLICITY OF BECOMING

1. See Catherine Keller, *From A Broken Web: Separation, Sexism and Self* (Boston: Beacon Press, 1988).

2. J. Halberstam, *In a Queer Time and Place: Transgender Bodies, Subcultural Lives* (New York: New York University Press, 2005), 2.

3. Stephen D. Moore and Joseph Marchal, eds., *Sexual Dis/Orientations: Queer Temporalities, Affects, Theologies* (New York: Fordham University Press, forthcoming).

4. Carl Schmitt, *Political Theology* (Chicago: University of Chicago Press, 2006), 5.

5. See "Crusade, Capital, and Cosmopolis: Ambiguous Entanglements," chap. 8 in my recent *Cloud of the Impossible: Negative Theology and Planetary Entanglement* (New York: Columbia University Press, 2015).

6. See "Broken Touch: Ecology of the Im/possible," chap. 9 in Keller, *Cloud of the Impossible*.

7. Elizabeth Freeman, *Time Binds: Queer Temporalities, Queer Histories* (Durham, NC: Duke University Press, 2010), xxiii. See also, Judith Butler, *Gender Trouble: Feminism and the Subversion of Identity* (New York: Routledge, 1990), 186–89.

8. Freeman, *Time Binds*, 62.

9. Ibid., 78.

10. Ibid., 62.

11. Ibid.

12. See especially the work of Delores Williams and Karen Baker-Fletcher.

13. Kelly Brown Douglas, *Stand Your Ground: Black Bodies and the Justice of God* (New York: Maryknoll, 2015).

14. Jacques Derrida, *The Politics of Friendship*, trans. George Collins (New York: Verso Books, 1994), 155. See also Clayton Crockett, *Radical Political Theology: Religion and Politics after Liberalism* (New York: Columbia University Press, 2013), 177.

15. Schmitt, *Political Theology*, 64.

16. Schmitt posited that, through American influence, politics would reduce to economics. Carl Schmitt, *The Nomos of the Earth in the International*

Law of the Jus Publicum Europaeum, trans. G. L. Ulmen (Candor, NY: Telos Press, 2003).

17. Jasbir Puar, *Terrorist Assemblages: Homonationalism in Queer Times* (Durham, NC: Duke University Press, 2007), 9.

18. Giorgio Agamben, *State of Exception* (Chicago: University of Chicago Press, 2005), 23.

19. Puar, *Terrorist Assemblages*, 14.

20. Joseph Marchal, "How Soon Is (This Apocalypse) Now? Queer Velocities after a Corinthian Already and a Pauline Not Yet," in Moore and Marchal, *Sexual Dis/Orientations*.

21. José Esteban Muñoz, *Cruising Utopia: The Then and There of Queer Futurity* (New York: New York University Press, 2009), 20. Emphasis added.

22. Muñoz, *Cruising Utopia*, 1.

23. Karen Barad, "Agential Realism: How Material-Discursive Practices Matter," chap. 4 in *Meeting the Universe Halfway: Quantum Physics and the Entanglement of Matter and Meaning* (Durham, NC: Duke University Press, 2007). See also, "Spooky Entanglements: The Physics of Nonseparability," chap. 4 in Keller, *Cloud of the Impossible*.

24. Karen Barad, "Nature's Queer Performativity," *Kvinder, Kon and Forskning* 1–2 (2012).

25. See essays by John Cobb Jr., Jeffrey W. Robbins, Christopher Demuth Rodkey, and Clayton Crockett, in *Resurrecting the Death of God: The Origins, Influence, and Return of Radical Theology*, ed. Daniel J. Peterson and G. Michael Zbaraschuk (New York: SUNY Press, 2014).

26. Alfred North Whitehead, *Process and Reality: An Essay in Cosmology*, ed. D. R. Griffin and S. Sherburne (New York: Free Press 1929/1978), 343. See also this volume's "Toward a Political Theology of the Earth."

27. John B. Cobb Jr., *Christ in a Pluralistic Age* (Louisville, KY: Westminster John Knox Press, 1975).

28. Lynne Huffer, *Mad for Foucault: Rethinking the Foundations of Queer Theory* (New York: Columbia University Press, 2010), 256.

29. Marcella Althaus-Reid, *The Queer God* (New York: Routledge, 2007), 4.

30. Marcella Althaus-Reid, quoted by Eliane Brum in an interview for the Brazilian magazine *Época*. Eliane Brum, "Teologia Indecente: Polêmica e provocadora, a professora de Ética Cristã da Universidade de Edimburgo reivindica um Cristo bissexual," *Epoca* 329 (June 9, 2004), http://revistaepoca.globo.com/Revista/Epoca/0,,EDR66302-6060,00.html. I found this quotation in Genilma Boehler's "The Queer God: The God We Must Free from the Mirror of Our Own Ideologies," http://ofld.mccchurch.org/download/Garner-Institute/Boehler%20-%20The%20Queer%20God%20-%20English.pdf.

31. Linn Marie Tonstad, *God and Difference: The Trinity, Sexuality and the Transformation of Finitude* (New York: Routledge, 2015), 277.

32. Ibn Arabi, quoted in William Chittick, *The Sufi Path of Knowledge* (Albany: SUNY Press, 1989), 303. In Arabic *naph* is connected to breath, *ruH* to wind.

33. Whitney Bauman, *Religion and Ecology: Developing a Planetary Ethic* (New York: Columbia University Press, 2014), 172.

34. See Matthew T. Riley, "A Spiritual Democracy of All God's Creatures: Ecotheology and Animals of Lynn White, Jr.," in *Divinanimality: Animal Theory, Creaturely Theology*, ed. Stephen D. Moore, 241–60 (New York: Fordham University Press, 2014).

35. Muñoz, *Cruising Utopia*, 189.

INDEX

Abrahamic monotheism, incarnation and, 4
absolute secret, 122–24; secret empire, 124–25
affirmative materialization, negative theology and, 76
"After the Death of God the Father" (Daly), 20
agape and reciprocity, 30
agential realism, 67
Alcoff, Linda Martin, *Feminism, Sexuality, and the Return of Religion*, 15
All That Is, 44
Althaus-Reid, Marcella, 24; *mesianismo*, 141; *Queer God*, 206; *Religion and Ecology*, 207
Altizer, Thomas J. J., 20
anatheism, 7; theopoetics and, 106
androcentrism, 170–71
anglobalization, 200
Anglo-Saxon exceptionalism, 200
anima mundi, 26
anointment, messianic indeterminacy and, 138
anthropocentrism: androcentrism and, 170–71; climate and, 177–78; material sensibilities and, 169–70; materialism and, 168–70; omnipotence theodicy and, 172–73; radical, modernism and, 167–68; universalism and, 171
apocalypse: the absolute secret and, 122–24; catastrophe, 181; Derrida on, 120–22, 230n5; feminist, 16; Messiah's secret name, 125–26; mourning and, 129–30; reterritorialization and, 181–82; secret empire, 124–25
apophasis: apocalypsis and, 13; carnal apophasis, 25–27; deconstruction and, 22; of gender, 40–41
apophatic entanglement, 39–40, 116

apophatic materialism, 74–77; nomadic polyamoury of place, 79
apophatic mysticism, Dickinson and, 38
apophatic theology, Gregory of Nyssa, 108–9
aporia, porosity, 28–29, 32–33
Apuleius, *The Golden Ass*, 87–90
Arendt, Hannah, natality and Augustine, 103
Armour, Ellen, 23
asymmetrical reciprocity, 29–30
Augustine: *Aeneid* and, 88; *Confessions*, 83–84; contemporaries and female biographies, 90; conversion, writing past, 85–86; conversion and his mother, 85; forms, 98–99; Heaven of Heaven, 100–1; immortality, 100–1; Monica, 83–94; mourning, 95–99; Scripture as Lady Wisdom, 86–87; wife, 91–93; woman's Life and, 84; woman's Life and his own Life, 92–93; writing and his mother, 84–85
avant-garde artists: bourgeois morality and, 50; *Faculty Paintings* of the Vienna Secession, 54–55; Jugendkunst, 51; naked truth, 50; nudes as symbols, 54; painter as outcast prophet, 55. *See also* Klimt, Gustav

Barad, Karen, 10, 60; intra-activity of the world, 67; philosophical physics, 62
Bauer, Gero, 193
Bauman, Whitney, 62; polyamory of place, 80, 207; queering nature, 79
becoming, 68; belonging and, 203–5; Christian exceptionalism, 109–10; coming and, 145; ecosmopolitics and, 70; incarnation and all becoming divine, 108; and interruption of being, 145; intra-active, 68; Irigaray, Luce,

becoming (*continued*)
109; and materialization of its world, 68; sovereign Being and, 145
belonging, becoming and, 203–5
Bennett, Jane, 60; Nicene Creed and, 76
Blackwell, Antoinette Brown, *The Making of the Universe: Evolution the Continuous Process Which Derives the Finite from the Infinite*, 42–43
Blanchot, Maurice, 125
Bloch, Ernst, *Principle of Hope*, 182
Blockadia, 191
body, universe as God's body, 43
Boff, Leonardo, 169
bourgeois morality, sexuality and, 50
boys club of religious leadership, 19
Brock, Rita Nakashima, 40
Buddha: Dharma of Innumerable Meanings, 154–55; spiritual egalitarianism, 148. See also *Lotus Sutra*
Burrus, Virginia, 10–11
Butler, Judith: cosmopolitanism and, 165; embarrassed etc., 41–42; *Gender Trouble*, 194–95; messianic redemption, 142–43; messianism of nonrealizability, 142–43
Bynum, Caroline Walker, 63
Byzantine iconoclasm, 51–52
Byzantine icons, participation in transfiguration, 63

Cancun Declaration of Like-Minded Megadiversity Countries, 171, 241n26
capitalism, prosperity gospel and, 61
Caputo, John D.: *Feminism, Sexuality, and the Return of Religion*, 15; *Insistence of God*, 113; radical theology, 112–13
Cardenal, Ernesto, 117; *Cosmic Canticle*, 117–18
carnal apophasis, 25–27
carnality, incarnation and, 26
Carter, J. Kameron, 4–5
catastrophe, Apocalypse and, 181
censorship by God, 24–25
Christ, regifting, 25
Christian exceptionalism, becoming and, 109–10
Christian imperialism, globalization and, 172
Christian materialism, 61; biblical incarnationalism and, 61–62; Opus Dei, 61; prosperity gospel, 61; relics, 63; supernaturalism, 79; Žižek, Slavoj, 65
Christianity: consolidation of many, 3; Dickinson, 37; as eschatology, 183; material Christianity, 63; prophetic, 21, 28; women becoming as men, 162–63. See also prophetic Christianity
Christo-sovereignty, 181
chronomormativity, 195, 198; queer exceptionalism and, 203
climate: anthropocentrism and, 177–78; entanglement and, 199; human exceptionalism and, 197; national emergency, 244n24; and political theology of the earth, 175; Pope Francis, 191
Cloud of the Impossible (Keller), 116
Cobb, John, *For the Common Good*, 190
Combahee River Collective, 42
coming: becoming and, 145; Derrida, 125, 131–32; Moltmann, 134
communion, 81
communitarian cosmopolitanism, 165
comparative messianisms, 137–38; messianic imperialism, 141; messianic redemption, 142; mindful unknowing, 144; mysticism, 144; Paul and, 139; political theology and, 139–40
comparative theology: Abrahamic modality, 12; political theology and, 11; relationist pluralism, 141
Confessions (Augustine), 10–11; conversion and his mother, 85; double climax, 85–86; forms, 98–99; *The Golden Ass* and, 87–90; Heaven of Heaven, 98–100; immortality, 100–1; Monica, 83–84; Monica's choice for wife, 91–93; Monica's death, 93–97; mourning, 95–99; tears, 94–98; waters, 100–3; as woman's Life, 84; woman's Life and his own Life, 92–93; writing past conversion, 85–86
Connolly, William, 189–90; *The Fragility of Things*, 69; pluralism, 143
contemplative gaze of *Nuda Veritas*, 56–58
Conway, Anne, 42
corporate sovereignty, deterritorialization, 181
Cosmic Canticle (Cardenal), 117–18
cosmic rule of incarnation, 26
cosmology: decolonial cosmology, 166–73; *docta ignorantia* (Nicholas of

Cusa), 73; eco-cosmic multiplicity in *Lotus Sutra*, 156–58; entanglement and transfeminist theology, 43–44; self and, 42–43
cosmopoetics, 114–15
cosmopolitanism: Butler, Judith, 165; communitarian cosmopolitanism, 165; dialogical cosmopolitanism, 165; Dussel, Enrique, 165; Habermas, Jürgen, 165; imperial cosmopolitanism, 165–66; Mignolo, Walter, 165; process theology and, 164–65; universality and, 165–66; West, Cornel, 165
cosmopolitics, cosmos and, 69–70
cosmovision, 169
Crenshaw, Kimberlé, 42
A Critique of Postcolonial Reason (Spivak), 169

Daly, Mary, 40; "After the Death of God of the Father," 20
death of God, 106; theopoetics and, 111
decolonial cosmology, 166–73; deconstructed anthropocentrism and, 173; human responsibility and, 173
deconstruction, negative theology and, 22
Deleuze, Gilles: body without organs, 43, 219n20; geophilosophy, 177; infinite speed, 57; Leibnizian fold, 116; neoliberalism, 180; process cosmos, 116; repetition, 32
democratization of politics, 186–87
dependent co-arising, 45
Derrida, Jacques: and the Apocalypse, 120–22, 230n5; coming, 125, 131–32; faith and, 120–21; "Faith and Knowledge," 130–31; heterogeneity of origin, 132; the "I," 135; and Messiah anecdote, 125; Messiah of the Apocalypse, 125–27; messianic eschatology, 133; messianic performative, 134–35; messianicity without messianism, 125; pure attestation, 122; *Specters of Marx*, 128; techno-tele-iconicity, public space and, 130–31; turn, 128
Derrida and Religion: Other Testaments (Sherwood and Hart, eds.), 119
desert eschatology, 132; orthodox theology and, 133–34
d'Espagnat, Bernard, 69

Dharma of Innumerable Meanings, 154–55
dialogical cosmopolitanism, 165
Dickinson, Emily, 10; apophatic mysticism and, 38; Christianity and, 37; compound vision, 37; dashes, 37–38, 41; divine ignorance and, 38; multiplicity of truth, 39; unknowing, 38–39
dis-incarnation, 61
divine ignorance, 38
divine multiplicity, 4
divinity: distribution, 4; multiplicity and, 45
docta ignorantia, 38
docta ignorantia (Nicholas of Cusa), 73
drag performance, 198
Dragon Princess, 161–62
Driesch, Hans, 78
Dussel, Enrique, cosmopolitanism and, 165

earthbodies, 177
Eckhart, Meister, 115
eco-cosmic multiplicity, 156–58
ecofeminist theology, 26, 42; radical democracy and, 186
ecological theology, sovereignty and, 184
economics: and globalism, 183; liberal, neutralizing politics, 186–87; neutralization of politics, 184
ecosmopolitics, 70
ecotheology, 175; process relational cosmology and, 190
Edelman, Lee, 203
egalitarianism, Buddha, 148
embarrassed etc., 41–42
enchantment of life, 63
entangled difference, 6; pluralism and, 71
Entangled Worlds: Science, Religion and Materiality (Keller and Rubenstein, eds.), 60
entanglement, 36; apophatic entanglement, 39–40, 116; climate change and, 199; exceptionalism and, 197–98; Gaia, 178–79; intersectionality and, 199; quantum entanglement, 43–44, 81–82; simultaneity and, 199; solidarity and, 199; transfeminist theology and, 43–44
Ephrem of Syria, 107–8
eros, reciprocity and, 30
Eros of the universe, 205–6

eschatology: Christianity as, 183; reterritorialization as apocalypse, 182
Escrivá, Josemaría, 61
Espejo, Paulina Ochoa, 190
exceptionalism: Anglo-Saxon, 200; Christian, and sovereign exceptionalism, 196–97; entanglement and, 197–98; human, 197, 199; human and climate change, 197; incarnational, 1; nationalized, 194; nationalized, sovereign politics and, 194; queer, 202–3; queer, chrononormativity and, 203; racialized, 194; racialized, sovereign politics and, 194; sexual, 202; US, 200; US exceptionalism, 200

Facing Gaia (Latour), 178–79
Faculty Paintings of the Vienna Secession, 54–55
faith: Derrida, 120–21; the secret and, 122–24
"Faith and Knowledge" (Derrida), 130–31
female Wisdom: Heaven of Heaven, 100–1; Monica and, 100–1
Feminism, Sexuality, and the Return of Religion (Alcoff and Caputo, eds.), 15
feminist apocalypse, 16
Feminist Interpretations of Augustine (Stark, ed.), 83
feminist theology, 9; ambivalence, 17; apocalyptic hysteria and, 21; Her Coming and, 16; inclusive language, 18; language limits and, 17–18; legacy, 9–10; masculine theos and, 16–17; second-wave feminism and, 40; secularization and, 17; and sovereign exceptionalisms, 197; whitefeminist theology, 23
feminist theory, queer theory supersession, 195–96
For the Common Good (Cobb), 190
forms, Augustine, 98–99
The Fragility of Things (Connolly), 69
fundamentalism, imperial cosmopolitanism and, 165–66

Gaia, 176, 178–79; *Facing Gaia* (Latour), 178–79; revenge, 179
Gebara, Ivone, 26, 169, 186; not-knowing, 44

gender: apophasis of, 40–41; construction of, 194; sex and, 195; sex/gender performativity, 23; transfeminism and, 36
Gender Trouble (Butler), 194–95
Genesis (Serres), 147, 150, 157
geophilosophy, 177
the gift: impure gift, 31; ingratitude, 31–32; purity, 29–31; reception, 30; reciprocity, 29–30; theme, 214n8
Global Fragments (Mendieta), 165
globalization: from above, 165; anglobalization, 200; anti-universalism and, 166; Christian imperialism and, 172; corporate sovereignty and, 181; corporation-led, 165; imperial cosmopolitanism and, 165–66; tele-technoscience, 130
God: mirroring back to ourselves, 113–14; omnisexuality, 24; renaming, 18–19; universe as God's body, 43. *See also* death of God
God and Difference (Tonstad), 206
God-talk, 22
The Golden Ass (Apuleius), and *Confessions*, 87–90
Goldenberg, Naomi, 20
Gospel of John, 3–4
grace, skillful means and, 152–53
Gregory of Nyssa: divine infinite, 108–9; Macrina and, 90
Griffin, David, 78; *Unprecedented*, 191
Guan Yin, 147; *Lotus Sutra*, 163
Guattari, Felix: body without organs, 43; geophilosophy, 177; neoliberalism, 180

Habermas, Jürgen, cosmopolitanism and, 165
Hadewijch, *Minne*, 33
Hartshorne, Charles, 26
Her Coming, feminist theology and, 16
heterogeneity, Derrida, 132
heteronormativity, constitutive exclusion and, 198
Hollein, Max, 47–48
homonationalism, 202
Hopper, Stanley, theopoetics term, 110–11
human as eroto-linguistic animal, 64
human dominion, sovereignty and, 177–78

Index

human exceptionalism: climate change and, 197; denaturalization, 199
human identity, separation from divine identity, 109

iconoclash, *Nuda Veritas*, 58–59
Iconoclash art exhibit, 58–59
iconoclasm, 10, 27; Byzantine, 51–52
icons: *In Defense of Icons* (John of Damascus), 52; iconophiles as materiophiles, 52; *versus* idols, 56–57; imitation of the divine, 53; as incarnation, 52; transfiguration of the gaze, 52–53
identitarian enclosure, 36
identity, human separated from divine, 109
identity politics, transfeminism and, 36
idoloclasm, 114
immortality, Augustine, 100–1
imperial cosmopolitanism, 165; fundamentalism and, 165–66
In Defense of Icons (John of Damascus), 52
incarnation: Abrahamic monotheism and, 4; all becoming divine, 108; carnality and, 26; as cosmic rule, 26; creation and, 2; dis-incarnation, 61; enchantment of life, 63; as exception to human condition, 108; icons as, 52; polyamorous body and, 24–25; promiscuous incarnations, 8; sovereign exception, 108; sovereign Man and, 115
The Incarnation, 2
incarnational exceptionalism, 1
incarnatus interruptus, 26
inclusive language, 18–19
indecent theology, queer God, 24
ingratitude, 31–32
Insistence of God (Caputo), 113
intercarnation, 2, 32; becoming practices, 12–13; intra-carnation, 10; materialization and, 115; neologism of, 9; paleologism of, 9; viewer and viewed, 52; world relations and, 2–3
interdependence: dependent co-arising, 45; feminist meaning, 40; *Lotus Sutra*, 153; as relational ontology, 198; transfeminism and, 42
interreligiousness: interreligious receptivity, 141; transfeminism and, 45
intersectionality, 42, 199; conscious connection, 44

intra-activity of the world, 67; becoming and, 68
intra-carnation, 10
Irigaray, Luce, 39; becoming divine, 109; frozen femininity and Plato's cave, 102
Isherwood, Lisa, 35

James, William, *A Pluralistic Universe*, 143
Jantzen, Grace, 26
Jerome, 90
Jesus, Jewish body, separation from, 4–5
Jesus Sophia, 18
Jew, racialization of, 4–5
John of Damascus, *In Defense of Icons*, 52
John of Patmos, 25, 128–29, 182
Jugendkunst, 51

Kalaitzidis, Pantelis, *Orthodoxy and Political Theology*, 141
Keller, Catherine: *Cloud of the Impossible*, 116; *Entangled Worlds: Science, Religion and Materiality*, 60; "The Place of Multiple Meanings: The Dragon Daughter Rides Today," 147
Kirby, Vicki, *Quantum Anthropologies*, 81
The Kiss (Klimt), 58
Klein, Naomi, 191; Blockadia, 191; on environmental crisis, 186; *This Changes Everything: Capitalism vs the Climate*, 175
Klimt, Gustav: *The Kiss*, 58; murals, 53–54; *Nuda Veritas*, 48, 49; nudity in, 48. *See also* avant-garde artists
kosmos, 22

language: inclusive, 18–19; limits, 17–18; metaphoric, 19
Latour, Bruno, 174; *Facing Gaia*, 178–79; Gaia and, 176; Gifford Lectures, 174; political theology of nature, 174, 176, 178–80
leadership of religion, boys club, 19
lesbian feminists, queer theory and, 198–99
liberalism: economics neutralizing politics, 186–87; *versus* radical theology, 185
liberation theology, 61, 80; ecological thinking and, 169; Latin American, 169

location, relativity and, 68–69
Logic of the One, 39
logos, 22
Lotus Sutra, 147–48; arhatism and, 152; Dharma of Innumerable Meanings, 154–55; Dragon Princess, 161–62; eco-cosmic multiplicity, 156–58; Guan Yin, 163; integration strategy, 151; interdependence and, 153; material form, multiplicity, 158; multiplicative matrix, 154–55; multiplicity, 149–63; *versus* orthodoxy, 160; parable of the rich man, 153; repetitions, 150–51; skillful means, 151–52; "The Sutra of Innumerable Meanings," 148; transformation and multiplicity, 159–60; wisdom, 160; women becoming as men, 162–63; women in, 161–62
love: being of, 33–34; reciprocity of the gift, 29–31; of the stranger, 28–29; unreserved *versus* deferred, 16

Mahmood, Saba, *Politics of Piety*, 185–86
Makart, Hans, 54
The Making of the Universe: Evolution the Continuous Process Which Derives the Finite from the Infinite (Blackwell), 42–43
Mankind, woman and, 194
Marcos, Sylvia, 169
Marion, Jean-Luc, 27; idol *versus* icon, 56–57
masculine theos, 16–17
material Christianity, 63; relics, 63
materialism, 2, 60; anthropocentrism and, 168–70; apophatic, 74–77; Christian materialism, 61–63; human as eroto-linguistic animal, 64; Milbank, 64; realistic pluralism and, 67; religious bodies and, 62; theological materialism, 61; Whitehead's rejection, 73–74; Žižek, Slavoj, 64–65
materialization: Gospel of John, 4; icons as materializations, 63; sacramental significance, 72; theopoetics and, 114–18
matter: apophatic bodies, 75; apophatic materialism and, 74–75; naming, 74–75; negative theology and, 76; Whitehead, 73–74
McFague, Sallie, 26; universe as God's body, 43
Mendieta, Eduardo, *Global Fragments*, 165

mesianismo, 141
the Messiah: of the Apocalypse, 125–27; mindful unknowing, 144; the Monster and, 129; secret name, 125–26
messianic eschatology, 133; messianic time, 146
messianic imperialism, 141
messianic indeterminacy, 137–38; anointment and, 138; interreligious receptivity, 141
messianic redemption, 142
messianicity: and purity, 133; without messianism, 125
metaphoric language about God, 19
metaphors of personhood, 27
metaphysics of substance, 65; Whitehead and, 66–67
Mignolo, Walter, cosmopolitanism and, 165
Milbank, John: asymmetrical reciprocity, 29–30; materialism, 64
militarism, imperial cosmopolitanism and, 165–66
mindful unknowing, messianism and, 144
Minne (Hadewijch), 33
modernism in female flesh, 55
modernization as radicalized anthropocentrism, 167–68
Moltmann, Jürgen: Christianity as eschatology, 183; coming, 145; the coming, 134
Mondzain, Marie-José, 50–51; on icons, 51–52
Monica (*Confessions*), 83–84; Augustine's conversion and, 85; Augustine's wife, 91–93; death, 93–97; *The Golden Ass* and, 87–90; Scripture as Lady Wisdom, 86–87; transformation in text, 91
monotheism, incarnation and, 4
monster, the messiah and, 127–29
Moore, Stephen, 11; *Untold Tales from the Book of Revelation: Sex and Gender, Empire and Ecology*, 119
Mother Sophia, 18
mourning, Augustine, 95–99
multiplicative matrix in the *Lotus Sutra*, 154–55
multiplicity, 5–7, 36; Dharma of Innumerable Meanings, 154–55; Dickinson, 39; divinity and, 45; eco-cosmic multiplicity in *Lotus Sutra*, 156–58; *Lotus Sutra*, 149–63; relationalism and,

Index 255

42; Serres, Michel, 150; of spirits, 8; and transformation, 159–60; of truth, 36, 39–40; Whitehead, 149, 151
Muñoz, José Esteban, 203
mutual immanence, 7, 42; relation and, 68
mysticism: messianism and, 144; participatory, 107–8

naked truth, 47–48; avant-garde artists, 50; Latour, Bruno, 58; the unknowable and, 52
naming, 40–41
Nancy, Jean-Luc, the image in painting, 57
nationalized exceptionalism, sovereign politics and, 194
negative theology, 39–40; affirmative materialization and, 76; deconstruction and, 22; divine ignorance and, 38; Gregory of Nyssa, 108–9; matter and, 76; silence and, 45
neoliberalism, 183; deterritorialization of the earth and, 108; sovereignty and, 180–81
neologism of intercarnation, 9
new materialism, 60–61; theology and, 61; vibrant matter, 67
Nicholas of Cusa: cosmo-theology, 115–16; the divine infinite, 115; *docta ignorantia*, 73
The Nomos of the Earth in the International Law of the Jus Publicum Europaeum (Schmitt), 184
Northcott, Michael, *A Political Theology of Climate Change*, 184
Nuda Veritas (Klimt), 48, *49*; as act of protest, 53; as allegory of Truth, 55; contemplative gaze, 56–58; gaze, 51–52; mirror, 56; Schiller quote, 55; and self-recognition, 50, 56
nudity: and evil, 48–49; in Klimt, 48; nudes as symbols, 54; post-modernity and, 50; realism and, 47–48; truth and religion, 50

omnipotence theodicy, anthropocentrism and, 172–73
omnisexuality of God, 24
the One, 148; over the many, 149
ontological relationism: Barad, Karen, 68; Butler, Judith, 224n47
Opus Dei, 61
Opus Earth, 79

orthodoxy: desert eschatology and, 133–34; divine sovereignty and, 133; versus *Lotus Sutra*, 160; transfeminism and, 36; truth and, 36
Orthodoxy and Political Theology (Kalaitzidis), 141

palelogism of intercarnation, 9
panentheism, 190; *versus* pantheism, 78; superpositional christology, 79–80
pan-experientialism, 78
pantheism *versus* panentheism, 78
participatory mysticism, 107–8
particularity, 5
paternalism, return, 21
patriarchy, return of, 20
perfection, theopoiesis and, 108–9
personhood metaphors, 27
philosophical physics, 62
philosophy of organism, 67
physics, philosophical physics, 62
"The Place of Multiple Meanings: The Dragon Daughter Rides Today" (Keller), 147
planetary emergency, 184
planetary politics, 12
plat, 56
plural religious belonging, 138, 140–41
pluralism, 143; comparative theology and, 138; Eastern thought, 149; entangled difference and, 71; relational, process theology and, 72
A Pluralistic Universe (James), 143
pneumatology, 207
poiesis, 11; theopoiesis, 11
political theology: of antagonism, 182; Christian dominion, 194; comparative messianism and, 139–40; comparative theology and, 11; ecotheology and, 175; entangled difference, 207; German theologians and, 183; messianic imperialism, 141; of nature, Latour, 174, 176, 178–80; Schmitt on sovereignty, 175; sovereign power and, 200
A Political Theology of Climate Change (Northcott), 184
political theology of the earth, 175; climate and anthropocentrism, 177–78; earthbodies, 177; geophilosophy and, 177
politico-religious right, 21
politics, democratization, 186–87

Politics of Piety (Mahmood), 185–86
polyamorous body, 24–25
polyamorous God, 207
polyamorous panenthesim, 77–81
polyamory of place, 80, 207; becoming and, 207–8
polydoxy: Dickinson and, 39; process theology and, 72
Polydoxy (Thatamanil), 45
porosity of the aporia, 28–29, 32–33
postfeminism, 34; transfeminism and, 35
poststructuralism, 120
potentiality, Whitehead, 69
prehension, 116
Principle of Hope (Bloch), 182
Process and Reality (Whitehead), 69, 110, 189
process cosmology, 43
process relational cosmology, ecotheology and, 190
process theology, 40, 62, 72; cosmopolitanism and, 164–65; Griffin, 78; iconography, 189; political theory in the postsecular, 189–90; polydoxy and, 72; sovereign omnipotence, 189
promiscuous incarnations, 8
pronouns, 18
prophetic Christianity, 21, 28
prosperity gospel, 61, 70
psychosomatic universe, 77
Puar, Jasbir, *Terrorist Assemblages*, 201–2
public space, techno-tele-iconicity and, 130–31
public things, 130–31
pure attestation, apocalypse and, 122
purity: of the gift, 29–30; messianicity and, 133

Quantum Anthropologies (Kirby), 81
quantum entanglement, 10, 43–44, 69, 81–82
queer exceptionalism, 202; chrononormativity and, 203
Queer God (Althaus-Reid), 206
queer performativity of nature, 204
queer relationalism, 203
queer temporality, 195
queer theology, classical trinitarianism, 206
queer theory: Edelman, 203; human exceptionalism and denaturalization, 199; lesbian feminists and, 198–99;

Muñoz, 203; superseding feminist theory, 195–96

racialization of Jews, 4–5
racialized exceptionalism, sovereign politics and, 194
radical democracy, ecofeminism and, 186
radical political theology, 184
radical theology: *versus* liberalism, 185; politics and, 187; and theopoetics, 112–13
realism: agential, 67; nude female body and, 47–48; truth and, 47–48
realistic pluralism, materialism and, 67
reciprocity: agape and, 30; eros and, 30; the gift and, 29–30
redeemer, woman redeemer, 16
Reeves, Gene, 148; *Lotus* dharma as middle way, 151
regifting of Christ, 25
relational pluralism, process theology and, 72
relationalism: Barad, Karen, 68; cosmology, 42–43; multiplicity and, 42; opacity, 44
relics, 63
religion: plural religious belonging, 138, 140–41; and tele-technoscience, 130–31
Religion and Ecology (Althaus-Reid), 207
religious leadership, boys club, 19
renaming of God, 18–19
res cogitans, 68
return: of the gift, 18–20; of patriarchy, 20
returning God, return of religion and, 17–20
revenant, 21
Robbins, Jeffrey: messianic time, 146; radical political theology, 184; theopolitical fatalism, 187
"The Roots of our Environmental Crisis" (White), 177–78
Rubenstein, Mary-Jane, *Entangled Worlds: Science, Religion and Materiality*, 60
Ruether, Rosemary Radford, 186

Schmitt, Carl, 175; the exception, 188; *The Nomos of the Earth in the International Law of the Jus Publicum Europaeum*, 184; secularized theology, 185
Schneider, Laurel, 8; logic of the one, 32, 39

Index

science: as derivative from medieval theology, 72; Nicholas of Cusa, 73
Scripture, Augustine and, 86–87
second-wave feminism, feminist theology and, 40
the secret: absolute secret, 122–24; secret empire, 124–25; secret name of Messiah, 125–26
secular liberation, 5–6
secular progressivism, 21–22
secularization, feminist theology and, 17
secularized theology, Schmitt and, 185
self-recognition, *Nuda Veritas* (Klimt), 50, 56
Serres, Michel: chaos theory, 157; *Genesis*, 147, 150
sex/gender performativity, 195
Sexual Dis/orientations: Queer Temporalities, Affects, Theologies (Moore and Marchal, eds.), 195
sexual exceptionalism, 202
sexuality: bourgeois morality and, 50; censorship, 24–25; omnisexuality of God, 24
Shanzer, Danuta, on Augustine, 85–86, 88
silence: negative theology and, 45; before truth, 45
simultaneity, 42, 199
skillful means, 152
Smith, Zadie, *White Teeth*, 23–24
solidarity, entanglement and, 199
Sophias, 18
sovereign Man, and incarnation, 115
sovereign politics, exceptionalism and, 194
sovereignty: Cancun Declaration, 241n26; Christian imperialism, 172; Christo-sovereignty, 181; corporate, deterritorialization, 181; ecological theology and, 184; emergency and, 175; the exception, 188, 196; incarnation and, 53; neoliberalism and, 180–81; omnipotence and process theology and, 189; omnipotent lawgiver, 176; orthodoxy and divine sovereignty, 133; paternal norm and, 201; political theology, 200; and secularized theology, 185; and theology of human dominion, 177–78
Specters of Marx (Derrida), 128; hauntology and, 131

spectropoetics, 128, 130
Spirit Sophia, 18
spirits, 8
Spivak, Gayatri: *A Critique of Postcolonial Reason*, 169; Derrida's turn, 128
Stapp, Henry, 77
Stark, Judith Chelius, *Feminist Interpretations of Augustine*, 83
Stevens, Wallace, 111
the stranger, love of, 28–29
strict father paradigm, 21
supernaturalism, Christian materialism, 79
superpositional christology, 79–80
supersessionism, 195–96
superstition, 62–63; enchantment of life, 63

tears: Augustine, 94–99; waters, 100–3
temporality: chrononormativity, 195, 198; queer temporality, 195
Terrorist Assemblages (Puar), 201–2
Thatamanil, John, *Polydoxy*, 45
theological materialism, 61; Milbank, 64
theology: comparative theology, 11–12, 141; of death of God, 7; ecofeminist theology, 26, 42, 186; ecological theology, 184; indecent, 24; liberation theology, 61, 80, 169; new materialism and, 61; *versus* theopoetics, 111–14. See also feminist theology; negative theology; political theology; process theology
Theopoetic (Wilder), 110–11
Theopoetic Folds: Philosophizing Multifariousness (Faber & Frankenthal eds.), 105
theopoetics, 40; anatheism and, 106; death of God and, 111; as discursive strategy, 106; God-boundary and, 106; materialization and, 114–18; and radical theology, 112–13; term coinage, 110–11; *versus* theology, 111–14; *versus* theopoetry, 111; theopoiesis and, 107
theopoiesis, 11; Hellinestic Christianity and, 107; negative theology and, 109–10; perfection and, 108–9
theos, 22
theosis, 107; divine infinite, 108–9
This Changes Everything: Capitalism vs the Climate (Klein), 175
Tonstad, Linn Marie, *God and Difference*, 206

transfeminism, 34–35; Dickinson, Emily, 37–39; entanglement and, 43–44; identity politics and, 36; interdependence and, 42; interreligiousness, 45; orthodoxy and, 36; postfeminism and, 35
transfiguration: icon viewer's gaze, 52–53; *versus* reassemblage, 63
transformation and multiplicity, 159–60
transubstantiation, 81
truth: connection to All That Is, 44; ignorance and, 38; interdependence and, 42; multiplicity, 39–40; The Naked Truth, 47–48; *Nuda Veritas* (Klimt), 55; nudity and, 50; orthodoxy and, 36; realism in art, 47–48; silence before, 45
truth talk, 44–45

universality: anthropocentrism and, 171; cosmopolitanism and, 165–66
universe as God's body, 43
unknowing, 36, 44–45; Bohr, 75; Dickinson, 38–39; naked truth and, 52; science and religion, 78
Unprecedented (Griffin), 191
Untold Tales from the Book of Revelation: Sex and Gender, Empire and Ecology (Moore), 119
US exceptionalism, 200

Vattimo, Gianni, 28
vibrant matter, new materialism and, 67
the Vienna Secession, 47–48; *Faculty Paintings*, 54–55; painter as outcast prophet, 55
vitalism, 63

Walker, Alice, 44
Waters, Monica *(Confessions)*, 100–3
West, Cornel, 21; cosmopolitanism and, 165
Western revolution, Hebrew eschatology and, 182–83
White, Lynn, Jr., "The Roots of Our Environmental Crisis" (White), 177–78
White Teeth (Smith), 23–24
whitefeminist theology, 23
Whitehead, Alfred North: Barad, Karen, and, 62; Eros of the universe, 205–6; materialism rejection, 73–74; matter, 73–74; misplaced concreteness, 69–70; multiplicity, 149, 151; mutual immanence, 7, 42; philosophy of organism, 67; potentiality, 69; prehension, 116; *Process and Reality*, 69, 110, 189; simple location, 66–67; split of science and religion, 72–74; substance metaphysics, 66–67
Wilder, Amos, *Theopoetic*, 110–11
woman and Mankind, 194
woman redeemer, 16
womanism, 44
women becoming as men, 162–63
Word Made Skin, 9
world relations, intercarnation and, 2–3

Xiang, Zairong, 193

Zhi Yi, *Lotus Sutra* and, 148
Žižek, Slavoj: materialism and, 64–65; messianism, 140